W9-BLY-984

THE COMPLETE PERSONALIZED PROMISE BIBLE ON

FINANCIAL INCREASE

EVERY SCRIPTURE PROMISE OF PROVISION,

PERSONALIZED AND WRITTEN

AS A PRAYER JUST FOR YOU

by

James R. Riddle

Harrison House

Tulsa, OK

Unless otherwise indicated all verses are taken from the *King James Version* of the Bible. Used by permission.

Verses marked NIV are taken from the *Holy Bible: New International Version*®. NIV®. Copyright © 1973, 1978, Zondervan Publishing House. All rights reserved.

10 09 08 07 06   10 9 8 7 6 5 4 3

The Complete Personalized Promise Bible on Financial Increase:
Every Scripture Promise of Provision, Personalized and Written as a Prayer Just for You
ISBN-13: 978-157794-779-0
ISBN-10: 1-57794-779-7
Copyright © 2006 by James R. Riddle
6930 Gateway East
El Paso, Texas 79915

Published by Harrison House, Inc.
P.O. Box 35035
Tulsa, Oklahoma 74153

Printed in the United States of America. All rights reserved under International Copyright Law. Contents and/or cover may not be reproduced in whole or in part in any form without express written consent of the Publisher.

DEDICATION

I dedicate this book to my loving wife, Jinny.
You have been my financial partner through both
triumph and tragedy. Through it all, we took our
stand together and made an open display of
the truths in this book. Buckle your seatbelt,
sweetheart, because the best is yet to come!

CONTENTS

Dear Father, open the eyes of their understanding that they may know Your great love and the exceeding greatness of Your power that is within them. Show them Your heart, Lord. Make them see the life You want them to live.

—James R. Riddle

INTRODUCTION

We all want to do our best *for* God, but we sometimes forget that our best can only be achieved *with* God.

As I was praying over this book, I sensed the Lord telling me to just share my heart.

I want to tell you that *I know the heart of God toward you.* His eyes never leave you. He holds you close to His chest and sets your dwelling place between His shoulders. He is passionate for your fellowship and wants you to have all the best things in life. If you catch even a glimpse of His love for you, the power of fear will be broken over you forever. I want to see our Father rejoice over your success. I want to sense His gladness as you break the bonds of poverty and dance into the realm of prosperity. I want to see the church arise and become the body they were intended to be.

The truths found in this book are the avenue of financial blessing in your life. However, if left on the page, they will do you no good. I know that from experience. No matter how much we believe, it does us no good if we do not put it into practice. God sets a choice before all of us. We can choose His way and be blessed, or we can remain in the realm of the curse. It all comes down to a choice. Stop right now and think about that. What will you choose? Tell the Father right now that from here on out you will choose to take Him at His Word. Make your choice an unwavering one. Make your choice in the face of all of your circumstances. No matter what things look like, what you feel like, or what you've experienced in life, you will believe. Don't read another word until you have that settled in your heart.

The first thing that we need to remember is that God intends for us to use His Word as our steadfast guide. I believe in the power of the Word and that it is the only avenue with which God produces miracles in our lives. It is alive and powerful and sharper than any two-edged sword. It is spirit and it is life. Therefore, it is my sincere and resolute belief that the Bible is the only foundation for successful prayer.

I don't think that any of us should believe for things that aren't found in the Word. That makes it too much of a guessing game. We end up praying, "Lord, if it be Thy will, please give me...." Then we walk away not really knowing if God wants us to have it or not. We hope He does, but we have no foundation to give any substance to that hope. There is no certainty in it. That means it has no faith value and cannot be pleasing to God. (Heb. 11:1-6.) Therefore, in order for our prayers to be successful, we should know of a certainty that God wants us to have what we are praying for.

My study of the Word has led me to believe that God *loves it* when his kids have *a lot* of money. What breaks His heart is when they have it but refuse to do good with it. He blesses us, not only for our sakes, but for the sake of others. We are blessed to be a blessing. (Gen. 12:1-3.)

I believe the reason most Christians do not prosper is because of either selfishness or self-righteousness.

The selfish are only seeking blessings for themselves. They have a "That's mine!" mentality and never a thought for how they can bless others with what they receive. It's hard for them to take in the big picture and see why God wants them to be blessed. God is conforming us to be just like Him. Does He ever say, "No! That's mine!"? No, He freely gives us all things to enjoy. He wants us to live in comfort and prosperity just like He does, and He wants us to share what we are given so that others can experience His goodness as well.

Then there are the self-righteous. These individuals do not see that they are living in the time of God's grace. They are doing everything they can to receive God's blessings but come up short because they are trusting in their works. When they don't receive, they think that maybe they haven't prayed enough or that sin has cancelled their blessing. In reality, they have fallen from grace by turning to the Law. (Gal. 5:4.) It is important that we understand that God's blessings come to us by grace through faith and not because we are living right. Of course we need to live right, but that does not make us right, or keep us right, with God. Every blessing of God comes to us because of Jesus alone and not by our works. That is exactly why we pray in *His* name.

So the questions are raised, what exactly *does* God want us to have, and how should we pray over our finances? I believe the Word gives us the perfect balance. We should pray according to what God has promised. Furthermore, we should pray in accordance with *everything* that He has promised and not just those areas that our itching ears like to hear.

As you read the promises in this book, I think you will come to agree with me that God is only concerned with whom we are serving and what our motives are in that service. So many people in the church are serving money, and they don't even know it. We need to renew our minds and put an end to such misplaced allegiance. We need to stop trusting in money and understand that if we are relieved when we get money, then we are in reality praising and honoring it. Our relief should be found in the promise of God and not in the receiving of money.

Money is just a tool to achieve a purpose. It is God's gift to you. Don't praise the gift—praise the giver. Don't glorify the gift—glorify the giver. Don't serve the gift—serve the giver. If you trust and serve money, you will live a life of fear and uncertainty; but if you trust and serve God, you will live a life of peace, contentment, and security.

The devil has duped so many people in the area of money. If he can't get us to be afraid of not having it, he tries to get us to be afraid of having it. *Loving* money is the root of all evil but *having* money is not. Used as a tool, it often provides the solution to our problems. As Solomon said, "Money answers all things." (Eccl. 10:19.) The problem, as always, is in the heart of the holder. God doesn't have a problem with giving us money if our heart is in the right place.

Never allow your financial circumstances to cause you to be afraid in any way. No matter what situation you are in, God is still God. He is your provider and caregiver. He is your loving Father, and you are His child. Your faith should be completely in Him and not in what your bank account looks like or what is going on in the stock market. If your finances ever make you nervous, you are showing that your faith is not in God. We all need to have the attitude that Paul had when he said that even if all that he had were taken from him, he would still possess all things. (2 Cor. 6:10.) He fully understood that as an heir of God, his provision would never fail.

That brings me to my final point. To prepare you for these prayers, I want to remind you of who you really are. It is imperative that you understand that you are a prince, or princess, in the Royal Family of God. You have an address in heaven. As a child of God, you are not of this world but you are born from above. You have forces working on your behalf that others can't even fathom. This is not who you are going to be. This is who you are right now. Your inheritance is more vast and wonderful than you can possibly imagine. This very moment you have more riches than any billionaire on the planet. As a matter of fact, all of the material things that the wealthy of the world are now enjoying actually belong to *your* Father. They may be gathering it all up, but what they have gathered, *you* will possess!

Keep all of this in mind, because in this life there is another reality that cannot be escaped. It is a reality that many preachers choose to ignore. That reality is this: even though you are not *of* the world, you are still *in* the world, which means that you are subject to the tribulations of the world. Some of you may have lost your jobs, or maybe your house is about to be foreclosed on. You may be about to reap a harvest from unfaithful seeds that you have sown. Or—and this is the most troubling of all—maybe you've done your very best; you've done all that you know to do and have stayed in faith, but things still seem to be falling apart around you. No matter what you are up against, remember who you are. You are a child of the King and live in a reality that is far above what the natural eye can see. Your provision is still there. I'm not saying to believe for the bad things to happen, but don't worry about it if they do. Know in your heart that you can never be overcome by the things of this world. You cannot be destroyed because God Himself is upholding you with His right hand.

Whatever your circumstance may be, when you picked up this book the tide turned. You have made the move that will set things back in your favor.

You see, your Father has not willed that you be weighed down by tribulations. By faith you can overcome them. As you pray these promises, provision will be set in motion. You will begin to see changes around you. If they take your house or car, you will not be concerned or afraid. You know the One in whom you have put your trust. You are content within your present situation because you know that your Lord is with you. He will never leave you nor forsake you. That is what gives you the edge at all times and in every circumstance. That is what makes you a winner. That is what places you among the elite of the world. If you will stand in faith, before this thing is over, the world will look upon you with wonder and envy because of the abundance that has been poured into your life.

HOW TO USE THIS BOOK

In this book there are hundreds of Scripture verses that deal with how to receive your financial miracle. Meditate on them. Speak them to yourself. Ask your Father to enlighten the eyes of your understanding. Know them thoroughly and do them religiously.

Each Scripture is followed by a prayer and a Declaration of Faith based upon the given verse. Read the Scripture verse to build your faith, pray the prayer from your heart, and speak the Declaration of Faith aloud as a positive affirmation of that promise for your life.

Each prayer is a relationship prayer. They speak to God on a very personal level. They will bring you into closeness with your Father. You will be at His very throne pouring your heart out to Him. Elaborate all you want. Tell Him how you feel, how much you love Him and appreciate all that He has done. Stay in faith and know that He is with you at all times.

You will notice that each Declaration of Faith is fully cross-referenced. Each of these references are added so you can understand how the verse harmonizes with the overall message of the Bible. For instance, we may read Genesis 13:2 and see how Abraham was rich in livestock and gold, but not see how that applies to us. Therefore, the cross-references of Galatians 3:6-14, etc., are added so we can see that we are to be blessed in the same ways that Abraham was blessed. These cross-references are extremely powerful in establishing key concepts of the Word into our lives. The Bible says, in the mouth of two or three credible witnesses let every word be established. (Deut. 19:15.) Therefore, each personalized text is complete with at least two establishing cross-references.

It is important that you do not skip over the Word and go straight to the prayers and declarations——they are not what will generate faith. Faith comes by hearing and meditating on the Word. If you only pray the prayers and speak out the declarations, you will hinder your harvest.

It is also important that you pray and speak out the entire book. You don't have to do it in one sitting, in a day, or in a week, just be consistent. You need to get a clear view of God's purpose in your finances. If you read, pray, and speak out the promises in Genesis and never get to Proverbs, you will miss some of the most important concepts that God wants you to know and thus hinder your financial harvest. You must realize that this is not a magic trick. It is a process. It is a system. It is a pattern of living that puts God first in all things. It is a way of living that opens the floodgates of abundance into your life.

Now read the promises, pray the prayers, and speak aloud the Declarations of Faith from your heart. Fellowship with your Father. Don't hold anything back. Tell Him how you feel. Tell Him what frustrates you and how much you need His help. Commit your way to Him completely. Choose to believe. Don't waiver. Don't allow doubt to hinder you. Even if the doubts come, and they will come, don't dwell on them or let them get you down. Your seed is still out there. Your periods of doubt will never destroy the seeds you have sown in faith. Don't listen to Satan's lies. You have not lost a thing. God will restore all that he has taken. Remove the doubt and stand in faith once again. Your harvest is coming. You are about to see miracles happen. You have your Father's Word on it!

BEGINNING PRAYER

Heavenly Father, I present myself before Your throne in Jesus' name and by His precious blood. Father, it is a privilege and an honor to be able to present myself before You like this. I don't take it for granted. I know that it is Your love that has brought me here. You have embraced me as Your child, and I find my dwelling place between Your shoulders. I stand boldly before You because of Your grace and mercy. I have no fear because I know You, Father, and I trust in Your love.

Father, I know that You have given me Your Word to bring me into the life that You have called me to live. I make my choice right now, before You and all of heaven; I will believe Your Word without reservation. You are not a man that You should lie, nor the son of man that You should repent of what You have said. You said it and that settles it.

Father, I know that there are more that are on my side than what my eyes can see. I know that what I see is not the whole truth. Therefore, no matter what I see, no matter what the circumstances are showing, I will continue in faith. I know that You are on my side no matter what I am facing. You are my comforter and my unfailing provider. I refuse to trust in my bank account, my credit rating, my paycheck, or anything else of this world. My trust is in You. You alone are deserving of all praise, honor, and glory. Your Word says that Your eyes look throughout the earth for someone to whom You can show Yourself strong. Here I am, Father. Show Yourself strong in me. I believe in You. I know that You will prosper me as I meditate on Your promises and speak them to you in faith. I believe that I am about to experience prosperity like I've never known before. I believe this, because I believe Your Word. I present it to You now in Jesus' name.

CHAPTER ONE

GENESIS

GENESIS 8:22

While the earth remaineth, seedtime and harvest, and cold and heat, and summer and winter, and day and night shall not cease.

~ PRAYER ~

Father, I thank You for the system of seedtime and harvest that You have set in place. You have given me an abundance of seeds to sow. I can sow favor seeds and reap a harvest. I can sow love seeds and reap a harvest. I can sow cash seeds and reap a harvest. I commit myself to recognize that I will reap what I sow. From now on I will recognize that I always have a seed of blessing that I can sow into another person's life.

——— DECLARATION OF FAITH ———

While the earth remains, I can absolutely count on seedtime and harvest, cold and heat, summer and winter, and day and night.

These fixed and certain laws remain in the earth. Therefore, I know beyond a shadow of doubt that I will reap what I have sown.

When I sow my seed, I can count on a harvest.

(2 Corinthians 9:6-10; Galatians 6:7,8; Matthew 13:24-32; Mark 4:2-20)

GENESIS 12:1-3

Now the Lord had said unto Abram, Get thee out of thy country, and from thy kindred, and from thy father's house, unto a land that I will shew thee: And I will make of thee a great nation, and I will bless thee, and make thy name great; and thou shalt be a blessing: And I will bless them that bless thee, and curse him that curseth thee: and in thee shall all families of the earth be blessed.

~ *PRAYER* ~

Father, I thank You for separating me from my old life. The old things have passed away and all things are become new. I now bind myself to You as my first and most vital necessity. I commit my way to You, for I know that You are directing my paths.

I am fully aware that I am blessed with father Abraham. You bless me and make my name great. You shower me with Your abundance and make me a blessing in this earth. I give freely of my substance and do what I can to bless the people around me. I thank You, Father, that You bless those who bless me and curse those who curse me. Through me, everyone in my circle of influence is blessed.

———— *DECLARATION OF FAITH* ————

I have been called by God to fulfill the destiny that He has for my life. He has made me great and has blessed me with an abundance of all good things. All of my needs and desires are fully met in Him.

If I honor God, He has promised to promote me to a position of prominence.

I am blessed and I am a blessing. In this awesome prosperity that I enjoy from my heavenly Father, I have plenty for myself, with an abundance left over so that I can be a blessing to others.

God blesses those who bless me and curses those who curse me.

He brings me to the place of abundant favors and confers on me happiness and prosperity.

(Jeremiah 29:11; Hebrews 12:1-3; 2 Corinthians 9:8,9; Exodus 23:20-22; Psalm 23)

GENESIS 13:2

And Abram was very rich in cattle, in silver, and in gold.

~ PRAYER ~

Father, I recognize Your covenant and the reasons for my prosperity. I know that if I follow Your way, I will increase more and more. I understand that it is Your will that I have extreme abundance so that I can be a blessing in this earth. The things I produce on the job are saturated with Your anointing. You have placed your command of blessing upon all that I set my hand to do, and the result is an abundance of silver, gold, and their like.

———— DECLARATION OF FAITH ————

I am blessed just like Abraham because I serve the same God. He is my Provider, and He is in lack of nothing. God is a God of abundance who rejoices in my prosperity. In Him, I have an abundance in all things.

(Genesis 30:43; 1 Corinthians 2:9; 2 Corinthians 6:10; 8:9; Deuteronomy 8:8-18; Psalm 35:27; Galatians 3:6-14)

GENESIS 13:5,6

And Lot also, which went with Abram, had flocks, and herds, and tents. And the land was not able to bear them, that they might dwell together: for their substance was great, so that they could not dwell together.

~ PRAYER ~

Father, I clearly see the abundance of Your provision. I see no competition among my brethren, because Your provision is both endless and everlasting. With You, there is no shortage of supply. You see no problem with increasing my borders. I receive Your increase. As I increase, expand my borders and move me to new territory. There is no sense in allowing the abundance of my provision to become cluttered on a small patch of land. I welcome the change as You give it, Father. Increase my borders in accordance with Your will.

———— DECLARATION OF FAITH ————

I am anointed to produce an abundance in my life. It is the Lord's perfect will for me to increase my substance and expand my borders.

(1 Chronicles 4:9,10; 2 Corinthians 9:8)

GENESIS 15:1

After these things the word of the Lord came unto Abram in a vision, saying, Fear not, Abram: I *am* thy shield, *and* thy exceeding great reward.

~ PRAYER ~

I am not afraid, Father, for I know that You are always with me. You are my shield and my exceeding great reward. You protect me from evil men, and You bless me with Your abundance.

———— DECLARATION OF FAITH ————

I am afraid of nothing! God, the Creator of the universe, is my shield. He grants me abundance to the extreme. My reward, in Him, is exceedingly great.

(2 Timothy 1:7; Joshua 1:5-9; Psalm 3:3; 5:12; Deuteronomy 28:1-14; 2 John 8)

GENESIS 15:13,14

And he said unto Abram, Know of a surety that thy seed shall be a stranger in a land *that is* not theirs, and shall serve them; and they shall afflict them four hundred years; And also that nation, whom they shall serve, will I judge: and afterward shall they come out with great substance.

~ PRAYER ~

Father, I fully understand that it is not Your will that I suffer under the yoke of bondage. You have set me free and have bid me to enjoy Your prosperity. You will not allow oppression to reign over me. You always remember our covenant. Therefore, no matter what I endure in this life, I know I will emerge from it with great substance from Your treasuries of abundance.

——— DECLARATION OF FAITH ———

When my enemies rise against me, I am not afraid. My Father is always with me. In Him, I am indeed a stranger in a strange land. I am a different breed – born in the blood of the Lamb. I live above the confines of the world system. No matter what my oppressors do to me, I shall emerge triumphant with great substance as my reward.

(Psalm 58:11; Deuteronomy 28:7,8; Ecclesiastes 2:10)

GENESIS 24:34,35

And he said, I *am* Abraham's servant. And the Lord hath blessed my master greatly; and he is become great: and he hath given him flocks, and herds, and silver, and gold, and menservants, and maidservants, and camels, and asses.

~ PRAYER ~

Father, I thank You that You have blessed me greatly. You bless my substance and my employment. You promote me to positions of leadership and give me employees that are loyal and wise. My production increases continually, and my salary is blessed by Your anointing.

——— DECLARATION OF FAITH ———

The Lord has blessed me with His abundance. He has placed upon me the mark of heavenly nobility and has granted me the ability to produce a surplus in my life. I always have much more than what I need and I abound to every good work.

(Deuteronomy 8:6-18; 28:1-14; Genesis 12:1-3; 13:2; Malachi 3:10-12; 2 Corinthians 8:9; 9:6-15)

GENESIS 24:40a

And he said unto me, The Lord, before whom I walk, will send his angel with thee, and prosper thy way;

~ *PRAYER* ~

Father, I thank You for the angel that is assigned to me. I recognize that he is here with me as a ministering spirit. He is here to help me in my finances and every area of my life. You are good to me, Father. Thank You for sending me an angel to prosper me in my way.

——— *DECLARATION OF FAITH* ———

I walk in the ways of the Word and never fail to recognize the help that I am given. My angel is preparing the way to make me prosperous and successful in everything that I set my hand to do. This very moment he is taking the words that I speak and bringing them to pass in my life.

(Hebrews 1:13,14; Exodus 23:20; Psalm 103:20)

GENESIS 26:2-5

And the Lord appeared unto him, and said, Go not down into Egypt; dwell in the land which I shall tell thee of: Sojourn in this land, and I will be with thee, and will bless thee; for unto thee, and unto thy seed, I will give all these countries, and I will perform the oath which I sware unto Abraham thy father; And I will make thy seed to multiply as the stars of heaven, and will give unto thy seed all these countries; and in thy seed shall all the nations of the earth be blessed; Because that Abraham obeyed my voice, and kept my charge, my commandments, my statutes, and my laws.

~ *PRAYER* ~

Father, I know that the oath you swore unto my father Abraham is given unto me. I have Your unfailing Word that I am blessed to be a blessing. You are with me at all times and in every circumstance. You bless both me and my children after me. You have given me Your Word, and You perform it on my behalf. You once looked unto Abraham as a man who would take You at Your Word. Now look unto me, Father. I believe You. I will keep Your charge, and I will walk in Your ways.

———— *DECLARATION OF FAITH* ————

I remain in perfect fellowship with the Lord and He guides me in all that I do. I am quick to obey His commands. He is with me in times of trouble and never fails to deliver me. He blesses both me and my children after me. He is my faithful and trusted friend who honors His every promise. I will trust His Word and not be afraid.

(2 Corinthians 13:14; Deuteronomy 12:28; 28:1-14)

GENESIS 26:12-14

Then Isaac sowed in that land, and received in the same year an hundredfold: and the Lord blessed him. And the man waxed great, and went forward, and grew until he became very great: For he had possession of flocks, and possession of herds, and great store of servants: and the Philistines envied him.

~ *PRAYER* ~

Father, I thank You that I will receive the maximum yield from my seed in the same year that I sow it. You bless me continually and make my name great. You give me a great store of people who offer me their services, and You bless all of my production. Because of Your anointing, my substance increases so much that my enemies look upon me with jealousy and envy.

———— *DECLARATION OF FAITH* ————

The Lord has blessed me with abundance.
His favor finds a home in me.
He receives the seed that I have sown and blesses it so that it will bring forth the maximum yield.
He has taken hold of me in His powerful arm and promoted me. In Him, I find wealth and position. I have been separated from the world. He has placed within me special and unique supernatural qualities. My supply is great with His blessing in my life.

(Romans 4:17; Philippians 4:19; 2 Corinthians 9:6-11; Mark 4:13-20; Deuteronomy 8:6-18; Daniel 1:20)

GENESIS 27:28,29

Therefore God give thee of the dew of heaven, and the fatness of the earth, and plenty of corn and wine: Let people serve thee, and nations bow down to thee: be lord over thy brethren, and let thy mother's sons bow down to thee: cursed *be* every one that curseth thee, and blessed *be* he that blesseth thee.

~ *PRAYER* ~

Father, thank You for all of Your goodness. You are so good to me. You give me the dew of heaven and the fatness of the earth. Your desire is to give me the best of all that the earth can yield. You give me heaven's anointing to cause me to thrive in the earth. I am a child of plenty. My provision never fails. Many are they who assist me in my calling. I have the favor of heaven and the favor of earth. Those who try to curse me only bring harm on themselves, and those who bless me receive Your blessing in return.

——— DECLARATION OF FAITH ———

The Lord is ever with me to bless me. He gives me abundance in every area of my life. Those who curse me, curse only themselves; and those who bless me are blessed with God's own endowment of abundance.

(Deuteronomy 28:1-14; 33:27-29; Psalm 46:1; 54:4; Genesis 12:1-3; 39:5)

GENESIS 28:3,4

And God Almighty bless thee, and make thee fruitful, and multiply thee, that thou mayest be a multitude of people; And give thee the blessing of Abraham, to thee, and to thy seed with thee; that thou mayest inherit the land wherein thou art a stranger, which God gave unto Abraham.

~ *PRAYER* ~

Father, I recognize that it is You who have blessed me. You make me fruitful in every way and cause me to increase in this earth. My children enjoy the bounty of Your abundance. The blessing of Abraham is upon me, and all those around me are blessed with me.

───── DECLARATION OF FAITH ─────

The Lord blesses me and makes me fruitful. He increases me in His abundance so that the cup of my life overflows with His goodness. In Him, I enjoy the very blessing of Abraham. Like Abraham, the Lord makes me rich!

(Genesis 12:1-3; 13:2; Galatians 3:13,14)

GENESIS 28:20-22

And Jacob vowed a vow, saying, If God will be with me, and will keep me in this way that I go, and will give me bread food to eat, and raiment to put on, So that I come again to my father's house in peace; then shall the Lord be my God: And this stone, which I have set *for* a pillar, shall be God's house: and of all that thou shalt give me I will surely give the tenth unto thee.

~ PRAYER ~

Father, I commit myself to You wholly. You are my God and Father. My provision comes from You alone. I do not trust in riches or the strength of my arms. I trust in You. You alone are the provider of my food and clothing. Your goodness and mercy surround me, and I find rest in Your tender care. Therefore, I will gladly give back a tenth of my increase.

───── DECLARATION OF FAITH ─────

Jesus has become my Rock. He is with me wherever I go and provides for my every need. He keeps me in safety at all times. He continually watches over me, giving me food to eat and clothes to wear. Therefore, I will not fail to pay Him the tithe of all of my continual, God-given increase.

(1 Corinthians 10:3,4; Philippians 4:11-19; Psalm 5:11,12; 23; Matthew 6:25-33; Malachi 3:8-12)

GENESIS 30:27-30

And Laban said unto him, I pray thee, if I have found favour in thine eyes, *tarry: for* I have learned by experience that the Lord hath blessed me for thy sake. And he said, Appoint me thy wages, and I will give *it*. And he said unto him, Thou knowest how I have served thee, and how thy cattle was with me. For *it was* little which thou hadst before I *came*, and it is *now* increased unto a multitude; and the Lord hath blessed thee since my coming: and now when shall I provide for mine own house also?

~ *PRAYER* ~

Father, I thank You for blessing others for my sake. My employers and associates are blessed because of the anointing You have placed on my life. They seek my favor and call me a blessing. Increase them, Father. Make me Your example. Use me to show them how wonderful You really are.

———— DECLARATION OF FAITH ————

Those whom I serve (employers, pastors, family, etc.) are blessed because of me. Their possessions increase and multiply because of the anointing on my life. The Lord showers them with favor and blessings for my sake.

(Ephesians 6:5,6; Titus 2:9,10; Genesis 39:2-5)

GENESIS 31:13

I *am* the God of Bethel, where thou anointedst the pillar, *and* where thou vowedst a vow unto me: now arise, get thee out from this land, and return unto the land of thy kindred.

~ *PRAYER* ~

Father, I will serve You all the days of my life. Wherever You bid me to go, I will go. You are my Rock of Bethel. I look to You alone to satisfy my every need and desire.

———— DECLARATION OF FAITH ————

The Lord is my God of Bethel. He has made His home in my heart. He is with me in all that I do and His Word never fails me. I will walk in

His ways and obey His every command. With Him at the lead, I am destined to succeed!

(1 Corinthians 3:16; Isaiah 55:11; Joshua 1:8)

GENESIS 36:6,7

And Esau took his wives, and his sons, and his daughters, and all the persons of his house, and his cattle, and all his beasts, and all his substance, which he had got in the land of Canaan; and went into the country from the face of his brother Jacob. For their riches were more than that they might dwell together; and the land wherein they were strangers could not bear them because of their cattle.

~ PRAYER ~

Father, I know that You have provided more than enough for everyone to live with plenty. Riches are from You. Increase my borders and fill me with Your abundance. Lift me and all of my brothers and sisters out of the land of poverty that we might dwell richly in the realm of prosperity.

—— DECLARATION OF FAITH ——

I will not let religious traditions guide me in my walk with God. I am intelligent enough to know that it takes money to advance God's kingdom. Therefore, I humble myself under His mighty hand knowing that He shall exalt me. I fully expect to move on to bigger and better things in my life.

(Matthew 15:3,6; 1 Peter 5:6; 1 Chronicles 4:9,10)

GENESIS 39:2-6

And the Lord was with Joseph, and he was a prosperous man; and he was in the house of his master the Egyptian. And his master saw that the Lord *was* with him, and that the Lord made all that he did to prosper in his hand. And Joseph found grace in his sight, and he served him: and he made him overseer over his house, and all *that* he had he put into his hand. And it came to pass from the time *that* he had made him overseer in his house, and over all that he had, that the Lord blessed the Egyptian's house for Joseph's sake; and the blessing of the Lord was upon all that he had in the house, and in the field. And he left all that he had in Joseph's hand; and he knew not ought he had, save the bread which he did eat. And Joseph was *a* goodly *person*, and well favoured.

~ *PRAYER* ~

Father, I thank You that You are always with me. You are always there to make me prosperous and successful. You place people of importance in my path to grant me favor and to bring me to the place You have ordained for me to be. I find grace in their sight, and they go out of their way to do nice things for me. I serve them well because of the anointing You have given me. By Your favor, they lift me to positions of authority, and I prosper in whatever position I am given. Everything I set my hand to do is prosperous and successful. I thank You that You bless them for my sake, Father. Everything that they have is blessed because of the favor they have given me. You pour out upon them an anointing for prosperity, and they enjoy the bounty of Your riches. Help me to serve them well, Father. Help me to be a person of integrity and admirable character so that You will be praised in all that I do.

DECLARATION OF FAITH

The Lord is always with me to make me prosperous and very successful.

Those who have been appointed as my supervisors can clearly see that the Lord is with me. They see how He makes everything that I set my hand to do to thrive and prosper.

He grants me abundant favor with those in authority over me. They look upon me as one who is called to lead, and the Lord blesses them for my sake. For my sake, all that they have is blessed.

(Genesis 30:29,30; Deuteronomy 8:6-18; 28:1-14; Daniel 1:20; Acts 7:9,10)

GENESIS 39:20-23

And Joseph's master took him, and put him into the prison, a place where the king's prisoners *were* bound: and he was there in the prison. But the Lord was with Joseph, and showed him mercy, and gave him favour in the sight of the keeper of the prison. And the keeper of the prison committed to Joseph's hand all the prisoners that *were* in the prison; and whatsoever they did there, he was the doer *of it*. The keeper of the prison looked not to any thing *that was* under his hand; because the Lord was with him, and *that* which he did, the Lord made *it* to prosper.

~ *PRAYER* ~

Father, I know that my gift will make a way for me. No matter what happens in my life, You are with me. If I am falsely accused and unjustly judged, it cannot stop Your anointing. I prosper wherever I am and whatever my situation. Your favor resides with me at all times. Even those who have been set against me end up granting me favor. No matter what situation I am in, I will recognize Your presence, Father. Everything I set my hand to do prospers because You are with me. When things look grim, I'll just keep right on going. Nothing can get me down, because my partner is the Lord of all.

——— *DECLARATION OF FAITH* ———

No matter what the circumstances may be in my life, I prosper, for the Lord is with me to show me mercy, loving-kindness, and an abundance of favor with all of those I come in contact with. I have favor with my employers, my pastors, my teachers, and my administrators. They see that I am called to be a leader, and the Lord makes everything that I am put in charge of to prosper.

(Psalm 1:1-3; 5:11,12; 23; Genesis 12:1-3; 30:29,30; 39:2-5; Deuteronomy 28:1-14)

GENESIS 48:15,16

And he blessed Joseph, and said, God, before whom my fathers Abraham and Isaac did walk, the God which fed me all my life long unto this day, The angel which redeemed me from all evil, bless the lads; and let my name be named on them, and the name of my fathers Abraham and Isaac; and let them grow into a multitude in the midst of the earth.

~ PRAYER ~

Father, I thank You that You are caring for me every day. You give me unfailing provision for every area of my life. Your angel guards me and redeems me from every trial that I face. The name of my father Abraham is upon me, and I rest secure in our covenant. In You, Father, my success is forever guaranteed.

———— DECLARATION OF FAITH ————

The Lord has been the shepherd of my life from the day I was born until now, and He will continue to be my shepherd throughout all of eternity.

He continually sends His angel to deliver me from all harm.

He blesses me, makes my name great, and increases me upon the earth in a shower of His abundance.

(Psalm 23; 34:7; 91:11; Genesis 12:1-3; Deuteronomy 16:14-17; Malachi 3:10)

GENESIS 49:22-26

Joseph is a fruitful bough, even a fruitful bough by a well; whose branches run over the wall: The archers have sorely grieved him, and shot at him, and hated him: But his bow abode in strength and the arms of his hands were made strong by the hands of the mighty God of Jacob: (From thence is the shepherd, the stone of Israel:) Even by the God of thy father, who shall help thee; and by the Almighty, who shall bless thee with blessings of heaven above, blessings of the deep that lieth under, blessings of the breasts, and of the womb: The blessings of thy father have prevailed above the blessings of my progenitors unto the utmost bound of the everlasting hills: they shall be on the head of Joseph, and on the crown of the head of him that was separate from his brethren.

~ *PRAYER* ~

Father, You cause everything that I do to prosper and become successful. Even when my enemies attack, they are thwarted before my face. You strengthen me in the power of Your might and shield me within the hedge of Your protection. I praise You for Your anointing which burns like a fire within me. With You on my side, I fear no enemy. You lead me in triumph and cause me to reap the spoils of war. You bless me with the blessings of heaven, the blessings of earth, and the blessings of the breast and the womb. What is enjoyed in heaven, I enjoy on this earth. The provision that You have supplied on earth is given to me in abundance. My children remain secure under Your relentless care and protection. I am perfectly blessed by the best God in existence. No one compares to You, Father. Others may trust in the might of their hands, the prestige of their education, or the favor of men; but I trust in You. You are my strength and my portion forever!

———— DECLARATION OF FAITH ————

I am a fruitful branch of the Vine. My branches scale walls and cover them. I remain steady in the midst of adversity. My strong arms remain at ready, for the hand of my Lord—my shepherd, my Rock—helps me.

The Almighty blesses me with blessings that come down from heaven, blessings that come up from the earth. My Father's blessings are greater than all, and His bounty mocks the bounty of kings.

(James 1:2-4; John 15:1-8; 1 Corinthians 15:58; Genesis 28:11-22; Zechariah 8:12; Psalm 24:1-6)

CHAPTER TWO

EXODUS

EXODUS 3:21,22

And I will give this people favour in the sight of the Egyptians: and it shall come to pass, that, when ye go, ye shall not go empty: But every woman shall borrow of her neighbour, and of her that sojourneth in her house, jewels of silver, and jewels of gold, and raiment: and ye shall put *them* upon your sons, and upon your daughters; and ye shall spoil the Egyptians.

~ *PRAYER* ~

Father, You are so awesome! Even my enemies can't help but grant me favor because of Your presence in me. No matter what I endure in life, I walk away blessed. Your favor surrounds me like a shield so that I never have to go without. Therefore, I never hesitate to negotiate. I ask and I receive, and I am blessed in all that I do. I spoil the camp of the enemy and walk away with a grin. No matter what the enemy brings against me, I emerge from it as more than a conqueror because of You, Father. Praise be to Your holy name!

——— DECLARATION OF FAITH ———

The Lord gives me favor in the sight of my enemies. God will give me abundance where I once had lack and prosperity where I once had poverty. The enemy will be forced to give back to me all he has stolen and much more.

(Ephesians 6:12; Genesis 39:5; Numbers 31; Psalm 5:11,12; Proverbs 19:14; 2 Chronicles 20:15-24)

Exodus 12:36

And the Lord gave the people favour in the sight of the Egyptians, so that they lent unto them *such things as they required.* And they spoiled the Egyptians.

~ *PRAYER* ~

Father, Your favor is such a blessing to me. I know why You bid me to ask. It is because of the anointing of favor that You have placed on my life. I ask and receive that my joy may be full. Through Your favor I spoil the camp of the enemy!

──── DECLARATION OF FAITH ────

My Father has placed the anointing of favor on my life. Therefore, I fully expect to receive favor from others. I will not reject favor because of false humility. To the contrary, I know that through favor I am amply supplied with all that I need and more.

(Psalm 5:11,12; Genesis 39:2-5; Colossians 2:18)

CHAPTER THREE

LEVITICUS

LEVITICUS 19:9,10 (23:22)

And when ye reap the harvest of your land, thou shalt not wholly reap the corners of thy field, neither shalt thou gather the gleanings of thy harvest. And thou shalt not glean thy vineyard, neither shalt thou gather *every* grape of thy vineyard; thou shalt leave them for the poor and stranger: I *am* the Lord your God.

~ PRAYER ~

Father, thank You for giving me a proper perspective for my finances. My pursuit of prosperity is not for myself alone but for others as well. I know that I am blessed so that I may be a blessing. I will remember the poor and the stranger. I will help when I can and be a blessing in this earth.

——— DECLARATION OF FAITH ———

I am a provider in this earth. I know that I am blessed so that I can be a blessing to others. In me, the poor in the land find provision and hope for the future.

(Galatians 2:10; Genesis 12:1-3)

LEVITICUS 23:10

Speak unto the children of Israel, and say unto them, When ye be come into the land which I give unto you, and shall reap the harvest thereof, then ye shall bring a sheaf of the firstfruits of your harvest unto the priest:

~ *PRAYER* ~

Father, I choose to honor You with my tithes. You are the Lord of my harvest. I have no harvest at all, except that which You have given me. Therefore, I will gladly give the tenth back to You.

———— *DECLARATION OF FAITH* ————

I am a reaper of many harvests, and I am faithful to tithe on every one. I will not forget who has given me what I have. It is not my own hand that has gotten me this wealth. It came to me by the power of the Lord.

(Deuteronomy 8:17,18; Zechariah 4:6; Malachi 3:6-12)

LEVITICUS 26:3-13

If ye walk in my statutes, and keep my commandments, and do them; Then I will give you rain in due season, and the land shall yield her increase, and the trees of the field shall yield their fruit. And your threshing shall reach unto the vintage, and the vintage shall reach unto the sowing time: and ye shall eat your bread to the full, and dwell in your land safely. And I will give peace in the land, and ye shall lie down, and none shall make *you* afraid: and I will rid evil beasts out of the land, neither shall the sword go through your land. And ye shall chase your enemies, and they shall fall before you by the sword. And five of you shall chase an hundred, and an hundred of you shall put ten thousand to flight: and your enemies shall fall before you by the sword. For I will have respect unto you, and make you fruitful, and multiply you, and establish my covenant with you. And ye shall eat old store, and bring forth the old because of the new. And I will set my tabernacle among you: and my soul shall not abhor you. And I will walk among you, and will be your God, and ye shall be my people. I *am* the Lord your God, which brought you forth out of the land of Egypt, that ye should not be their bondmen; and I have broken the bands of your yoke, and made you go upright.

~ PRAYER ~

Father, my way of life is to do that which You have called me to do and to be the person You have created me to be. I choose to be a doer of the Word. I am blessed because I do things Your way. Your precepts bring me life and abundance. I thank You that You prosper me on the job and in everything I set my hand to do. I never fail to yield a proper increase. I reap a harvest even as I sow my seed. I eat and drink to the full and dwell in safety in the land. I have no cause for fear, for You are with me at all times. You establish Your covenant with me. I live in peace and prosperity. When my enemies rise against me, they are smitten before my face. I easily chase them away and put them to flight.

You are the greater One who dwells within my heart. We now walk together as Father and son/daughter. Bondage for me is a thing of the past. You have broken my bonds and set me free. With You on my side, I never have cause to be afraid. I am now living in the realm of Your blessings where I regularly have to clear out the old to make room for the new.

Father, it is awesome to think that You have respect unto me. You make me a fruitful branch of the Vine. You multiply me in all things and never forget that I am Your covenant child. I am sealed into a covenant relationship that guarantees my success now and forevermore.

———— DECLARATION OF FAITH ————

I shall keep the anointing of the Holy Spirit burning within me continually. I am as a lamp of pure gold. The oil of the Spirit is ever full within me, and my light shall never go out.

I thresh the fruit of my harvest from the time of gathering through the time of gathering through to the time of planting. I never go without. I live my life blessed with God's abundance. In Jesus, I have all that I desire and dwell in safety in the land.

The peace of God has filled my life. I fear nothing. I lie down in peace. Nothing, absolutely nothing, can fill me with dread; and no enemy can make me afraid.

I chase down my enemies, and they fall before me. I am on the offensive in the army of God. It is not in my nature to maintain a defensive posture. I am an attacker, and I go forward with my brothers and sisters in Christ to conquer in the nature of Jesus. Five of us chase a hundred, and a hundred of us put ten thousand to flight.

The Lord looks upon me with favor. He causes everything that I do to be fruitful and prosperous. He multiplies me in all good things and in every good way. He sets me apart unto Himself, establishing and ratifying His covenant with me. I am living in the fullness of His abundance. My increase is continual, so that I must regularly clear out the old to make room for the new.

The Lord has set His dwelling place within me and has given me His Word that He will never leave me nor forsake me. His Spirit is ever with me and is indeed within me. He walks with me, and His presence surrounds me. He is my closest companion in this earth.

The Lord is my God and Father, and I am His son/daughter. He has broken the bars of the yoke of slavery that were once on my shoulders. He dashed them to pieces and declared that I am free! He has enabled me to walk with my head held high, free of all bondage. He has made me His own son/daughter and an heir to His kingdom.

(Ephesians 5:18; Matthew 5:14-16; 25:1-13; 28:18-20; 1 Peter 2:12; 2 Corinthians 9:6-11; Psalm 5:11,12; 112:1-9; Philippians 4:19; Deuteronomy 8:6-18; 28:1-14; 32:30; Genesis 13:2; 15:11; 39:2-5; Joshua 1:5-9; 2:24; 8:1; 2 Timothy 1:7; Isaiah 43:1-3; 1 Timothy 6:12; Romans 8:14-17, 37; Hebrews 8:6; 13:5,6; 1 Corinthians 3:16; John 10:10; Galatians 4:4-6; 5:1)

LEVITICUS 27:30

And all the tithe of the land, *whether* of the seed of the land, *or* of the fruit of the tree, *is* the Lord's: *it is* holy unto the Lord.

~ *PRAYER* ~

Father, I know that my tithe is important. It is holy to You. Therefore, I give it without reservation. Through my tithe, I am declaring that You alone are my source of supply. Without You, Father, I would have nothing.

—————— *DECLARATION OF FAITH* ——————

I honor the Lord with the tithe of all of my increase. It is the Lord's, and it is holy to Him. I pay it without reservation.

(Malachi 3:6-12; Deuteronomy 14:22-29; Nehemiah 10:37,38; Proverbs 3:9,10)

CHAPTER FOUR

NUMBERS

NUMBERS 6:22-27

And the Lord spake unto Moses, saying, Speak unto Aaron and unto his sons, saying, On this wise ye shall bless the children of Israel, saying unto them, The Lord bless thee, and keep thee: The Lord make his face shine upon thee, and be gracious unto thee: The Lord lift up his countenance upon thee, and give thee peace. And they shall put my name upon the children of Israel; and I will bless them.

~ PRAYER ~

Father, I thank You that You bless me and keep me. You make Your face to shine upon me, and You are gracious unto me. You lift up Your countenance upon me, and You give me peace. Your name is upon me, and You have blessed me. In You I have favor and blessings in abundance. It is so awesome to be called by Your name, Father. I rest in the shadow of Your wings.

——— DECLARATION OF FAITH ———

The Lord has conferred upon me every blessing that heaven has to offer.

His eyes are trained upon me, and He relentlessly watches over me to ensure my safety.

He is my ever-present helper who supports me in all that I do.

His face shines upon me to enlighten my way and show me mercy, kindness and an abundance of favor.

In Jesus, He has given me His permanent stamp of approval and has granted me continuous peace.

I bear His name as His own child, and He blesses me with all good things

(Psalm 5:11,12; 23; 84:11; Proverbs 3:3,4; Nehemiah 1:5,6; Ephesians 1:3-14; 2:14)

NUMBERS 22:12

And God said unto Balaam, Thou shalt not go with them; thou shalt not curse the people: for they *are* blessed.

~ PRAYER ~

Father, I thank You that You have commanded Your blessing upon me. No weapon, sorcery, or divination can prosper over me. I am under the commanded blessing of almighty God!

—— DECLARATION OF FAITH ——

The Lord has set His face against anyone who would curse me, for He has declared that I am to be blessed.

(Genesis 12:1-3; 22:17; Exodus 23:22; Numbers 23:20; Ephesians 1:3)

NUMBERS 23:19,20

God *is* not a man, that he should lie; neither the son of man, that he should repent: hath he said, and shall he not do *it?* or hath he spoken, and shall he not make it good? Behold, I have received *commandment* to bless: and he hath blessed; and I cannot reverse it.

~ PRAYER ~

Father, I fully trust Your Word. I do not mentally assent to it but fully trust it. I do not say that I believe and then allow my actions to display mistrust. I know that You make good on everything You have promised me. I understand that there is more to the situation than what my eyes can see. You have given Your command of blessing. It cannot be reversed. Therefore, I am blessed. Period.

—— DECLARATION OF FAITH ——

My Father is not a man that He would lie to me. He does not shrink back from any of His promises. What He has said, He does. What He has spoken comes to pass in my life. No enemy has any power to hinder the Lord's commanded blessing. Therefore, no matter what my situation is, or who comes against me, I will continue to prosper and reap harvests in abundance.

(Isaiah 55:11; 2 Corinthians 1:20; Psalm 119:89,90,138-140,160-162; Mark 11:22-25)

NUMBERS 30:2

If a man vow a vow unto the Lord, or swear an oath to bind his soul with a bond; he shall not break his word, he shall do according to all that proceedeth out of his mouth.

~ PRAYER ~

Father, I choose to be a man/woman of my word. If I say it, I will do it. When I make a pledge, I pay it. I will not go back on any vow. I will keep my word.

────── DECLARATION OF FAITH ──────

I will be honest in all of my dealings, whether with God or with men. When I give my word, I intend to keep it.

(1 Kings 9:4,5; Psalm 26:1,2)

CHAPTER FIVE

DEUTERONOMY

DEUTERONOMY 2:7

For the Lord thy God hath blessed thee in all the works of thy hand: he knoweth thy walking through this great wilderness: these forty years the Lord thy God *hath been* with thee; thou hast lacked nothing.

~ PRAYER ~

I thank You, Father, for being my unfailing provider. You know all that I endure in this life. You know every hardship and trial. In all situations, You are always there for me. You always cause me to prosper in whatever I set my hand to do. You see to it that I am fed and clothed. You never fail to provide for me. Because of You, I shall never want.

——— DECLARATION OF FAITH ———

The Lord my God blesses all the works of my hands.

My walk in this earth is as if I am walking through a great wilderness. The world system is so contrary to my new nature that I am like a stranger in a strange land. But this is not a fearful thing for me, for my Father blesses me abundantly in the land, and I lack no good thing.

(Deuteronomy 28:12; Hebrews 11:13-16; 13:5,6; 1 John 2:15; Psalm 34:10)

DEUTERONOMY 6:5-12

And thou shalt love the Lord thy God with all thine heart, and with all thy soul, and with all thy might. And these words, which I command thee this day, shall be in thine heart: And thou shalt teach them diligently unto thy children, and shalt talk of them when thou sittest in thine house, and when thou walkest by the way, and when thou liest down, and when thou risest up. And thou shalt bind them for a sign upon thine hand, and they shall be as frontlets between thine eyes. And thou shalt write them upon the posts of thy house, and on thy gates. And it shall be, when the Lord thy God shall have brought thee into the land which he sware unto thy fathers, to Abraham, to Isaac, and to Jacob, to give thee great and goodly cities, which thou buildedst not, And houses full of all good *things*, which thou filledst not, and wells digged, which thou diggedst not, vineyards and olive trees, which thou plantedst not; when thou shalt have eaten and be full; *Then* beware lest thou forget the Lord, which brought thee forth out of the land of Egypt, from the house of bondage.

~ *PRAYER* ~

Father, I truly love You with all of my heart. You are the first love of my life. Nothing that I desire compares with You. Knowing You is more important to me than any other pursuit. Therefore, I commit myself to Your Word. I will speak of it morning, noon, and night. It shall encompass all of my conversations. I will speak of it when I sit in my house, when I lie down, when I rise up, and when I walk by the wayside. I will teach it diligently to my children and my grandchildren. It shall be as a sign upon my hand and as frontlets before my eyes. I make my commitment before You to make Your Word the final authority in my life.

Father, I thank You that through Your Word You cause me to inherit great wealth. My houses are filled with good things. I enjoy abundant provision in the land You have given me. I reap the work of others as an inheritance from You. I will not forget that You alone cause me to possess these things. All that I have is from Your hand. I thank You for it all, Father. Praise be to Your holy name!

—— DECLARATION OF FAITH ——

I love my heavenly Father with all of my mind, all of my spirit, and all of my physical strength.

His Word is implanted and deeply rooted in my mind and in my heart.

I whet and sharpen the Word within me that it may pierce through to my mind and my spirit.

I impress the statutes of my God diligently upon the minds of my children. I talk of them when I sit in my house, when I walk by the wayside, when I lie down, and when I rise up. I bind them as a sign on my hand and as an ornament before my eyes. I write them on the door posts of my house and upon my gates.

By these statutes I receive an abundance of blessings.

By the promise of the Lord, I am brought into a prosperous dwelling. Through Him, my home is supplied with an abundance of good things.

All that I have has been given to me by His grace.

It is the Lord who prospers me and gives me an inheritance of things that I did not provide.

I will not forget what He has done for me.

(Deuteronomy 4:29; 8:6-18; Ephesians 3:17; Mark 4:13-20; Psalm 112:1-3; Romans 5:1,2,17; 8:14-17; Philippians 4:19)

DEUTERONOMY 8:10-18

When thou hast eaten and art full, then thou shalt bless the Lord thy God for the good land which he hath given thee. Beware that thou forget not the Lord thy God, in not keeping his commandments, and his judgments, and his statutes, which I command thee this day: Lest *when* thou hast eaten and art full, and hast built goodly houses, and dwelt *therein*; And *when* thy herds and thy flocks multiply, and thy silver and thy gold is multiplied, and all that thou hast is multiplied; Then thine heart be lifted up, and thou forget the Lord thy God, which brought thee forth out of the land of Egypt, from the house of bondage; Who led thee through that great and terrible wilderness, *wherein were* fiery serpents, and scorpions, and drought, where *there was* no water; who brought thee forth water out of the rock of flint; Who fed thee in the wilderness with manna, which thy fathers knew not, that he might humble thee, and that he might prove thee, to do thee good at thy latter end; And thou say in thine heart, My power and the might of *mine* hand hath gotten me this wealth. But thou shalt remember the Lord thy God: for *it is* he that giveth thee power to get wealth, that he may establish his covenant which he sware unto thy fathers, as *it is* this day.

~ PRAYER ~

Father, I bless You for all that You have done for me. I refuse to take any of Your blessings for granted. I know that You alone are my provider and that I would have nothing if it were not for You. You have led me through some very hard times, and I have emerged victorious. I know that no matter where I am in life, You are there to raise me to prominence. You never fail to give me direction and purpose. I recognize that it is You who have promoted me in life. You have given me raises and caused me to advance. It is You who have blessed my bank accounts. It is You who have prospered everything I have set my hand to do. It is You who have given me power to create wealth that You may establish Your covenant with me. I humble myself under Your mighty hand, Father, and I move forward in Your powerful anointing. I am blessed to be a blessing. I have power to create wealth so that I may be a blessing in this earth, and I do not forget to give You the praise, honor, and glory for it.

──── DECLARATION OF FAITH ────

I am careful to keep my Father in my mind at all times. I am resolved to be God-inside minded. When I build magnificent dwellings to live in, I remember Him. As my silver and gold multiplies, I recognize Him. As all that I have increases, I give Him credit. As I dwell in the realm of abundance that He has provided for me, I praise Him.

I always take notice of my provider and recognize that it is He who has brought me out of bondage. He has led me through the wilderness, trampling down the fiery serpents and scorpions along the way.

He has brought me water from the rock and fed me with the manna of heaven. All that He does for me, or to me, is for good. He is good to His children. He is good to me.

I know that it is not my own power that has brought me into the land of abundance. It is God who has given me power and supernatural ability to create wealth in order that He may establish His covenant with me.

I am a wealth creator. Day and night I am given unfailing ideas for the production of wealth in my life.

God expects me to take part in His gracious provision. He wants me to have material things. It is the way I'm supposed to live.

I will never forget Him or take Him for granted. I will never fail to recognize how my wealth has been achieved.

To God be the glory!

(1 John 4:4; Deuteronomy 6:5-13; 28:1-14; Genesis 13:2; 1 Timothy 6:17; Luke 10:19; Nahum 1:7; Galatians 4:5,6; John 10:10; Psalm 34:8-10; 35:27; 91:9-13; 112:1-9; 1 Corinthians 3:16; 10:4)

Deuteronomy 11:13-15

And it shall come to pass, if ye shall hearken diligently unto my commandments which I command you this day, to love the Lord your God, and to serve him with all your heart and with all your soul, That I will give *you* the rain of your land in his due season, the first rain and the latter rain, that thou mayest gather in thy corn, and thy wine, and thine oil. And I will send grass in thy fields for thy cattle, that thou mayest eat and be full.

~ *PRAYER* ~

Father, I hearken diligently to Your commands and precepts. I set You as the first and most vital necessity in my life. I trust in You alone as my provider. You give me the first rain and the latter rain to water the seed that I have sown. You see to it that I have all that I need and more. Everything under my care is covered with Your anointing. I am never without provision, because You are the Lord of my harvest.

—— *DECLARATION OF FAITH* ——

The Lord gives rain to my land in its season, and He blesses all the work of my hands. Every area of my life is saturated in God's blessing and anointing.

The early and the latter rain never let me down. I gather my harvest without fail and my barns always remain full.

(Deuteronomy 28:1-14; Genesis 27:28: Proverbs 3:9,10)

DEUTERONOMY 11:18-28

Therefore shall ye lay up these my words in your heart and in your soul, and bind them for a sign upon your hand, that they may be as frontlets between your eyes. And ye shall teach them your children, speaking of them when thou sittest in thine house, and when thou walkest by the way, when thou liest down, and when thou risest up. And thou shalt write them upon the door posts of thine house, and upon thy gates: That your days may be multiplied, and the days of your children, in the land which the Lord sware unto your fathers to give them, as the days of heaven upon the earth. For if ye shall diligently keep all these commandments which I command you, to do them, to love the Lord your God, to walk in all his ways, and to cleave unto him; Then will the Lord drive out all these nations from before you, and ye shall possess greater nations and mightier than yourselves. Every place whereon the soles of your feet shall tread shall be yours: from the wilderness and Lebanon, from the river, the river Euphrates, even unto the uttermost sea shall your coast be. There shall no man be able to stand before you: *for* the Lord your God shall lay the fear of you and the dread of you upon all the land that ye shall tread upon, as he hath said unto you. Behold, I set before you this day a blessing and a curse; A blessing, if ye obey the commandments of the Lord your God, which I command you this day: And a curse, if ye will not obey the commandments of the Lord your God, but turn aside out of the way which I command you this day, to go after other gods, which ye have not known.

~ *PRAYER* ~

Father, I make it my habit in life to meditate on Your Word. It shall never depart from my lips. I speak of it when I walk by the wayside, when I lie down, and when I rise up. I teach it to my children and my children's children. I keep it on my mind constantly. It encompasses all of my conversations so that I may think and say the right things at all times. By Your Word, Father, my days and the days of my children are multiplied, and I live as the days of heaven even while on the earth.

Father, I commit myself to the keeping of Your Word. I make it the final authority in all circumstances. I know that what You have promised is true. I cling to You with all that I am, Lord. I declare that nothing shall keep me from what You desire for me to have. My purpose is to please You in every way. Increase me in strength, Lord. Make me a strong and powerful man/woman of influence in this earth. Guard my back against the attacks of the ungodly. Put the fear and dread of me on the hearts of my enemies. May they hear Your report of me and flee in stark terror.

You have given me the choice of living under Your blessings or living under the curse. The choice is mine. Therefore, I choose the blessings. Through Your Word, I choose the abundant life that You have called me to live.

———— DECLARATION OF FAITH ————

I give my whole heart, soul, and mind in submission to the Word of God. I meditate upon it in its entirety. I bind all of His statutes as if they were a sign upon my hand and an ornament before my eyes. I write them on the doorposts of my houses and upon my gates.

By the Word of my Father, the days of my children are multiplied.

I love Him and walk in all of His ways.

I am resolved to attach myself to Him in love.

He is my example and is ever with me.

He drives out my enemies from before me and dispossesses them.

Every place that the sole of my foot treads is mine. I hereby claim it for the kingdom of God.

There is not a soul in all of creation who has the ability to triumph over me.

He sets before me the choice of living under His blessing or living under the curse. The choice is mine. I can be blessed if I choose to believe in and adhere to His Word and the statutes therein, or I can be cursed if I choose to reject them.

I choose the blessing!

(Deuteronomy 2:25; 6:4-13; Joshua 1:8; 2:9-11; 24:15; Ephesians 6:1-3; Exodus 14:14; 23:20-30; Romans 8:31; James 4:7)

DEUTERONOMY 14:22-29

Thou shalt truly tithe all the increase of thy seed, that the field bringeth forth year by year. And thou shalt eat before the Lord thy God, in the place which he shall choose to place his name there, the tithe of thy corn, of thy wine, and of thine oil, and the firstlings of thy herds and of thy flocks; that thou mayest learn to fear the Lord thy God always. And if the way be too long for thee, so that thou art not able to carry it; *or* if the place be too far from thee, which the Lord thy God shall choose to set his name there, when the Lord thy God hath blessed thee: Then shalt thou turn *it* into money, and bind up the money in thine hand, and shalt go unto the place which the Lord thy God shall choose: And thou shalt bestow that money for whatsoever thy soul lusteth after, for oxen, or for sheep, or for wine, or for strong drink, or for whatsoever thy soul desireth: and thou shalt eat there before the Lord thy God, and thou shalt rejoice, thou, and thine household, And the Levite that *is* within thy gates; thou shalt not forsake him; for he hath no part nor inheritance with thee.

At the end of three years thou shalt bring forth all the tithe of thine increase the same year, and shalt lay *it* up within thy gates: And the Levite, (because he hath no part nor inheritance with thee,) and the stranger, and the fatherless, and the widow, which *are* within thy gates, shall come, and shall eat and be satisfied; that the Lord thy God may bless thee in all the work of thine hand which thou doest.

~ *PRAYER* ~

Father, I choose to be known to You as a tither. You are the Lord of my harvest. Therefore, I gladly give You a tenth of my increase. I will not expect

Your prosperity without honoring You for what You have already given me. I know that my tithe guarantees Your partnership with me in all of my financial endeavors. For me it is a seed of strength that fills me with Your anointing. By following the precepts of Your system, I enjoy favor and power so that I am successful in everything I set my hand to do. Father, I am so grateful that Your desire for me is to love life and see good days. Through Your blessing I enjoy good things of every kind. I thank You that it is Your perfect will that I drive a nice car and live in a beautiful home. You want me to have the best things in life. You bless my family, friends, pastors, and associates for my sake. The poor and needy find provision through me. What an awesome, wonderful God You are! You make life so satisfying for me, Father. All praise be to Your holy name.

——— DECLARATION OF FAITH ———

I am faithful to pay a tithe on all of my God-given increase. It is holy to the Lord, and I will not rob Him of it.

It is my tithes and offerings that provide for the work of the gospel.

As I provide for the gospel, God provides for me. When I tithe, I have His promise that He will prosper all of the work of my hands. It is a declaration that my finances are under the rulership and guardianship of almighty God!

(Malachi 3:6-12; Nehemiah 10:37-39; Deuteronomy 28:12; Proverbs 3:9,10)

DEUTERONOMY 15:4-6

Save when there shall be no poor among you; for the Lord shall greatly bless thee in the land which the Lord thy God giveth thee *for* an inheritance to possess it: Only if thou carefully hearken unto the voice of the Lord thy God, to observe to do all these commandments which I command thee this day. For the Lord thy God blesseth thee, as he promised thee: and thou shalt lend unto many nations, but thou shalt not borrow; and thou shalt reign over many nations, but they shall not reign over thee.

~ *PRAYER* ~

Father, I thank You that You are a good Father and that You take good care of Your children. You are an unfailing provider. Any time in my life that I have suffered lack was my own doing and not Yours. You have placed within me all of the ability I need to be prosperous and successful. You have made Your promise to me that if I will do things Your way, I will be a lender and not a borrower. I will be promoted to positions of authority and responsibility. Father, I expect these things in my life. I know that You make good on Your Word and that I am blessed to be a blessing in this earth.

———— *DECLARATION OF FAITH* ————

There is no one who is poor in the family of God. I am not, nor will I ever be, poor. My Father has blessed me and has given me an inheritance to possess now in this life. It is an ever-present provision for me that I can draw upon in times of need.

I am careful to keep all of my Father's statutes, and He blesses me just as He has promised. I lend to many and borrow from none.

I will not be the slave of a lender. I am not called to be in bondage but to lead. My Father has ordained that I be the head and not the tail, above only and not beneath.

(Revelation 2:9; 2 Corinthians 8:9; Psalm 37:25; Philippians 4:19; Deuteronomy 28:12-14; Proverbs 22:7)

DEUTERONOMY 15:7-11

If there be among you a poor man of one of thy brethren within any of thy gates in thy land which the Lord thy God giveth thee, thou shalt not harden thine heart, nor shut thine hand from thy poor brother: But thou shalt open thine hand wide unto him, and shalt surely lend him sufficient for his need, *in that* which he wanteth. Beware that there be not a thought in thy wicked heart, saying, The seventh year, the year of release, is at hand; and thine eye be evil against thy poor brother, and thou givest him nought; and he cry unto the Lord against thee, and it be sin unto thee. Thou shalt surely give him, and thine heart shall not be grieved when thou givest unto him: because that for this thing the Lord thy God shall bless thee in all thy works, and in all that thou puttest thine hand unto. For the poor shall never cease out of the land: therefore I command thee, saying, Thou shalt open thine hand wide unto thy brother, to thy poor, and to thy needy, in thy land.

~ *PRAYER* ~

Father, I will not judge my brethren harshly. Those who are poor can find assistance with me. By Your wisdom, Father, I give them what is sufficient for their need. My focus is to bring them out of poverty. My desire is to make sure they are fed, clothed, and given shelter. My goal is to show them the way to prosperity so that they will never suffer lack again. I will not turn my ear or my eye away from them when they ask for my help. I know that when I give to the poor, I am lending to You, Father; and You are faithful to repay me. I am a carrier of Your anointing, and everything I set my hand to do prospers. Therefore, I know that when I give to the poor, I have not lost any of my substance. To the contrary, I have gained favor and blessing because You see all and bless me in return.

———— *DECLARATION OF FAITH* ————

I give to the poor in the land freely and without reservation. Because of this, my Father blesses all of my work. Everything that I set my hand to do prospers, and all of my enterprises are brought to unfailing success. It is my Father's great pleasure to grant me an abundance of good things, and I willingly share my bounty with the poor in the land.

(2 Corinthians 8:2-5; 9:5-8; Genesis 39:1-5; Psalm 41:1-3; 84:11; Luke 12:32; Proverbs 19:17)

DEUTERONOMY 16:17

Every man *shall give* as he is able, according to the blessing of the Lord thy God which he hath given thee.

~ PRAYER ~

Father, I know that You have given me a purpose in life. All that I have is for that purpose. Therefore, I will give as I am able so that my purpose will be fulfilled.

─────── DECLARATION OF FAITH ───────

I am always able to give. The Lord's blessing is ever with me and I am faithful to support His church.

(Malachi 3:6-12; 2 Corinthians 8:12-15)

DEUTERONOMY 18:4,5

The firstfruit *also* of thy corn, of thy wine, and of thine oil, and the first of the fleece of thy sheep, shalt thou give him [your priest/pastor]. For the Lord thy God hath chosen him out of all thy tribes, to stand to minister in the name of the Lord, him and his sons for ever.

~ PRAYER ~

Father, I know that it is not up to me as to how to distribute my tithe. You have placed me in the church as a prince/princess who provides. My tithe goes to the pastor appointed over me so that he/she may use the funds as he/she sees fit.

─────── DECLARATION OF FAITH ───────

I am wise and discerning of the ways of the Lord. He has set a specific system for finances in this earth and I intend to align myself with it. Therefore, I commit 10 percent of my income to the church. I give it without reservation into the hands of my pastor, God's chosen minister, and I fully trust that the right thing will be done with it.

(Malachi 3:6-12; 2 Corinthians 8:1-15)

DEUTERONOMY 23:5

Nevertheless the Lord thy God would not hearken unto Balaam; but the Lord thy God turned the curse into a blessing unto thee, because the Lord thy God loved thee.

~ PRAYER ~

Father, thank You for loving me. I rest completely secure in Your tender care. When my enemies rise against me to curse me and to do me harm, You turn their curses into blessings. You have commanded that I am blessed; and in Jesus, nothing can change that.

—— DECLARATION OF FAITH ——

I am precious to my Father. He does not allow the curses of the ungodly to overtake me. Instead, He turns their every curse into a blessing. God has commanded His blessing on all of my storehouses and accounts. As I follow His ways, they are blessed without fail.

(Deuteronomy 8:18; 28:8; 2 Corinthians 9:6; Psalm 112)

DEUTERONOMY 23:19,20

Thou shalt not lend upon usury to thy brother; usury of money, usury of victuals, usury of any thing that is lent upon usury: Unto a stranger thou mayest lend upon usury; but unto thy brother thou shalt not lend upon usury: that the Lord thy God may bless thee in all that thou settest thine hand to in the land whither thou goest to possess it.

~ PRAYER ~

Father, I refuse to have a heart full of greed and selfishness. I keep my personal relationships separate from my business relationships. I do not look to get rich by taking the wealth of my brothers and sisters. My thoughts are to bless them, not take what they have. I am blessed to be a blessing, not a selfish miser. Father, I know that all that I set my hand to do is blessed because I remain generous and do things the way You want me to do them.

——— *DECLARATION OF FAITH* ———

I keep a clear head in all of my financial dealings. A heart full of greed shall never be found in me. When my brother or sister in Christ is in need, I do not see an opportunity to make money. My concern is that their need is met and that they get back on their feet. God blesses me so that I can be a blessing, not to make me a rich, pitiful miser.

(Proverbs 3:7-10; Proverbs 14:21,31)

DEUTERONOMY 23:21

When thou shalt vow a vow unto the Lord thy God, thou shalt not slack to pay it: for the Lord thy God will surely require it of thee; and it would be sin in thee.

~ *PRAYER* ~

Father, when I vow a vow to You, I will keep my word. I will not carry the sin of a broken vow in my heart. When it is in my hand to pay it, I will pay it.

——— *DECLARATION OF FAITH* ———

I know that my reputation is contained in the words that I speak. Therefore, my word is precious to me. When I give it, I intend to keep it. When I make a vow, I pay it without fail.

(Psalm 65:1; Ecclesiastes 5:4,5)

DEUTERONOMY 24:19-22

When thou cuttest down thine harvest in thy field, and hast forgot a sheaf in the field, thou shalt not go again to fetch it: it shall be for the stranger, for the fatherless, and for the widow: that the Lord thy God may bless thee in all the work of thine hands. When thou beatest thine olive tree, thou shalt not go over the boughs again: it shall be for the stranger, for the fatherless, and for the widow. When thou gatherest the grapes of thy vineyard, thou shalt not glean *it* afterward: it shall be for the stranger, for the fatherless, and for the widow. And thou shalt remember that thou wast a bondman in the land of Egypt: therefore I command thee to do this thing.

~ *PRAYER* ~

Father, I will not forget all that You have done for me and how far You have brought me in life. You have taught me to be good to others and to remain generous to those who are in need. My hands are open wide to the widow, the orphan, and the stranger. Bless them through me, Father. Bless the work of my hands and increase my substance that I may have an abundance to share with others.

———— *DECLARATION OF FAITH* ————

I will not forget what the Lord has done for me. I know that without Him I would be little more than a poor, pitiful, blind, and naked beggar in His sight. But I am not without Him. He has raised me up and seated me with the royalty of heaven. He gives me His unfailing provision and bids me to be a blessing in the earth. Therefore, I shall remember the poor, the stranger, the widow, and the orphan. My harvest is not for myself alone, but to be a blessing and provide for those in need.

(Psalm 72:12-14; Proverbs 19:17; Isaiah 10:1,2)

Deuteronomy 28:1-13

And it shall come to pass, if thou shalt hearken diligently unto the voice of the Lord thy God, to observe *and* to do all his commandments which I command thee this day, that the Lord thy God will set thee on high above all nations of the earth: And all these blessings shall come on thee, and overtake thee, if thou shalt hearken unto the voice of the Lord thy God. Blessed *shalt* thou *be* in the city, and blessed *shalt* thou *be* in the field. Blessed *shall be* the fruit of thy body, and the fruit of thy ground, and the fruit of thy cattle, the increase of thy kine, and the flocks of thy sheep. Blessed *shall be* thy basket and thy store. Blessed *shalt* thou *be* when thou comest in, and blessed *shalt* thou *be* when thou goest out. The Lord shall cause thine enemies that rise up against thee to be smitten before thy face: they shall come out against thee one way, and flee before thee seven ways. The Lord shall command the blessing upon thee in thy storehouses, and in all that thou settest thine hand unto; and he shall bless thee in the land which the Lord thy God giveth thee. The Lord shall establish thee an holy people unto himself, as he hath sworn unto thee, if thou shalt keep the commandments of the Lord thy God, and walk in his ways. And all people of the earth shall see that thou art called by the name of the Lord; and they shall be afraid of thee. And the Lord shall make thee plenteous in goods, in the fruit of thy body, and in the fruit of thy cattle, and in the fruit of thy ground, in the land which the Lord sware unto thy fathers to give thee. The Lord shall open unto thee his good treasure, the heaven to give the rain unto thy land in his season, and to bless all the work of thine hand: and thou shalt lend unto many nations, and thou shalt not borrow. And the Lord shall make thee the head, and not the tail; and thou shalt be above only, and thou shalt not be beneath; if that thou hearken unto the commandments of the Lord thy God, which I command thee this day, to observe and to do *them*:

~ PRAYER ~

Thank You, Father, for the provisions of our covenant. You have freely given me all that I need for success in life. I trust Your Word. I know that all of Your blessings have come upon me, and they shall overtake me. I am blessed in the city and blessed in the country. My children are blessed at my side. My production increases unfailingly under Your anointing. Everything in my care is fruitful and multiplies. I am blessed when I come in and blessed when I go out. When my enemies rise against me they are smitten before my face. They rise against me one way but flee from me in seven ways. You have commanded blessings on all of my storage places and my accounts. They must increase, for You have commanded Your blessings upon them. I am set apart unto You, Father. You alone are my provider. You have charge of my life. You open to me Your good treasure to give rain to my land and to bless all of the works of my hands. Everything I set my hand to do is brought to unfailing success. I have no fear of any job I am given. Your anointing is upon me to see me through. I do all things in Your name; and because of Your anointing, I do all things well. I shall lend to many and borrow from none. I am the head and not the tail, above only and not beneath. I am Your covenant child, Father, and You have blessed me beyond measure.

—————— *DECLARATION OF FAITH* ——————

I heed the voice of the Lord my God. I keep all of His statutes and forever hold His Word dear to my heart, for by the Word of the Lord I am set high above all worldly people.

All of these blessings come upon me and overtake me.

I am blessed (given divine favor, good fortune, happiness, prosperity, and good things of every kind) in the city, and I am blessed (given divine favor, good fortune, happiness, prosperity, and good things of every kind) in the country.

Blessed are my children, my animals, and my garden.

Blessed are the increase of my cattle and the offspring of my flocks.

Blessed are my produce and my gatherings.

I am blessed when I come in and blessed when I go out.

The Lord causes my enemies who rise up against me to be defeated before my face. They rise up against me in one direction but flee from me in seven directions.

The Lord commands blessings on all of my treasuries and on everything that I set my hand to do. He gives me abundant prosperity in the land, which He has given me.

My heavenly Father establishes me before the world as a holy person that He has set apart unto Himself. He makes His declaration that I am His and under His guardianship. This is His promise to me if I hold fast to His Word and walk in His ways.

All of the people of the world clearly see that I am called by the name of the Lord. They recognize that I am in His family. I am His son/daughter and heir, and His blessings are evident in my life. This fact sparks terror in the hearts of my enemies.

The Lord gives me a tremendous surplus of prosperity for my home and family. The fruit of my body, the young of my cattle, and the produce of my ground are blessed with His abundance.

My Lord gives rain to my land precisely when I need it. He has opened to me His heavenly treasury. With perfect timing, He rains it down upon me and blesses all the work of my hands.

He has made me a lender and not a borrower. I shall lend to many and borrow from none.

I am the head and not the tail, above only and not beneath. I am destined to take the lead in any enterprise I undertake. My Father has placed me at the top and never at the bottom, for I keep His Word; and I am careful to adhere to His statutes.

I do not reject any of my Father's requirements. I do not steer away from them even a little to the right or to the left. I set them firm in my heart and place my complete trust in them regardless of what my eyes may see or what other gods may offer.

The righteous requirement of the Law is fulfilled in me. I do not live my life in habitual sin but in holiness before the Lord.

I have been made the very righteousness of God in Christ Jesus.

My trust is firmly planted in Him.

(Genesis 12:1-3; 13:2; 39:2-5; Leviticus 26:9; Ephesians 2:6; 6:12; 2 Corinthians 5:21; Deuteronomy 2:25; 8:18; 11:25; Psalm 1:1-3; 5:11,12; 112:1-3; Philippians 4:17-19; Isaiah 43:1,2; John 15:7; Romans 8:4; Malachi 3:10; 1 John 3:9; Proverbs 3:5,6)

DEUTERONOMY 29:9

Keep therefore the words of this covenant, and do them, that ye may prosper in all that ye do.

~ PRAYER ~

Father, I will keep Your Word and do Your will. I am resolved to walk in Your anointing of prosperity all the days of my life.

───── *DECLARATION OF FAITH* ─────

I remain in God's Word and adhere to the statutes of His covenant, for by them I deal wisely in the affairs of this life and prosper in all that I set my hand to do.

(John 15:7; Joshua 1:8; Psalm 1:1-3; 119:97-101; 105-107; Deuteronomy 28:12)

DEUTERONOMY 30:19

I call heaven and earth to record this day against you, *that* I have set before you life and death, blessing and cursing: therefore choose life, that both thou and thy seed may live:

~ *PRAYER* ~

Father, may it be known to all of heaven and earth that I choose life and blessing so that both me and my seed may live.

───── *DECLARATION OF FAITH* ─────

Heaven and earth are watching to see what life I will choose to live, and they are ready to back me in whatever decision I make. Therefore, I choose life and blessing. I will follow the ways of the Word and live my life under the commanded blessing of Almighty God!

(Psalm 112; Deuteronomy 28:8; Joshua 24:15)

DEUTERONOMY 33:11

Bless, Lord, his substance, and accept the work of his hands: smite through the loins of them that rise against him, and of them that hate him, that they rise not again.

~ *PRAYER* ~

Father, bless my substance. Prosper all the work of my hands. Remove my enemies from me and destroy all that they have set against me. Remove them, Father, so that they may never rise against me again.

——— DECLARATION OF FAITH ———

My substance is blessed of the Lord. All that I have is covered in His anointing. When my enemies rise to steal, kill, or destroy what I have obtained, they are smitten before my face. No enemy has the power to overrun me, for the Lord Himself is my shield and unfailing defense.

(Deuteronomy 28:7; John 10:10; Isaiah 41:10-14)

CHAPTER SIX

JOSHUA

Joshua 1:7-9

There shall not any man be able to stand before thee all the days of thy life: as I was with Moses, *so* I will be with thee: I will not fail thee, nor forsake thee. Be strong and of a good courage: for unto this people shalt thou divide for an inheritance the land, which I sware unto their fathers to give them. Only be thou strong and very courageous, that thou mayest observe to do according to all the law, which Moses my servant commanded thee: turn not from it *to* the right hand or *to* the left, that thou mayest prosper whithersoever thou goest. This book of the law shall not depart out of thy mouth; but thou shalt meditate therein day and night, that thou mayest observe to do according to all that is written therein: for then thou shalt make thy way prosperous, and then thou shalt have good success. Have not I commanded thee? Be strong and of a good courage; be not afraid, neither be thou dismayed: for the Lord thy God *is* with thee whithersoever thou goest.

~ PRAYER ~

Thank You, Father, for never leaving me nor forsaking me. I trust in You with all of my heart. I know that You will never fail me. I have the shield of Your protection and the power of Your anointing in every situation I face. Because of You, no one is able to succeed against me. Therefore, I will be strong and of good courage at all times. I will not allow the ignorance of fear to prevail in my life. I observe Your Word and act on it. I meditate on it day and night so that I may do what its precepts tell me to do. Through Your Word, Father, I prosper wherever I go and in whatever task I undertake. I have good success and deal wisely in all of the affairs of life. Therefore, I am not afraid to step out in faith and take hold of what You have given me.

──── *DECLARATION OF FAITH* ────

Through all the days of my life, not one of my enemies will be able to stand against me.

My Father is with me. Even more so, He has taken up residence inside of me.

Therefore, I will be strong and courageous. I have complete confidence in His ability to give me the victory. I encounter danger and difficulties with firmness and without fear. I am bold, brave, and resolute. I fulfill my calling in a spirit of valor and determination that overcomes any obstacle that the enemy would put in my path.

I do not turn from God's Word. I make it the cornerstone of my life so that I may prosper in all that I do.

I speak the Word continually. I meditate upon it day and night so that I may do all that is written therein. By this, I make my way prosperous, have good success, and deal wisely in all of the affairs of my life.

I do not shrink back from God's Word. I am faithful, strong, vigorous, bold, and very courageous. Fear has no place in my life, for the Lord is with me wherever I go!

(Romans 8:31-37; Ephesians 3:16-19; Hebrew 6:12; Deuteronomy 31:6,7; Psalm 1:1-3; Isaiah 41:10)

JOSHUA 22:8

And he spake unto them, saying, Return with much riches unto your tents, and with very much cattle, with silver, and with gold, and with brass, and with iron, and with very much raiment: divide the spoil of your enemies with your brethren.

~ *PRAYER* ~

Father, through all of the battles of life, I know that You have made me more than a conqueror. I know how to fight the war over my finances and bring home the spoils of victory. You train me thoroughly, Father, and I always emerge triumphant. I set myself firmly on the task of creating wealth. I rummage through the camp of the enemy, take back the riches he has stolen, and divide the spoil with my brethren.

——— *DECLARATION OF FAITH* ———

I spoil the enemy and take back what is rightfully mine. I return from battle with great wealth and riches, with an abundance of livestock and a plentiful supply of silver, gold, bronze, iron, and fine clothing. I return with an abundance of riches and divide the spoils with the church.

(Numbers 31:27; 1 Samuel 30:24; Exodus 12:36; Joel 2:25,26; 2 Corinthians 6:10; 8:9)

CHAPTER SEVEN

JUDGES

❖

JUDGES 18:5

And they said unto him, Ask counsel, we pray thee, of God, that we may know whether our way which we go shall be prosperous.

~ PRAYER ~

Father, I will not pursue gain without Your counsel and approval. I know that only by following Your lead am I guaranteed success.

—— DECLARATION OF FAITH ——

I will not move forward in any financial endeavor unless I have sought the counsel of God on the matter. He is my partner in all things, not just the one who fixes my mistakes. I will not do anything without His guidance, but will remain focused on His will and purpose for my life.

(Joshua 9:1-27; Proverbs 3:32; 12:15; 19:21)

CHAPTER EIGHT

RUTH

RUTH 2:12

The Lord recompense thy work, and a full reward be given thee of the Lord God of Israel, under whose wings thou art come to trust.

~ PRAYER ~

Father, I give You all the praise, honor, and glory for my harvest. You recompense my work and give me a full reward. I will trust You unwaveringly and rest in the shadow of Your wing.

———— DECLARATION OF FAITH ————

I have taken refuge under my Father's wings, and He has given me a full reward. Though I was not a part of His family, He has adopted me, recreated me so that I am actually born again as His own son/daughter, and has given me all of the rights and privileges of an heir to His kingdom. He has comforted me and given me abundant favor in His sight.

(1 Samuel 24:19; Psalm 17:8; 36:7; 58:11; 91:1-4; Galatians 4:4-6; Romans 8:14-17; 2 Corinthians 1:3,4; 5:17)

CHAPTER NINE

1 SAMUEL

1 Samuel 2:7-9

The Lord maketh poor, and maketh rich: he bringeth low, and lifteth up. He raiseth up the poor out of the dust, *and* lifteth up the beggar from the dunghill, to set *them* among princes, and to make them inherit the throne of glory: for the pillars of the earth *are* the Lord's, and he hath set the world upon them. He will keep the feet of his saints, and the wicked shall be silent in darkness; for by strength shall no man prevail.

~ PRAYER ~

Father, You are the God of my promotion. Promote me according to Your Word. Lift me up above the heads of my enemies. Make me the head and not the tail, above only and not beneath. Raise me up from my situation. You are my Father, and I am Your heir. I am an heir to the throne of glory. Set me among princes. Deliver me from the beggarly elements of life. My strength is in You, Father. Keep my feet set on the path of Your prosperity.

——— DECLARATION OF FAITH ———

My Father has raised me from the dust (the place where I am easily driven by the wind).

He has delivered me from the dunghill (the place of deep and filthy poverty). He has separated me from the beggarly elements of life and has seated me with kings and nobles.

He has made me righteous in the earth.

He guards all of my ways and gives me strength to do His will.

My Father thunders from heaven, and my adversaries are defeated.

He gives me strength to walk in His victory and continually intensifies His burden-removing, yoke-destroying power within me.

(Ephesians 4:14; 2 Corinthians 8:9; Romans 5:17; Psalm 18:1-19; 1 John 2:27; 5:18)

CHAPTER TEN

2 SAMUEL

─── ✛ ───

2 SAMUEL 6:11,12a (1 CHRONICLES 13:14)

And the ark of the Lord continued in the house of Obededom the Gittite three months: and the Lord blessed Obededom, and all his household.

And it was told king David, saying, The Lord hath blessed the house of Obededom, and all that *pertaineth* unto him, because of the ark of God.

~ PRAYER ~

Father, in Your presence are blessing and power. You dwell within me and cause all that I do to prosper. Everything around me is affected by Your anointing. All that I have increases because of Your presence, and everyone in my circle of influence enjoys the blessing as well.

──── DECLARATION OF FAITH ────

The presence of God is within me and all around me. Every place I go, God goes. He is my partner in all things. I live for His will and count it a privilege to be a part of what He is doing in the earth.

(1 Corinthians 3:9-16; 2 Corinthians 6:1)

2 SAMUEL 7:28,29

And now, O Lord GOD, thou *art* that God, and thy words be true, and thou hast promised this goodness unto thy servant: Therefore now let it please thee to bless the house of thy servant, that it may continue for ever before thee: for thou, O Lord God, hast spoken *it*: and with thy blessing let the house of thy servant be blessed for ever.

~ *PRAYER* ~

Father, what You have promised is true. Not one word that has gone from Your lips goes unfulfilled. You have promised me blessings and goodness. Therefore, I expect blessings and goodness in my life. I know that it pleases You to bless my house and to prosper my family. With Your blessing, my family and I are blessed forever.

——— *DECLARATION OF FAITH* ———

I know that the Word of the Lord is faithful and true. Nothing that He has promised me fails to come to pass in my life. It pleases Him to bless me with good things of every kind. I fully trust that His blessing is upon my house now and forevermore!

(1 Samuel 20:15; 2 Samuel 23:5; Isaiah 56:5)

CHAPTER ELEVEN

1 KINGS

1 KINGS 2:2,3

I go the way of all the earth: be thou strong therefore, and show thyself a man; And keep the charge of the Lord thy God, to walk in his ways, to keep his statutes, and his commandments, and his judgments, and his testimonies, as it is written in the law of Moses, that thou mayest prosper in all that thou doest, and whithersoever thou turnest thyself:

~ PRAYER ~

Father, I purpose in my heart to be a mature son/daughter. I will not be a child who whines and complains, nor will I let circumstances cause me to cower. Instead I will remain strong and trust in Your Word. I will keep Your charge and walk in Your ways. Your precepts shall be on my lips all the days of my life. Prosper me according to Your promises, Father. Prosper me in every task I undertake.

——— DECLARATION OF FAITH ———

I am girded with the strength of almighty God. I walk in the power of His might and show myself to be His son/daughter. I walk in all of His ways and keep all of His statutes. His precepts and testimonies are forever on my lips.

I am a child of discernment, sound judgment, and discretion. I am enlightened with supernatural ability to learn. God's ways are opened to me; and I am bold, shrewd, and wise in all of the ways of life.

In all that I set my hand to do, I am found to be successful and prosperous.

(Deuteronomy 28:12; 29:9; 31:7; Joshua 1:7,8; 1 Chronicles 22:12,13; Daniel 1:17,20)

1 KINGS 3:11-13 (2 CHRONICLES 1:11,12)

And God said unto him, Because thou hast asked this thing, and hast not asked for thyself long life; neither hast asked riches for thyself, nor hast asked the life of thine enemies; but hast asked for thyself understanding to discern judgment; Behold, I have done according to thy words: lo, I have given thee a wise and an understanding heart; so that there was none like thee before thee, neither after thee shall any arise like unto thee. And I have also given thee that which thou hast not asked, both riches, and honour: so that there shall not be any among the kings like unto thee all thy days.

~ PRAYER ~

Father, I will keep my mind stayed on Your will and purpose for my life. I will not involve myself in a greedy pursuit of riches. Teach me what is important, and give me wisdom to make righteous judgments. Give me a wise and understanding heart that I may know You thoroughly and do Your will without uncertainty. Enlighten the eyes of my understanding so that I may prosper in accordance with Your will.

———— DECLARATION OF FAITH ————

The Lord has given me wisdom and understanding of all of His ways. Through His wisdom I keep a proper focus in my pursuit of prosperity. I am not one who greedily seeks riches and honor for myself. First and foremost I seek the advancement of God's kingdom. It is His will for my life that I pursue and not my own. He gives me the ability to create wealth that He may establish His covenant with me. I will not forget this precious fact.

(Matthew 6:19-33; Deuteronomy 8:17,18; Proverbs 8:13-19)

CHAPTER TWELVE

1 CHRONICLES

1 Chronicles 4:9,10

And Jabez was more honourable than his brethren: and his mother called his name Jabez, saying, Because I bare him with sorrow. And Jabez called on the God of Israel, saying, Oh that thou wouldest bless me indeed, and enlarge my coast, and that thine hand might be with me, and that thou wouldest keep *me* from evil, that it may not grieve me! And God granted him that which he requested.

~ PRAYER ~

Father, I choose to be honorable in Your sight. I don't hold on to false humility that never asks anything of You. I desire tremendous blessing. I cannot be a blessing if I am not blessed myself. Therefore, Father, prosper me and make my name great. Bless me and enlarge my borders. Place Your hand upon me in power and increase all of my substance. Keep me from evil so that my holdings will remain secure. Bless me, Father, and I will be a blessing to honor Your name.

———— DECLARATION OF FAITH ————

I refuse to listen to false and disparaging reports that are contrary to what God says that I am. I am now a born-again child of the living God. I am bold to ask my Father for the deepest desires of my heart, and I lay claim to all that He has given me.

God's hand is ever with me, and His fellowship sustains me. When I enter His throne room, I remain completely honest and without pretentious-ness. Because of this, He gives me a place of high honor in His presence and pours out an unfailing endowment of abundance into my life. He enlarges my borders and shields me from all evil. Under my Father's tender care, I live a life free of worry and misery.

(Philippians 3:13,14; 4:8; Hebrews 4:16; Galatians 3:13; 4:5; 1 John 5:18; Psalm 103:1-18)

1 Chronicles 17:23-27

Therefore now, Lord, let the thing that thou hast spoken concerning thy servant and concerning his house be established forever, and do as thou hast said. Let it even be established, that thy name may be magnified for ever, saying, The Lord of hosts *is* the God of Israel, *even* a God to Israel: and *let* the house of David thy servant *be* established before thee. For thou, O my God, hast told thy servant that thou wilt build him an house: therefore *thy servant hath found in his heart* to pray before thee. And now, Lord, thou art God, and hast promised this goodness unto thy servant: Now therefore let it please thee to bless the house of thy servant, that it may be before thee forever: for thou blessest, O Lord, and *it shall be* blessed for ever.

~ *PRAYER* ~

Father, what You have blessed is blessed forever. David had a yearning to build You a house, and it touched Your heart. I too have a deep-seated desire to build Your house. I seek first the establishment of Your kingdom and Your righteousness. Therefore, look upon me and bless me as You did David. Make me a provider for Your kingdom and build my house as I build Yours. Increase me and prosper me as only You can. Establish me as a house built upon a rock. Bless me with Your blessing, and prosper me according to Your Word.

—— *DECLARATION OF FAITH* ——

The Word of the Lord concerning me has been established for all of eternity. Therefore, I can count on it being accomplished in my life.

I have confidence in my heavenly Father. He is on my side, and I have no reason to fear. I have His Word that He will build my house in safety. My family—all of my posterity—is blessed. I rejoice in God's blessings upon my family, for I have this confidence: what the Lord blesses is blessed forever!

(Isaiah 55:11; Proverbs 21:30; Psalm 4:8; 103:17; 119:89-93; 114-116; 2 Corinthians 1:20; Joshua 1:5-9; Romans 8:31; 1 Peter 5:5-7; Ephesians 1:3,13,14)

1 CHRONICLES 22:11-13

Now, my son, the Lord be with thee; and prosper thou, and build the house of the Lord thy God, as he hath said of thee. Only the Lord give thee wisdom and understanding, and give thee charge concerning Israel, that thou mayest keep the law of the Lord thy God. Then shalt thou prosper, if thou takest heed to fulfill the statutes and judgments which the Lord charged Moses with concerning Israel: be strong, and of good courage; dread not, nor be dismayed.

~ *PRAYER* ~

Father, I know that You are with me. You dwell within me in all of Your power and authority. Prosper me as I advance Your kingdom. Give me wisdom and understanding in the laws of increase. Enlighten my understanding of Your Word. I make my choice to believe. I will not fear or be dismayed under any circumstances. I remain strong and of good courage, for You have promised to prosper me; and You always honor Your Word.

—— *DECLARATION OF FAITH* ——

I am a child of wisdom and understanding. I have been anointed with an abundance of wisdom so that I may be greatly successful in my calling.

Everything that I set my hand to do prospers and is brought to unfailing success.

I refuse to give in to fear and doubt. I am not dismayed. I am strong and of good courage, for the Lord is always with me to shield me and to give me the victory.

(1 Corinthians 1:30: 2:6-16; 15:57; Daniel 1:17,20; Deuteronomy 28:12; Genesis 39:2-5; James 1:5-8; Joshua 1:5-9)

1 CHRONICLES 29:1-18

Furthermore David the king said unto all the congregation, Solomon my son, whom alone God hath chosen, *is yet* young and tender, and the work *is* great: for the palace *is* not for man, but for the Lord God. Now I have prepared with all my might for the house of my God the gold for *things to be made* of gold, and the silver for *things* of silver, and the brass for *things* of brass, the iron for *things* of iron, and wood for *things* of wood; onyx stones, and *stones* to be set, glistering stones, and of divers colours, and all manner of precious stones, and marble stones in abundance. Moreover, because I have set my affection to the house of my God, I have of mine own proper good, of gold and silver, *which* I have given to the house of my God, over and above all that I have prepared for the holy house, *Even* three thousand talents of gold, of the gold of Ophir, and seven thousand talents of refined silver, to overlay the walls of the houses *withal*: The gold for *things* of gold, and the silver for *things* of silver, and for all manner of work *to be made* by the hands of artificers. And who *then* is willing to consecrate his service this day unto the Lord? Then the chief of the fathers and princes of the tribes of Israel, and the captains of thousands and of hundreds, with the rulers of the king's work, offered willingly, And gave for the service of the house of God of gold five thousand talents and ten thousand drams, and of silver ten thousand talents, and of brass eighteen thousand talents, and one hundred thousand talents of iron. And they with whom *precious* stones were found gave *them* to the treasure of the house of the Lord, by the hand of Jehiel the Gershonite. Then the people rejoiced, for that they offered willingly, because with perfect heart they offered willingly to the Lord: and David the king also rejoiced with great joy.

Wherefore David blessed the Lord before all the congregation: and David said, Blessed *be* thou, Lord God of Israel our father, for ever and ever. Thine, O Lord, *is* the greatness, and the power, and the glory, and the victory, and the majesty: for all *that is* in the heaven and in the earth *is thine*; thine *is* the kingdom, O Lord, and thou art exalted as head above all. Both riches and honour *come* of thee, and thou reignest over all; and in thine hand *is* power and might; and in thine hand *it is* to make great, and to give strength unto all. Now therefore, our God, we thank thee, and praise thy glorious name. But who *am* I, and what *is* my people, that we should be able to offer so willingly after this sort? for all things *come* of thee, and of thine own have we given thee.

For we *are* strangers before thee, and sojourners, as *were* all our fathers: our days on the earth *are* as a shadow, and *there is* none abiding. O Lord our God, all this store that we have prepared to build thee an house for thine holy name *cometh* of thine hand, and *is* all thine own. I know also, my God, that thou triest the heart, and hast pleasure in uprightness. As for me, in the uprightness of mine heart I have willingly offered all these things: and now have I seen with joy thy people, which are present here, to offer willingly unto thee. O Lord God of Abraham, Isaac, and of Israel, our fathers, keep this for ever in the imagination of the thoughts of the heart of thy people, and prepare their heart unto thee.

~ *PRAYER* ~

Father, You are more important to me than anything. It is my desire to see my church filled with the best furnishings that money can buy. Your representative house should be an honorable house. Therefore, I give willingly to my church that I may honor You. My pastor does not have to beg me for money. I prepare my giving even before I get to church. Father, Yours is the greatness, the power, the glory, the victory, and the majesty. How can I not give to honor You? All that I have is Yours to begin with. You are exalted as head over all. I am not the proprietor of my finances. I am merely Your steward. All riches and honor come from You. In Your hand are all power and might. It is in Your hand to make great and give strength. So I thank You, Father. You turn to me and bless me for love's sake. I praise You for Your unfailing provision. All that I have is from You. Of Your own substance I give. Accept my offerings, Father. I give them willingly and in faith. I know that You will take what I give and multiply it back to me good measure, pressed down, shaken together, and running over. You are faithful, Father, and I will be faithful too.

DECLARATION OF FAITH

I give offerings to the Lord freely—an abundance of riches—with a willing heart. I consecrate myself to giving as one consecrates himself to the priesthood. For me, it is a lifelong commitment and a joy. I am a happy and hilarious giver!

I am a child of the kingdom where my Father reigns supreme. His is the greatness, the power, the glory, the victory, and the majesty in my life. All of the heavens and the earth are His, and He is exalted as head over all. He is my Father! It is He who grants me riches and honor—who makes me strong and causes me to become great.

God's name is my family name. I am His heir.

I know that all that I have comes from the Lord. All that I can give was His to begin with. Therefore, all of my strength and ability to give offerings comes from Him alone. I am humbled by the realization that I am a steward, not a proprietor.

Therefore, all of my boasting is in Him! All of my joy is in Him! I do not give grudgingly, but cheerfully. I consider it an honor and a privilege to be able to give for the support of the kingdom. My giving is a declaration that God alone is in charge of my prosperity.

My purpose in life is to live the kingdom way—in God's way of being and doing things. He is the director of my thoughts and purposes. He establishes my heart as loyal toward Him and gives me every ability to walk in the power of His anointing.

(2 Corinthians 8:2-5,12; 9:1,2,5-11; Exodus 35:21-35; Luke 6:38; 12:33,34; Galatians 4:5,6; 1 Timothy 1:17; Ephesians 1:17-23; Genesis 12:1-3; Romans 8:32; 14:17; Malachi 3:6-12; Matthew 6:33; Psalm 112)

1 CHRONICLES 29:28

And he died in a good old age, full of days, riches, and honour: and Solomon his son reigned in his stead.

~ PRAYER ~

Father, I purpose in my heart to be wise with my finances. I will remain faithful all the days of my life. I will treat my money with respect and use it as a tool to advance Your kingdom. Through faithfulness, I will leave this world at a ripe old age with riches and honor as an inheritance for my children.

—————— DECLARATION OF FAITH ——————

I live out my life in satisfaction with a full number of days and will die at a ripe old age with riches and honor as an inheritance for my posterity.

(Isaiah 46:4; Psalm 91:16; 112; 119:37; Job 5:26; 29:18; Proverbs 13:22)

CHAPTER THIRTEEN

2 CHRONICLES

2 CHRONICLES 17:3-6a

And the Lord was with Jehoshaphat, because he walked in the first ways of his father David, and sought not unto Baalim; But sought to the *Lord* God of his father, and walked in his commandments, and not after the doings of Israel. Therefore the Lord stablished the kingdom in his hand; and all Judah brought to Jehoshaphat presents; and he had riches and honour in abundance. And his heart was lifted up in the ways of the Lord:

~ PRAYER ~

Father, I choose to walk in Your ways and build my wealth according to Your standards. I will not seek selfish gain or look to cheat others to further my own prosperity. I seek You with all of my heart. I am a doer of Your Word and not a hearer only. Establish me in Your righteousness. Prosper me and increase my holdings according to the precepts and promises You have given. Bring to me riches and honor in abundance so that I may be a blessing in this earth. My heart is lifted up in Your ways, Father. Glory to Your name!

—— DECLARATION OF FAITH ——

My heart is filled with courage and joy in the ways of God. I closely follow the godly counsel that the Lord places in my life. I refuse to follow after the ways of evil men who seek prosperity at any cost. I do not tolerate the devil's presence in my life. His ways bring fear, sorrow, pain, and destruction.

I follow the ways of the Lord and cast the devil, and everything that he stands for, away from my presence!

(Psalm 1:1-3; 2 Timothy 1:7; James 4:7; Mark 16:17; Luke 9:1; 10:17-19)

2 CHRONICLES 20:15-25

And he said, Hearken ye, all Judah, and ye inhabitants of Jerusalem, and thou king Jehoshaphat, Thus saith the Lord unto you, Be not afraid nor dismayed by reason of this great multitude; for the battle *is* not yours, but God's. To morrow go ye down against them: behold, they come up by the cliff of Ziz; and ye shall find them at the end of the brook, before the wilderness of Jeruel. Ye shall not *need* to fight in this *battle*: set yourselves, stand ye *still*, and see the salvation of the Lord with you, O Judah and Jerusalem: fear not, nor be dismayed; to morrow go out against them: for the Lord *will be* with you. And Jehoshaphat bowed his head with *his* face to the ground: and all Judah and the inhabitants of Jerusalem fell before the Lord, worshipping the Lord. And the Levites, of the children of the Kohathites, and of the children of the Korhites, stood up to praise the Lord God of Israel with a loud voice on high.And they rose early in the morning, and went forth into the wilderness of Tekoa: and as they went forth, Jehoshaphat stood and said, Hear me, O Judah, and ye inhabitants of Jerusalem; Believe in the Lord your God, so shall ye be established; believe his prophets, so shall ye prosper. And when he had consulted with the people, he appointed singers unto the Lord, and that should praise the beauty of holiness, as they went out before the army, and to say, Praise the Lord; for his mercy *endureth* for ever. And when they began to sing and to praise, the Lord set ambushments against the children of Ammon, Moab, and mount Seir, which were come against Judah; and they were smitten. For the children of Ammon and Moab stood up against the inhabitants of mount Seir, utterly to slay and destroy *them*: and when they had made an end of the inhabitants of Seir, every one helped to destroy another. And when Judah came toward the watch tower in the wilderness, they looked unto the multitude, and, behold, they *were* dead bodies fallen to the earth, and none escaped. And when Jehoshaphat and his people came to take away the spoil of them, they found among them in abundance both riches with the dead bodies, and precious jewels, which they stripped off for themselves, more than they could carry away: and they were three days in gathering of the spoil, it was so much.

~ PRAYER ~

Father, I thank You that You personally fight my battles for me. You take up the battle as Your own and fight for me. It is therefore impossible for me to ever be defeated. No matter how strong the enemy looks, or how many forces he has on his side, I will not be afraid. You are on my side! I will stand my ground and sing aloud Your praises. Victory is mine in Jesus' name!

Father, I make my quality choice right now to believe in You. I know that in You I am firmly established. You give revelation to Your prophets, and I choose to believe. I prosper under my pastor's guidance. I give You praise and honor for the tremendous love You have shown me. I praise the beauty of Your holiness. I praise You for Your grace and mercy. I have no fear, because I know You are with me. I am surrounded by Your favor and blessings continually. In the midst of turmoil and battles, I praise Your holy name! Set an ambush on those who have come against me, Father. Set them to confusion and make them fall by a sword from their own camp. Let none of them escape.

I know I shall enjoy the fruit of Your victory. I emerge unscathed from every battle. I spoil the camp of the enemy and find riches in abundance. What the enemy leaves behind, I will possess.

Father, I exalt and magnify Your holy name! You always cause me to triumph so that I may enjoy the spoils of war.

———— DECLARATION OF FAITH ————

I have set my face like flint to be true to the Lord. I hold fast to His promises and trust in the security of our covenant. Therefore, I remain confident that when the enemy attacks me with a great horde of allies bent on my destruction, the Lord shall stand to His feet and make His proclamation, "This battle is Mine!"

Whom shall I fear? Who can defeat my Father in heaven? He is the Lord of Hosts. I shall not be afraid. I shall take my position and stand my ground!

I listen for my Father's commands. I take heed to the voice of His prophets, and I prosper in the midst of the turmoil. I praise His name for the victory even in the heat of the battle. I give Him glory, for His mercy and loving-kindness endure forever!

I shall see the enemy fall in a great destruction, for the battle belongs to the Lord! Despite the battles that I must endure, my Father showers me with an endless supply of blessings.

(Deuteronomy 1:29,30; 20:14; 1 Samuel 14:20; 17:47; Exodus 3:22; 14:13,14; Numbers 14:9; Isaiah 7:9; Judges 7:22; 2 Corinthians 1:20; Romans 8:31; Psalm 91; 136; Luke 10:17-19; Genesis 12:1-3)

2 Chronicles 26:5

And he sought God in the days of Zechariah, who had understanding in the visions of God: and as long as he sought the Lord, God made him to prosper.

~ PRAYER ~

Father, I thank You for giving me understanding of Your will and of Your ways. I will seek Your face continually and prosper in everything I set my hand to do.

——— DECLARATION OF FAITH ———

I stand on the Lord's promise that as long as I seek Him, He will give me success in all that I do.

(Matthew 6:33; Deuteronomy 28:1-14; Genesis 39:2-5; 2 Chronicles 20:20)

2 Chronicles 31:6-10

And *concerning* the children of Israel and Judah, that dwelt in the cities of Judah, they also brought in the tithe of oxen and sheep, and the tithe of holy things which were consecrated unto the Lord their God, and laid *them* by heaps. In the third month they began to lay the foundation of the heaps, and finished *them* in the seventh month. And when Hezekiah and the princes came and saw the heaps, they blessed the Lord, and his people Israel. Then Hezekiah questioned with the priests and the Levites concerning the heaps.

And Azariah the chief priest of the house of Zadok answered him, and said, Since *the people* began to bring the offerings into the house of the Lord, we have had enough to eat, and have left plenty: for the Lord hath blessed his people; and that which is left *is* this great store.

~ *PRAYER* ~

Father, I know I can never outgive You. You bless me continually and multiply back to me all that I have sown into Your kingdom. It is easy to give to such a loving Father. Your faithfulness is unfailing. Therefore, I give to You willingly, with a cheerful heart of faith. I know that in You I will always have enough with plenty to spare. I only ask that You increase me even more, Father. Increase my holdings so that I may give even more bountifully and be a blessing to others.

———— *DECLARATION OF FAITH* ————

The Lord continually increases my ability to give. He gives me seed to sow and bread to eat. As I faithfully sow into His kingdom, He causes my finances to increase to such measure that I can literally abound to every good work. Because I freely give my offerings in the church, I have enough to eat and plenty to spare. When money is needed, I have it to give, for the Lord has blessed me with an enormous blessing and has granted me an excessive bounty.

(2 Corinthians 9:6-11; Malachi 3:10,11; Proverbs 3:9,10; Exodus 36:2-7)

2 CHRONICLES 31:20,21

And thus did Hezekiah throughout all Judah, and wrought *that which was* good and right and truth before the Lord his God. And in every work that he began in the service of the house of God, and in the law, and in the commandments, to seek his God, he did *it* with all his heart, and prospered.

~ *PRAYER* ~

Father, You have all of my heart. All that I am and all that I do is in Your name. Prosper me according to Your Word. I give my life in service to Your cause.

─────── *DECLARATION OF FAITH* ───────

I choose to do what is good, right, and faithful before the Lord. In everything that I do, in my service to the church and obedience to God's ways, I work whole-heartedly, seeking the advancement of His kingdom. And in doing so, I prosper.

(Joshua 1:8; Matthew 6:33; 2 Kings 20:3; Psalm 1:1-3; Colossians 3:17)

2 CHRONICLES 32:27-30

And Hezekiah had exceeding much riches and honour: and he made himself treasuries for silver, and for gold, and for precious stones, and for spices, and for shields, and for all manner of pleasant jewels; Storehouses also for the increase of corn, and wine, and oil; and stalls for all manner of beasts, and cotes for flocks. Moreover he provided him cities, and possessions of flocks and herds in abundance: for God had given him substance very much. This same Hezekiah also stopped the upper watercourse of Gihon, and brought it straight down to the west side of the city of David. And Hezekiah prospered in all his works.

~ *PRAYER* ~

Father, I thank You for pouring out Your abundance into my life. You richly fill all of my storehouses and accounts. My substance increases more and more. You fill my treasuries with silver, gold, and precious stones. All of my work prospers under Your anointing. Your provision, Father, is always more than enough.

─────── *DECLARATION OF FAITH* ───────

In Christ, I have been granted a position of high honor and have been given great riches. As I draw upon His provision, my dwellings are well supplied. It is God's will that my home be arrayed in the finest that heaven has to offer.

I am a builder in life, and I continually increase. Everything that I set my hand to do prospers.

(Ephesians 1:3; 2:6; Philippians 4:17-19; 2 Corinthians 6:10; 8:9; Psalm 112:1-3; Genesis 13:2; 39:2-5; Galatians 3:9-14; Deuteronomy 8:6-18; 28:1-14)

CHAPTER FOURTEEN

NEHEMIAH

✦

NEHEMIAH 2:20a

Then answered I them, and said unto them, The God of heaven, he will prosper us; therefore we his servants will arise and build:

~ *PRAYER* ~

Father, I thank You for making me a builder in life. I shall advance Your kingdom. I long to be a part of building projects and every endeavor that causes Your kingdom to increase. Bless me financially, Father. Prosper me according to Your Word, and I will arise and build.

—— *DECLARATION OF FAITH* ——

My Father grants me success in all that I set my hand to do. He bids me to lay claim to my rightful inheritance in this earth.

(Genesis 39:2-5; Deuteronomy 28:12; Joshua 1:8; Galatians 4:5,6; Romans 8:17)

CHAPTER FIFTEEN

JOB

JOB 1:3

His substance also was seven thousand sheep, and three thousand camels, and five hundred yoke of oxen, and five hundred she asses, and a very great household; so that this man was the greatest of all the men of the east.

~ PRAYER ~

Father, Your blessing exceeds the blessing of kings. In You I have abundance to the extreme and enjoy a very great household. You bless me and make my name great so that I may be a blessing in this earth.

—— DECLARATION OF FAITH ——

The Lord causes my substance to increase continually. His undeniable blessing is evident in my life. The world cannot help but take notice of the love and favor He shows me.

(Psalm 112; Genesis 26:14)

JOB 1:10

Hast not thou made an hedge about him, and about his house, and about all that he hath on every side? thou hast blessed the work of his hands, and his substance is increased in the land.

~ PRAYER ~

Father, enclose me in the hedge of Your protection. Secure my home and all that I have. Guard me on every side. Bless the work of my hands and expand my borders. Increase my substance, Father, and make my influence felt throughout the earth.

———— *DECLARATION OF FAITH* ————

God has placed a hedge of protection around my family, myself, and everything that I have; and the enemy cannot penetrate it no matter how hard he tries.

The Lord blesses all of the work of my hands, making me prosperous and very wealthy.

(Psalm 5:11,12; 34:7; 112:1-3; Job 3:23; 1 John 5:18; Deuteronomy 8:18; 28:12)

JOB 8:6,7

If thou *wert* pure and upright; surely now he would awake for thee, and make the habitation of thy righteousness prosperous. Though thy beginning was small, yet thy latter end should greatly increase.

~ *PRAYER* ~

Father, I won't pay attention to what my eyes see. I know that there is more to the story than what is displayed in my circumstances. My beginnings may look small, but my latter end shall greatly increase. You are now causing my substance to increase immeasurably. My habitation is prosperous indeed.

———— *DECLARATION OF FAITH* ————

I live a pure and upright life before my heavenly Father. I continually look to Him as my sole provider. I call to Him, and He comes to my rescue. He restores me to my rightful place in this earth. Though my beginnings be humble, my latter end will be a powerful testimony of God's prosperity and success.

(Romans 12:1; Philippians 4:19; Genesis 22:14; Psalm 18:1-19; Job 42:12)

JOB 22:21-30

Acquaint now thyself with him, and be at peace: thereby good shall come unto thee. Receive, I pray thee, the law from his mouth, and lay up his words in thine heart. If thou return to the Almighty, thou shalt be built up, thou shalt put away iniquity far from thy tabernacles. Then shalt thou lay up gold as dust, and the *gold* of Ophir as the stones of the brooks. Yea, the Almighty shall be thy defence, and thou shalt have plenty of silver. For then shalt thou have thy delight in the Almighty, and shalt lift up thy face unto God. Thou shalt make thy prayer unto him, and he shall hear thee, and thou shalt pay thy vows. Thou shalt also decree a thing, and it shall be established unto thee: and the light shall shine upon thy ways. When *men* are cast down, then thou shalt say, *There is* lifting up; and he shall save the humble person. He shall deliver the island of the innocent: and it is delivered by the pureness of thine hands.

~ PRAYER ~

Father, it is so good to be acquainted with You. I am happy to be Your child. You are good to me, and Your mercy towards me is everlasting. I delight myself in You and lift up my face to receive Your presence. Peace floods my spirit as I fellowship with You. You cause good things to happen to me every day.

I receive Your Word, Father. I lay up Your precepts on the tablet of my heart. Build me up according to Your promise. Anoint me to lay up gold as dust in my accounts. Grant me plenty of silver. Fill my accounts with abundant provision, and be my defense against robbery and crooked individuals.

I am resolved to pay my vows. I do not promise and then go back on my word. Therefore, I decree a thing and trust that You will establish it. I decree that You will _____

_____

_____

_____ in honor of my vow. You shine light on all of my ways and cause me to fully understand the direction I must take. Your blessings on me shall pour into the lives of others. When others are cast down, I will say, "There is lifting up," and You shall save the humble person through me. In You, Father, there is deliverance from the snares of life. You deliver me from all poverty and lack, and You strengthen my hands so that I may deliver others.

——— *DECLARATION OF FAITH* ———

I am freely submitted to God to walk in all of His ways. There is peace between us; and by His divine enabling, He brings me to the place of abundant prosperity. I accept all of His instructions and lay up His words in the treasury of my heart.

My heavenly Father hears my every prayer, and I am faithful to pay all of my vows to Him. What I decide on is firmly established, and His light shines on all of my ways.

When I humble myself under His mighty hand, He exalts me in due time.

He delights in me as His own son/daughter and anoints me to do His will in the earth.

(1 Peter 5:5-7; John 10:10; Psalm 50:14,15; 119:11-16; Deuteronomy 28:1-14; Romans 5:1; 1 John 5:14,15; James 4:3; 5:14-16; Ezekiel 22:30; Galatians 4:4-7)

JOB 29:1-25

Moreover Job continued his parable, and said, Oh that I were as *in* months past, as *in* the days *when* God preserved me; When his candle shined upon my head, *and when* by his light I walked *through* darkness; As I was in the days of my youth, when the secret of God *was* upon my tabernacle; When the Almighty *was* yet with me, *when* my children *were* about me; When I washed my steps with butter, and the rock poured me out rivers of oil;

When I went out to the gate through the city, *when* I prepared my seat in the street! The young men saw me, and hid themselves: and the aged arose, *and* stood up. The princes refrained talking, and laid *their* hand on their mouth. The nobles held their peace, and their tongue cleaved to the roof of their mouth. When the ear heard *me*, then it blessed me; and when the eye saw *me*, it gave witness to me: Because I delivered the poor that cried, and the fatherless, and *him that had* none to help him. The blessing of him that was ready to perish came upon me: and I caused the widow's heart to sing for joy. I put on righteousness, and it clothed me: my judgment *was* as a robe and a diadem. I was eyes to the blind, and feet *was* I to the lame. I *was* a father to the poor: and the cause *which* I knew not I searched out. And I brake the jaws of the wicked, and plucked the spoil out of his teeth.

Then I said, I shall die in my nest, and I shall multiply *my* days as the sand. My root *was* spread out by the waters, and the dew lay all night upon my branch. My glory *was* fresh in me, and my bow was renewed in my hand. Unto me *men* gave ear, and waited, and kept silence at my counsel. After my words they spake not again; and my speech dropped upon them. And they waited for me as for the rain; and they opened their mouth wide *as* for the latter rain. *If* I laughed on them, they believed *it* not; and the light of my countenance they cast not down. I chose out their way, and sat chief, and dwelt as a king in the army, as one *that* comforteth the mourners.

~ PRAYER ~

Father, I trust in Your goodness. You always preserve me from harm and guide me through the dark paths of life. You share with me the hidden secrets and cause me to prosper no matter what is going on around me. You teach me to walk as a son of God. Every place that the sole of my foot treads is covered in Your presence. In You, I have unfailing provision. You anoint me to be a powerful influence in the earth. You cause people to recognize Your presence in my life, and they respect me for it. Even rulers and those in authority incline their ears to me. They bless me and court my favor. For You prosper everything I set out to do. You make me a deliverer to the poor and needy. You make me a champion to victims of abuse. I break the jaw of the wicked one and snatch his victims right from his teeth. The widow and the orphan are blessed because of me. I cause the widow's heart to sing for joy. I put on Your righteousness, Father, and it clothes me. My judgment is like a royal robe and a diadem. I am eyes to the blind and feet to the lame. I am a father to the poor to guide them in the ways of prosperity. When I need wisdom and understanding, You supply them to me liberally. Others see it and seek my counsel and advice. You ground me in the foundation of Your Word and hedge me in with Your favor on all sides. People wait for me as for the rain and long for the goodness that I bring them. They long to hear my good report. They know that the words I give them will bring them life. Father, You have even anointed my smile. When others are discouraged, my smile alone can lift their spirits. You cause me to live among the people as a king among his troops and as one who comforts those who mourn. You make me to be a good son/daughter, Father, and a true ambassador of Your kingdom.

―――――― *DECLARATION OF FAITH* ――――――

The Lord is my intimate friend. His companionship is a blessing to my household.

He holds His lamp before me to light my way in the darkness.

The Almighty is ever with me, and my children dwell in safety at my side. Everything that I do succeeds and nothing is too difficult for me to accomplish. When I enter the city and sit with my friends in the public square, people greet me with respect. I am honored by everyone in town because of my Father's favor.

When I speak, people listen and hang on my every word.

People who know me speak well of me, and my reputation goes before me to make my Father proud.

I am known for helping people in distress and for standing up for those who are in need.

My presence makes the widow's heart sing. She is overjoyed at all of my visits. All of my dealings with people are for good, and I am known as a fair and generous man/woman.

I am eyes to the blind and feet to the lame, a father/mother to the orphan, and a champion to victims of abuse.

I live a life deeply rooted and well watered.

My soul is covered in God's glory.

Men and women listen when I speak and afterwards ponder the words that God has given me. When I smile at them, their faces light up and their troubles take flight. I am a leader among them and set the pace by which they live.

I am the very image of my Father in heaven.

(John 15:14,15; James 2:23; Psalm 72:4; 90:16; 91:15; 103:17; 115:13,14; 119:105; Deuteronomy 28:9-13; Matthew 17:20; 1 Kings 4:34; 1 Corinthians 1:30; Acts 6:10; Proverbs 3:3,4; 29:7; James 1:27; Isaiah 61:1-3; Genesis 1:26,27; 12:1-3)

JOB 36:7-11

He withdraweth not his eyes from the righteous: but with kings *are they* on the throne; yea, he doth establish them for ever, and they are exalted. And if *they be* bound in fetters, *and* be holden in cords of affliction; Then he showeth them their work, and their transgressions that they have exceeded. He openeth also their ear to discipline, and commandeth that they return from iniquity. If they obey and serve *him*, they shall spend their days in prosperity, and their years in pleasures.

~ PRAYER ~

Father, I am humbled knowing that Your eyes never leave me. You keep watch over me as the apple of Your eye. In righteousness You establish me forever. When I turn the wrong way and enter the realm of bondage, You show me my mistake and guide me back on the path of freedom. Open the eyes of my understanding, Lord. Make me to clearly see the path of victory and prosperity.

Father, I commit myself to obey and serve You all the days of my life. Through Your anointing I will spend my days in prosperity and my years in pleasures.

DECLARATION OF FAITH

The Lord's eyes never leave me. He keeps watch over all that I do and is my ever-present help to ensure my success.

He corrects and disciplines me when I waiver and makes sure that I know what I have done wrong. He then sets me back on the path of His prosperity and sees to it that I spend my days in peace and contentment.

(Nehemiah 1:5,6; Psalm 33:18; 34:15; 46:1; 91:15,16; Hebrews 12:1-16; 13:5,6; Joel 2:25,26)

JOB 36:15,16

He delivereth the poor in his affliction, and openeth their ears in oppression. Even so would he have removed thee out of the strait *into* a broad place, where *there is* no straitness; and that which should be set on thy table *should be* full of fatness.

~ *PRAYER* ~

Father, I thank You for delivering me from poverty. I lack no good thing as I faithfully walk in Your ways. You have brought me out into a broad place. I am not confined by lack of provision. My table is supplied richly. All that is set on my table is full of richness and luxury.

—— *DECLARATION OF FAITH* ——

My Father coaxes me away from life's troubles. He speaks to me in the midst of them, drawing me out into a spacious place, free of restrictions, and bids me to eat at the table of His blessings.

(Isaiah 30:21; 1 John 1:3-7; Psalm 18:19; 23:5; 36:8; 112:1-3; 118:5)

JOB 42:10-12

And the Lord turned the captivity of Job, when he prayed for his friends: also the Lord gave Job twice as much as he had before. Then came there unto him all his brethren, and all his sisters, and all they that had been of his acquaintance before, and did eat bread with him in his house: and they bemoaned him, and comforted him over all the evil that the Lord had brought upon him: every man also gave him a piece of money, and every one an earring of gold. So the Lord blessed the latter end of Job more than his beginning: for he had fourteen thousand sheep, and six thousand camels, and a thousand yoke of oxen, and a thousand she asses.

~ PRAYER ~

Father, I thank You that You always turn my captivity. When I endure hardship, I always emerge with twice as much as what I started with. I cannot be destroyed, because You, Father, are upholding me with Your right hand. Therefore, I will keep my mind properly focused. I will not hold grudges or seek ill will on others. To the contrary, I pray for them that they might live good lives and enjoy Your salvation and prosperity.

Father, because of my generosity You cause others to give back to me good measure, pressed down, shaken together, and running over. My latter end is blessed far more than my beginning. I thank You for taking such good care of me.

──── DECLARATION OF FAITH ────

My Father lifts me up from the thief's attacks and brings forth my prosperity. He restores double what the enemy has taken and sets me on the path of ever-increasing abundance so that the latter part of my life is much greater than the former.

(John 10:10; Colossians 1:13; Deuteronomy 8:18; James 5:11; Exodus 22:4,7,9; Zechariah 9:11-13; Joel 2:25,26)

CHAPTER SIXTEEN

PSALMS

PSALM 1:1-3

Blessed *is* the man that walketh not in the counsel of the ungodly, nor standeth in the way of sinners, nor sitteth in the seat of the scornful. But his delight *is* in the law of the Lord; and in his law doth he meditate day and night. And he shall be like a tree planted by the rivers of water, that bringeth forth his fruit in his season; his leaf also shall not wither; and whatsoever he doeth shall prosper.

~ PRAYER ~

Father, I do not walk in the counsel of the ungodly, I do not participate in sinful activities, and I do not act scornfully towards others. My delight is in Your Word. In it I meditate day and night.

I thank You, Father, that Your anointing flows mightily through me. I am like a tree that is planted by rivers of water. I bring forth fruit in abundance. My leaf never withers, my accounts do not dwindle, and everything that I set my hand to do prospers.

──── DECLARATION OF FAITH ────

I move forward in life, in happiness, and in peace.

I follow the ways of the Word, and I am blessed in all that I do.

I do not follow the advice nor the pattern of living of those who spurn the guidance of my heavenly Father.

I withdraw myself from the sinful activities that the world accepts.

I refuse to take sides with fools and mockers who scoff at morality.

My delight, gratification, and satisfaction are in the Word of the living God. In it I meditate—speaking it to myself day and night—engrafting and rooting it deeply into my spirit. By this, my way is made prosperous; and I achieve tremendous success.

I am like a tree that is planted beside fresh water springs. I bear the best of fruit in my life.

Everything about me exudes life, and everything that I set my hand to do prospers.

(Proverbs 4:14; Jeremiah 15:17; Joshua 1:8; Psalm 119:14-16,23,24; Genesis 39:2-5)

PSALM 3:1-8

Lord, how are they increased that trouble me! many *are* they that rise up against me.

Many *there be* which say of my soul, *There is* no help for him in God. Selah.

But thou, O Lord, *art* a shield for me; my glory, and the lifter up of mine head.

I cried unto the Lord with my voice, and he heard me out of his holy hill. Selah.

I laid me down and slept; I awaked; for the Lord sustained me.

I will not be afraid of ten thousands of people, that have set *themselves* against me round about.

Arise, O Lord; save me, O my God: for thou hast smitten all mine enemies *upon* the cheek bone; thou hast broken the teeth of the ungodly.

Salvation *belongeth* unto the Lord: thy blessing *is* upon thy people. Selah.

~ PRAYER ~

Father, I know that You are faithful. You do not leave me at the mercy of others. You are a shield for me, my glory and the lifter of my head. You never fail to answer me when I call out to You. You are with me at all times and in every circumstance. You sustain me through the night hours, and I awake refreshed and ready to meet a new day. I have no fear, Father, for You are always with me. I am not afraid no matter how many people rise against me. No matter how strong they are, they are no match for You. You break their teeth and take them out of the equation. Their weapons are useless against me because You are the God of my salvation. Blessings are upon me and curses cannot cling to me, for You have commanded that I be blessed!

——— DECLARATION OF FAITH ———

When many rise against me to trouble me, saying, "There is no help for him/her in God," I will not throw down my faith. My heavenly Father is faithful. He is my shield against all trouble and persecution. He lifts my head in honor and covers me with His glory as a testimony to all of my enemies.

I stretch myself out to sleep in perfect peace, free of all anxiety.

When my rest is complete, I awake again and find the Lord at my side, keeping guard over my life. He is an ever-present sentinel who never fails to protect me from the attacks of my enemies. I will not fear even tens of thousands drawn up against me, for I am never alone. The Lord of Hosts is my companion and ally. He strikes my enemies down in a fierce display of His power. His mighty fist shatters their teeth.

So let the enemy bark all he wants. His bite is nothing to me.

(Leviticus 26:6, 13; Psalm 4:8; 9:13; 23:4; 27:3,6; 121; 127:2; Hebrews 10:35; Romans 1:16; 8:30-37; 2 Timothy 3:12; Exodus 23:20-30; 1 John 4:1-4)

PSALM 5:11,12

But let all those that put their trust in thee rejoice: let them ever shout for joy, because thou defendest them: let them also that love thy name be joyful in thee. For thou, Lord, wilt bless the righteous; with favour wilt thou compass him as *with* a shield.

~ PRAYER ~

Father, it is such a joy to know that You are always there to defend me. I am never alone. The very God of all creation is on my side! Knowing that I am called by Your name fills me with elation beyond description. Thank You so much for causing Your blessing to rain upon me. Thank You for causing Your favor to surround me in all of my endeavors. It covers me like a shield to ensure my success. There is no better life than a life lived in partnership with You.

————— DECLARATION OF FAITH —————

It is such a joy for me to be able to trust in the Lord. Knowing that His eyes never leave me and that He is always there to defend me fills my heart with elation! He has set me apart to bless me with His abundance and surrounds me with His favor as with a shield.

(Proverbs 3:3-6; Psalm 3:5,6; 11:4; 35:1; Nehemiah 1:5,6; 8:10; Genesis 12:1-3)

PSALM 23:1-6

The Lord *is* my shepherd; I shall not want. He maketh me to lie down in green pastures: he leadeth me beside the still waters. He restoreth my soul: he leadeth me in the paths of righteousness for his name's sake. Yea, though I walk through the valley of the shadow of death, I will fear no evil: for thou *art* with me; thy rod and thy staff they comfort me. Thou preparest a table before me in the presence of mine enemies: thou anointest my head with oil; my cup runneth over. Surely goodness and mercy shall follow me all the days of my life: and I will dwell in the house of the Lord forever.

~ PRAYER ~

Father, You are my shepherd and guardian. In You, I am never in need. I rest in green and fertile pastures. The security of Your provision rids me of all anxiety. You show me the path of least resistance and give me wisdom to know the direction I must take. You quiet the turmoil around me and give me a straight course and purpose in life. You lift me when I am downcast and renew my vitality. You lead me in the paths of righteousness for Your name's sake and not because of anything I have done. Even when I walk through the valley of the shadow of death, I have no fear. You are always with me. You never leave me nor forsake me. Your rod and Your staff give me comfort. They are always used for me and never against me. My enemies cannot prevail over me because I am protected by the Lord of all. You even prepare a table before me in the presence of my enemies. You make sure that they are there to see how You have blessed me. In the midst of their attacks, You place a shield of protection around me and set blessing after blessing before me to enjoy. You anoint my head with oil. You set me apart and fill me with Your Spirit. You give me power to overcome any trouble that I face. You cause my cup to overflow with Your provision. I have all that I need and more. I am so blessed. I am destined to enjoy your goodness and mercy all the days of my life, and I will dwell in Your house forever.

—— *DECLARATION OF FAITH* ——

The Lord is my Shepherd, a fierce guardian who watches over me with a relentless eye.

He fills all of my needs and desires so that I am in want of nothing.

He makes me to lie down in green pastures—a fertile land of abundance.

He leads me beside the still and quiet streams of life-giving water.

He restores my life to full vitality.

He guides me in the paths of righteousness for His name's sake alone and not by my own merits.

Even if I am walking in the midst of death's domain, I will fear no evil, for I know that the Lord is with me. The rod of His wrath and the staff of His power bring me comfort.

He prepares a table for me of the choicest portions of His bounty right in the presence of my enemies. They look on in humiliation as I feast upon His blessings.

He covers my head with His burden-removing, yoke-destroying power, and my prosperity flows from me in a shower of abundance.

His love and His mercy cling to me all the days of my life, and He calls me His own forevermore.

(John 10:7-14; Philippians 4:19; Ezekiel 34:14; Revelation 7:17; Psalm 5:8-12; 104:15; Isaiah 43:1,2; 2 Timothy 1:7; 1 John 2:27)

PSALM 34:4-10

I sought the Lord, and he heard me, and delivered me from all my fears. They looked unto him, and were lightened: and their faces were not ashamed.

This poor man cried, and the Lord heard *him*, and saved him out of all his troubles.

The angel of the Lord encampeth round about them that fear him, and delivereth them.

O taste and see that the Lord *is* good: blessed *is* the man *that* trusteth in him.

O fear the Lord, ye his saints: for *there is* no want to them that fear him.

The young lions do lack, and suffer hunger: but they that seek the Lord shall not want any good *thing*.

~ *PRAYER* ~

Father, no matter what happens to me, I know that You are faithful to deliver me. You have stationed Your angel beside me. He ministers to me wherever I go and delivers me from every trouble I find myself in.

Father, You truly are good to me. You are worthy of my trust. I am so blessed because of You. You are the God of my provision. The young lions do lack and suffer hunger, but I am always well supplied. I shall never be in want of any good thing.

DECLARATION OF FAITH

I seek the Lord with all of my heart and place His ways at the center of my thoughts.

He has become my refuge and deliverance from every fear.

He has made me to be radiant and to hold my head up high.

My confidence in Him is greatly rewarded, and I am never put to shame. He hears my every prayer and delivers me out of every trouble.

His angel has been assigned to me to minister to all of my needs and give me provision and abundance in every circumstance. He encamps about me and fulfills God's purposes for me.

Experience has proven that the Lord is good. I take my refuge in Him, and I am blessed. I have placed my steadfast confidence in Him, and I lack no good thing in my life. Even the strongest in the world can become weak and hungry, but I am sustained and given great strength to persevere in every situation.

(Deuteronomy 4:29; 6:4; Joshua 1:8; Psalm 91; Hebrews 1:14; 4:16; Exodus 23:20-23)

PSALM 35:27

Let them shout for joy, and be glad, that favour my righteous cause: yea, let them say continually, Let the Lord be magnified, which hath pleasure in the prosperity of his servant.

~ *PRAYER* ~

Father, I shout for joy in the knowledge of Your presence. I rejoice, for I am part of Your righteous cause. I magnify You, Father, for You take pleasure in my prosperity. You enjoy my success and are well pleased when my finances increase.

——— *DECLARATION OF FAITH* ———

The Lord is my mainstay. He delights in the abundance of my prosperity.
My tongue shall continually speak of His righteousness and sing His praises. May those who bear witness exalt His name forever.

(Isaiah 54:17; Jeremiah 29:11; Deuteronomy 6:7; Romans 12:15)

PSALM 37:1-6

Fret not thyself because of evildoers, neither be thou envious against the workers of iniquity. For they shall soon be cut down like the grass, and wither as the green herb. Trust in the Lord, and do good; *so* shalt thou dwell in the land, and verily thou shalt be fed. Delight thyself also in the Lord; and he shall give thee the desires of thine heart. Commit thy way unto the Lord; trust also in him; and he shall bring *it* to pass. And he shall bring forth thy righteousness as the light, and thy judgment as the noonday.

~ *PRAYER* ~

Father, I will not concern myself with the prosperity of evildoers. What they are doing cannot stop Your prosperity in my life. Evil people who compete against me will soon be cut down like the grass and wither as the green herb. Father, in all of my ways I will trust in You and do what is right. Feed me according to Your Word. Make me to dwell richly in the land. Increase my ability to advance Your Kingdom. Fill my storehouses as a witness against those who pursue prosperity through extortion and greed. Let them see the glory of kingdom living that they may be ashamed and turn from their wicked ways.

Father, Your presence brings me such joy and gladness. I truly delight myself in You. You are the first love of my life. I commit all of my ways to You. All that I have and all that I am are in Your hands. Bring me the desires of my heart. Give me what my spirit longs for and satisfy this yearning that You have placed within me. Make my righteousness shine like the dawn and my cause like the noon day sun!

DECLARATION OF FAITH

I do not become stressed out over the actions of evil men, nor do I envy those who do wrong. They will all fade like the grass in winter, and like the green plants, they will soon die away.

My purposes are set in the Lord to dwell in His spacious lands and enjoy the abundance of His pastures. I stand for what is good and right and trust in Him with unfailing loyalty. He is my comfort and my delight, and He gives me all the desires of my heart. My way is committed to Him, to trust in Him in every circumstance. He will make my righteousness shine like the dawn, and the justice of my cause will blaze like the noonday sun.

(1 Timothy 1:7; 1 Peter 5:5-7; Leviticus 5:1; Proverbs 3:5,6; 23:17; Psalm 90:5,6)

PSALM 37:12-27

The wicked plotteth against the just, and gnasheth upon him with his teeth.
The Lord shall laugh at him: for he seeth that his day is coming.
The wicked have drawn out the sword, and have bent their bow, to cast down
the poor and needy, *and* to slay such as be of upright conversation.
Their sword shall enter into their own heart, and their bows shall be broken.
A little that a righteous man hath *is* better than the riches of many wicked.
For the arms of the wicked shall be broken: but the Lord upholdeth the
righteous.

The Lord knoweth the days of the upright: and their inheritance shall be for ever.

They shall not be ashamed in the evil time: and in the days of famine they shall be satisfied.

But the wicked shall perish, and the enemies of the Lord *shall be* as the fat of lambs: they shall consume; into smoke shall they consume away.

The wicked borroweth, and payeth not again: but the righteous showeth mercy, and giveth.

For *such as be* blessed of him shall inherit the earth; and *they that be* cursed of him shall be cut off.

The steps of a *good* man are ordered by the Lord: and he delighteth in his way.

Though he fall, he shall not be utterly cast down: for the Lord upholdeth *him with* his hand.

I have been young, and *now* am old; yet have I not seen the righteous forsaken, nor his seed begging bread.

He is ever merciful, and lendeth; and his seed *is* blessed.

Depart from evil, and do good; and dwell for evermore.

~ *PRAYER* ~

Father, I have no fear, for You are with me. I always keep in mind that You are on my side. You have covered me in a hedge of Your protection. When the wicked plot against me, You laugh, for You see that their day is coming. When they seek my destruction, You take Your place as the sentinel and defender of my life. You turn their plans back on their own heads, and the very thing that they use against me becomes the source of their own destruction. You break the power of the wicked while upholding me in the strength of Your righteousness. With You as my faithful partner, no foe can succeed against me.

Father, You know my days thoroughly. I shall not be ashamed when hard times come. Through depression and famine, I am satisfied with Your provision. My inheritance is firmly established, and my supply never fails.

Guide my every step according to Your Word. Take delight in my way. Broaden the path beneath my feet. Make me steady and unwavering in the laws of increase that I may glorify You in all that I do.

Father, I know that when I fall, I am never utterly cast down for You uphold me with Your righteous right hand. Your grace is sufficient for me, and I always prosper in spite of my shortcomings. Because of You, I shall never be forsaken, and my children shall never beg for bread.

Your ways are now my ways, Father. I am merciful and giving, and my seed is anointed for abundant increase. Evil shall have no place in my life. I choose to do good and dwell in Your presence forever.

———— DECLARATION OF FAITH ————

The Lord knows all of my days and is attentive to my needs and desires. My inheritance shall endure forever. Nothing, nor anyone, can take it from me. When disaster strikes, I remain calm, for I know that my provision comes from the Lord. In the hardest of times—through depression or famine—even then, I will enjoy His abundance. I never cease to have plenty in my life.

I am not like the wicked who borrow and do not repay.

I give generously, with a happy and hilarious heart, and the Lord blesses me with His abundant provision. He has set aside a tremendous expanse of land as my inheritance.

My Father is overjoyed to spend His time with me. He rejoices as we walk this life together, and He sees to it that all of my steps stand firm. Even if I stumble, I will not fall, for the Lord will catch me with His hand. He will never forsake me all the days of my life, and my children shall never beg for a meal. I always have enough so that I may be generous and lend freely, and my children shall enjoy His abundance as well.

(Hebrews 9:15; 13:5,6; Philippians 10-20; 2 Chronicles 31:10; Exodus 36:5; Malachi 3:10; Philippians 4:; Jude 24; Psalm 40:2; 119:5; Proverbs 24:16; Deuteronomy 15:8)

Psalm 41:1,2

Blessed *is* he that considereth the poor: the Lord will deliver him in time of trouble.

The Lord will preserve him, and keep him alive; *and* he shall be blessed upon the earth: and thou wilt not deliver him unto the will of his enemies.

~ PRAYER ~

Father, I choose to show compassion to the poor. I choose to be generous and giving. I have shown myself to be merciful and kind to those in need. From my heart, I have advanced Your kingdom. Therefore, preserve me, Father, and keep me alive. Deliver me in times of trouble. Show Your blessings now in this life. Bless me upon the earth, and deliver me from the will of my enemies.

—— DECLARATION OF FAITH ——

The Lord delivers me out of every trouble and distressing situation. Because of this, I am a shield to those who lack the strength to stand against the devil's evil schemes.

He preserves my life from the attacks of the enemy and blesses me with His favor and abundance.

He sustains me when sickness comes to take me from His work. He restores me to my true, energetic, and healthy self.

(Psalm 5:11,12; 27:12; 103:1-5; 112:1-3; Isaiah 40:29-31; James 5:14-16)

Psalm 52:1-9

Why boastest thou thyself in mischief, O mighty man? the goodness of God
    endureth continually.

Thy tongue deviseth mischiefs; like a sharp razor, working deceitfully.

Thou lovest evil more than good; *and* lying rather than to speak righteous-
    ness. Selah.

Thou lovest all devouring words, O *thou* deceitful tongue.

God shall likewise destroy thee for ever, he shall take thee away, and pluck thee out of *thy* dwelling place, and root thee out of the land of the living. Selah.

The righteous also shall see, and fear, and shall laugh at him:

Lo, *this is* the man *that* made not God his strength; but trusted in the abundance of his riches, *and* strengthened himself in his wickedness.

But I *am* like a green olive tree in the house of God: I trust in the mercy of God forever and ever.

I will praise thee for ever, because thou hast done *it:* and I will wait on thy name; for *it is* good before thy saints.

~ PRAYER ~

Father, I know that Your goodness never fails. When the deceitful plot against me, Your Word is my stay. You maintain my course and see to it that I do not come to harm. You destroy the works of the wicked and raise me up to prominent positions. I laugh at the plots of the wicked, for I know the One in whom I have placed my trust. You are more mighty than any enemy, and Your protection never fails. I do not trust in money, but in Your goodness. I do not gain riches through deceit but by the precepts of Your Word. I am like a green olive tree in Your house, Father. I trust in Your mercy and loving-kindness forevermore. I praise You because it is You who have prospered me. Your power alone prospers all that I set my hand to do. All that I have, I have because of You. I am a servant called by Your name, and I dedicate my life to the advancement of Your kingdom.

—— DECLARATION OF FAITH ——

I do not concern myself with the strength of evil men. The goodness of God endures continually and there is nothing they can do to stop it. They may devise mischief and make deceitful plans against me, but their plans will come to nothing. The Lord never fails to defend me. He will pluck them out of my life and cause them to be as nothing in my presence.

As for me, I am like a green olive tree in the house of God. Everything that I do prospers, and I never fail to bear good fruit. I am a chosen vessel of

God's mercy and grace. Every bit of wrath that was reserved for me was placed on Jesus two thousand years ago. From this day to eternity, I can count on receiving nothing but blessing from my great Father God. All praise be to His holy name!

(Psalm 1:1-3; Isaiah 41:10-13; John 5:24; 15:1,2; Colossians 2:8-14)

PSALM 62:5-12

My soul, wait thou only upon God; for my expectation *is* from him.

He only *is* my rock and my salvation: *he is* my defence; I shall not be moved.

In God *is* my salvation and my glory: the rock of my strength, *and* my refuge, *is* in God.

Trust in him at all times; *ye* people, pour out your heart before him: God *is* a refuge for us.

Selah

Surely men of low degree *are* vanity, *and* men of high degree *are* a lie: to be laid in the balance, they *are* altogether *lighter* than vanity.

Trust not in oppression, and become not vain in robbery: if riches increase, set not your heart *upon them.*

God hath spoken once; twice have I heard this; that power *belongeth* unto God.

Also unto thee, O Lord, *belongeth* mercy: for thou renderest to every man according to his work.

~ *PRAYER* ~

Father, You are no respecter of persons. You see us all as equally able to prosper and enjoy success in life. Power belongs to You alone, Father. I will not trust in oppression to bring my increase, nor will I seek to gain riches through robbery. I seek You alone for power to gain wealth. And as my riches increase, Father, I will not set my heart on them. My wealth is not my ability to pay my bills. My ability is You, Father. You alone are my provider. You alone are the power that causes me to increase. I will sow my seed and reap an abundant harvest, because You, Father, are the Lord of my harvest. You show me mercy at all times and always prosper what I set my hand to do.

——— DECLARATION OF FAITH ———

Rest for my soul can be found in God alone. I will wait in silent submission and in great hope and earnest expectation of the wonders He will perform in my life. He alone is my Rock and my salvation. He is my deliverer who sets me in the place of highest honor.

I am an unshakable, immovable and ever-ready warrior in His army. My trust is in Him at all times; and my heart is laid bare before Him, crying out, "I am Yours forever!"

I cannot be found forcing men to give to me what is rightfully mine, nor do I need to steal and cheat my way to prosperity. Even if I have gained such an abundance of earthly riches that I am the envy of the world, I will not set my heart on them. My heart belongs to my heavenly Father. He shows His love for me by the rewards that I have received, and by them, I do rejoice; but my focus is on Him alone. He alone is the strength by which I live.

(Ephesians 2:6; Deuteronomy 8:6-18; Jeremiah 3:23; Isaiah 40:17; 1 Timothy 6:17)

PSALM 65:4

Blessed *is the man whom* thou choosest, and causest to approach *unto thee, that* he may dwell in thy courts: we shall be satisfied with the goodness of thy house, *even* of thy holy temple.

~ PRAYER ~

Thank You, Father, for choosing me to be Your child. You cause me to approach You boldly, and You have given me an eternal dwelling within Your courts. I shall be satisfied with the goodness of Your inheritance now and forevermore. Help me to stay focused, Father, that I may always walk in the awareness that the blessings of Your house are mine to enjoy.

——— DECLARATION OF FAITH ———

My Father has chosen me and adopted me as His own child. He has brought me near to Himself and has given me a place of honor in the courts of His palace. He fills me with all good things so that I am in need of nothing. All I have to do is ask, and He freely gives me all that He has.

(Galatians 4:5,6; Ephesians 1:4; 2:6; James 4:8; John 14:13,14; 16:27; Romans 8:32)

PSALM 68:17-20

The chariots of God *are* twenty thousand, *even* thousands of angels: the Lord *is* among them, *as in* Sinai, in the holy *place.*

Thou hast ascended on high, thou hast led captivity captive: thou hast received gifts for men; yea, *for* the rebellious also, that the Lord God might dwell *among them.*

Blessed *be* the Lord, *who* daily loadeth us *with benefits, even* the God of our salvation. Selah.

He that is our God *is* the God of salvation; and unto GOD the Lord *belong* the issues from death.

~ PRAYER ~

Father, I know that there are more on my side than what my eyes can see. Thousands of angels are ready at this very moment to minister to me and see to it that my prosperity flows like a geyser in a desert land. What's more, Father, is that You are in the midst of them. Your power and glory go forth to honor Your Word on my behalf. You carry my burdens for me and cause me to live in victory. You daily load me with Your benefits. You are the God of my salvation and my unfailing source of supply. With You as my covenant partner, I never have to go without.

———— DECLARATION OF FAITH ————

The great army of the living God is on my side. They have ascended from the great mountain of God to shield me on every side and to see to it that I am kept safe from the onslaughts of the enemy.

My heavenly Father takes up my every burden as His own. He bears them daily so that I may dwell in His presence in peace and comfort. He gives me a copious supply of daily provisions to fill all of my needs. He is my salvation from every trouble and my escape from the snares of death.

(2 Kings 6:15-17; Exodus 23:20-23; 1 Peter 5:5-7; Matthew 11:28-30; Deuteronomy 32:29; 33:2; Mark 16:19; Acts 1:8,9; Ephesians 4:8; Psalm 103:1-5; Romans 6:23)

PSALM 78:18-29

And they tempted God in their heart by asking meat for their lust.

Yea, they spake against God; they said, Can God furnish a table in the wilderness?

Behold, he smote the rock, that the waters gushed out, and the streams overflowed; can he give bread also? can he provide flesh for his people?

Therefore the Lord heard *this*, and was wroth: so a fire was kindled against Jacob, and anger also came up against Israel;

Because they believed not in God, and trusted not in his salvation:

Though he had commanded the clouds from above, and opened the doors of heaven,

And had rained down manna upon them to eat, and had given them of the corn of heaven.

Man did eat angels' food: he sent them meat to the full.

He caused an east wind to blow in the heaven: and by his power he brought in the south wind.

He rained flesh also upon them as dust, and feathered fowls like as the sand of the sea:

And he let *it* fall in the midst of their camp, round about their habitations.

So they did eat, and were well filled: for he gave them their own desire;

~ PRAYER ~

Father, I have it settled in my heart that I will trust You despite what my eyes may see. Your blessings never fail, and Your Word always rings true. I declare right now that You are God. You are all powerful and all knowing. Nothing is impossible for You. No matter what my situation is, You are well able to provide for me. I trust You with all of my heart and refuse to give in to the circumstances. I believe in You, Father. I will not cave in to doubt and unbelief.

Father, I recall all that You have accomplished in my life. You have done great and mighty works that defy explanation. I remember, Father. Thank You for always being there for me. I know You will always be there for me. You fill me with my heart's desires. I will never forget, nor take for granted, the goodness You have shown me.

I make it my life's commitment to live without greed or selfishness. I refuse to be self-centered. I seek profit that I may be a blessing and display Your goodness in all the earth.

———— DECLARATION OF FAITH ————

I trust in the Lord and lean not unto my own understanding. I know that He is with me at all times to prosper me and bring me to good success. His Word is my final authority in all circumstances.

I am not out to become rich in order to consume it with lust. It is God's will alone that I pursue. I receive what He wants me to receive and live the way that He wants me to live. My prayer is that His will be done on earth as it is in heaven. They live well in heaven; therefore I live well on earth. Far be it from me to take hold of false humility and not receive His wonderful blessings.

(Proverbs 3:4-10; Joshua 1:8; Isaiah 55:11; James 4:3; Matthew 6:10; 7:21; John 5:30)

PSALM 84:4-12

Blessed *are* they that dwell in thy house: they will be still praising thee. Selah.

Blessed *is* the man whose strength *is* in thee; in whose heart *are* the ways
    of them.

Who passing through the valley of Baca make it a well; the rain also filleth
    the pools.

They go from strength to strength, *every one of them* in Zion appeareth
    before God.

O Lord God of hosts, hear my prayer: give ear, O God of Jacob. Selah.

Behold, O God our shield, and look upon the face of thine anointed.

For a day in thy courts *is* better than a thousand. I had rather be a door-keeper in the house of my God, than to dwell in the tents of wickedness.

For the Lord God *is* a sun and shield: the Lord will give grace and glory: no good *thing* will he withhold from them that walk uprightly.

O Lord of hosts, blessed *is* the man that trusteth in thee.

~ PRAYER ~

Father, it is such a joy to dwell in Your presence. I am a child of God. I dwell in Your house and enjoy the provision of Your matchless treasuries. I have a good life!

I am so blessed, Father. You arm me with strength for every task. You anoint me with power and shield me in the hedge of Your protection. It is my pleasure to live by Your precepts. Your Word is life to me. It is provision and abundance.

Father, a day in Your house is better than a thousand days in the world. I would rather be a butler in Your house than to dwell as a king in the tents of wickedness. The riches and honor of this world are nothing compared to Your glorious provision. To be honored by You is my ambition. To please You is my life.

Father, all of the bitter things in life are turned sweet in Your presence. Your goodness rains down upon me daily. I am awed by such grace and mercy. I wrap my hands in Your garments and claim You as mine forever. You are my sun and my shield. Your grace and glory are mine evermore. No good thing will You ever withhold from me. With all of my heart, Father, I love You, believe in You, and trust You with unwavering confidence.

DECLARATION OF FAITH

I dwell in the very house of God, and I am blessed in every way.

My praises continually soar into His presence.

Through Him, I have strength to do the task He has set before me. My heart is set on a pilgrimage to do His will.

As I pass through the valley of weeping, I make it a place of joy. In my presence, it becomes a place of fresh water springs, and I shower blessings upon it like an autumn rain.

I press on from endeavor to endeavor and increase from strength to strength. I am a child of the Most High God, and I appear regularly at His throne.

My Father is my sun and my shield. He enlightens and enlivens me as I do His will, and He protects me from danger so that I remain secure.

He bestows on me His favor and honor, and I am held in high esteem by my peers.

No good thing will He withhold from me as I daily walk in His ways.

(Galatians 6:10; Ephesians 1:3; 2:6,19; Romans 11:29; Colossians 1:29; Proverbs 3:3,4;4:18; 2 Corinthians 3:18; Hebrews 4:16; Ezra 1:11-2:1; Psalm 23; 34:9,10; 1 Peter 5:5-7)

PSALM 85:12,13

Yea, the Lord shall give *that which is* good; and our land shall yield her increase. Righteousness shall go before him; and shall set *us* in the way of his steps.

~ *PRAYER* ~

Father, I know that You will give me that which is good. I shall yield an abundant increase from the seed that I have sown. Righteousness goes before me and sets me in the way of Your steps.

—— *DECLARATION OF FAITH* ——

The Lord never fails to give me an abundance of good things. His righteousness goes before me to prepare the way for my steps. My land shall indeed yield its harvest.

(Psalm 37:23; 84:11; 112:1-3; 2 Corinthians 9:5-11; James 1:17)

PSALM 104:24

O Lord, how manifold are thy works! in wisdom hast thou made them all: the earth is full of thy riches.

~ *PRAYER* ~

Father, You have provided more than enough for me to have an abundance in my life. How manifold are all of Your works! You knew from the beginning all that would be needed. Your provision has always been more than enough. I live in the land of plenty and enjoy the bounty of Your inheritance.

———— *DECLARATION OF FAITH* ————

I serve El Shaddai, the God who is more than enough! I think in terms of God's abundance, not the world's shortages. I enjoy the Lord's prosperity through both trouble and triumph. Nothing can stop His goodness in my life.

(Psalm 91; 112; Romans 8:35; Isaiah 58:11)

PSALM 106:3-5

Blessed *are* they that keep judgment, *and* he that doeth righteousness at all times.

Remember me, O Lord, with the favour *that thou bearest unto* thy people: O visit me with thy salvation;

That I may see the good of thy chosen, that I may rejoice in the gladness of thy nation, that I may glory with thine inheritance.

~ *PRAYER* ~

Father, I will keep Your Word and walk in Your ways. You have given me understanding of Your precepts, and they are a joy to perform.

I thank You that You always remember me with favor and never fail to visit me with Your salvation. Your thoughts toward me are always for good. You have paid my price fully and never hold me to account for my shortcomings. I continually experience the good of Your chosen. Happiness is my lot and I glory in Your inheritance.

———— *DECLARATION OF FAITH* ————

I am a happy and prosperous man/woman and consistently do what is right. I make justice a top priority in my life.

My Father continually shows me His favor and assists me in doing His will so that I may enjoy the prosperity and success of His chosen ones.

I share in the joy of the church and join them in heartfelt praises to our God.

(Psalm 5:11,12; 112:1-3; Joshua 1:8; Genesis 18:19; Nehemiah 8:10; Galatians 6:9)

Psalm 112:1-10

Praise ye the Lord. Blessed *is* the man *that* feareth the Lord, *that* delighteth greatly in his commandments.

His seed shall be mighty upon earth: the generation of the upright shall be blessed.

Wealth and riches *shall be* in his house: and his righteousness endureth for ever.

Unto the upright there ariseth light in the darkness: *he is* gracious, and full of compassion, and righteous.

A good man showeth favour, and lendeth: he will guide his affairs with discretion.

Surely he shall not be moved for ever: the righteous shall be in everlasting remembrance.

He shall not be afraid of evil tidings: his heart is fixed, trusting in the Lord.

His heart *is* established, he shall not be afraid, until he see *his desire* upon his enemies.

He hath dispersed, he hath given to the poor; his righteousness endureth forever; his horn shall be exalted with honour.

The wicked shall see *it*, and be grieved; he shall gnash with his teeth, and melt away: the desire of the wicked shall perish.

~ *PRAYER* ~

Father, I praise You and magnify Your holy name. I trust You with all of my heart and delight in Your commandments. They are peace to me, and I thank You for them. I enjoy living by Your precepts. Through them I am blessed beyond measure!

Your blessings flood down upon me, and I enjoy the bounty of Your inheritance. You cause my home to be filled with riches and lasting wealth. In Jesus, You make my righteousness shine like the dawn for all of eternity.

Father, I thank You that You cause my seed to be mighty upon the earth. You bless me and make my name great. My children are blessed at my side forevermore!

I thank You that You cause light to shine for me in dark places. You enlighten the way before me so that I can clearly see the path You have called me to take.

Father, I choose to be gracious and full of compassion. I will be good to those around me and not seek evil toward my fellow man. I choose to be good and righteous. I show others favor and remain generous to those in need. I guide all of my affairs with discretion and choose no path that is contrary to Your will.

I rest securely in Your tender care, Father. I shall not be moved. Throughout eternity I will be remembered as one who trusted in You with all of my heart. I am resolved to never give in to the circumstances or give up on Your Word. My heart is fixed upon You, Father. I will trust You and not be afraid. When evil reports come, I remain steadfast. My heart is established and unwavering. I have made my choice. I will trust in my Lord!

Father, I thank You for Your power and protection. My enemies cannot make me afraid. I shall see my desires upon them. I will win every battle and continually set the enemy to flight.

You have blessed me so that I can be a blessing. I have dispersed and have given to the poor. My righteousness will be remembered forever, and my horn shall be exalted with honor. I know that nothing that I do is in vain. You see all, Father, and You remember. You promote me according to my deeds. The wicked shall see it and be grieved. They shall gnash their teeth and all that they desire against me shall perish.

─────── DECLARATION OF FAITH ───────

I give proper reverence to my heavenly Father and find great delight in His precepts.

I am blessed in all that I do.

Wealth and abundance of riches are in my house, and my righteousness has no end.

I am gracious and compassionate, just like my Father.

Darkness turns to light in my presence. With me, there is no darkness at all.

Good things rain down upon me continually, for I have learned the blessings of generosity and give freely for the advancement of God's kingdom.

I am known as a just and righteous man/woman. I distribute gifts regularly to those in need, and the resulting righteousness endures forever. When bad news comes, I am not shaken. When the spirit of fear comes against me, I face it with courage. I know the One in whom my trust is set, and my victory in the end is absolutely certain.

(Deuteronomy 28:1-14; Psalm 1:1-3; 102:28; Proverbs 1:33; 3:16,24; 8:18; 10:7; Genesis 12:1-3; 13:2; Matthew 5:14-16; 6:19-33; Malachi 3:6-12; 2 Corinthians 9:5-11; 2 Timothy 1:7; Numbers 14:8; Hebrews 13:9; Isaiah 12:2)

PSALM 113:7,8

He raiseth up the poor out of the dust, *and* lifteth the needy out of the dunghill; That he may set *him* with princes, *even* with the princes of his people.

~ *PRAYER* ~

Father, I thank You for raising me out of the dust. You have lifted me from the dunghill and have made me a member of Your royal court. I now enjoy the wealth of Your house and take my place among the princes of Your people.

———— DECLARATION OF FAITH ————

God has lifted me out of the ash heap and has seated me with kings and princes. Where the devil brought me to destruction, God has raised me to the place of highest honor.

(Ephesians 2:6; Revelation 1:5,6; Colossians 1:13; Psalm 72:12; Job 36:7; Deuteronomy 7:14; Isaiah 54:1)

PSALM 115:11-16

Ye that fear the Lord, trust in the Lord: he *is* their help and their shield.
The Lord hath been mindful of us: he will bless *us*; he will bless the house of
  Israel; he will bless the house of Aaron.
He will bless them that fear the Lord, *both* small and great.
The Lord shall increase you more and more, you and your children.
Ye *are* blessed of the Lord which made heaven and earth.
The heaven, *even* the heavens, *are* the Lord's: but the earth hath he given to
  the children of men.

~ *PRAYER* ~

Father, I maintain a deep sense of accountability to You. I know that You are
with me and that You intend for me to fulfill the call You have placed on my
life. You are my partner in this. You are here right now to help me. You are
my shield and powerful ally.

I thank You for being ever mindful of me. You never stop thinking of me,
and all of Your thoughts of me are for good. You choose to bless me and
cause my name to be revered. You bless my house so that it is known as a
house of blessing. You increase me more and more, both me and my children. My resources do not dwindle but continually increase. You, Father, are
the maker of the heavens and the earth and have commanded Your blessing
upon me. You are the owner of all and have made me Your heir. The heavens
and the heaven of heavens belong to You: but the earth You have given to me
as an inheritance. Thank You for my part and my portion, Father. I shall take
charge of that which You have given me.

—— DECLARATION OF FAITH ——

*I am always on God's mind. He is continually finding ways to bless me.
My joy knows no bounds as He showers me with His wonderful gifts. He
makes both me and my children to increase so that we have an abundance of
all good things.*

*He has placed all of His creation into my hands so that I will never lack
the things that I need. Everything that my Father has created in this earth is*

put here for my provision. There is more than enough for all of us to draw upon so that we can live a life of wealth and abundance.

(Psalm 128:1-4; Hebrews 6:10; Genesis 12:1-3; 13:2; 14:9; 2 Chronicles 31:10)

Psalm 126:4-6

Turn again our captivity, O Lord, as the streams in the south.

They that sow in tears shall reap in joy.

He that goeth forth and weepeth, bearing precious seed, shall doubtless come again with rejoicing, bringing his sheaves *with him.*

~ PRAYER ~

Father, You have seen my tears. You know my hardships and the trials I've endured. I look upon them now and smile. No matter what has gone on in my life, Your Word has reigned supreme. Though I have sown in tears, I shall reap with joy! I have borne precious seed, and I have sown it into Your kingdom with no regrets. I know that I shall doubtless come again with rejoicing! I shall bring in the sheaves of my harvest. I shall reap in abundance and glory in Your matchless provision!

——— DECLARATION OF FAITH ———

My Father restores my fortunes like the raging streams of the Negev.

I have sown my seed and shall reap an abundant harvest. Through hardship and turmoil, I have gathered my seed; and I have sown it in the midst of life's troubles. But oh my latter end. What I have sown in tears I will reap with joy! My harvest will be gathered in bundles so large they cannot be carried!

(Psalm 85:1-3; Joel 2:25; 2 Corinthians 9:5-11; Galatians 6:9; Job 42:12; Isaiah 61:3; Malachi 3:10,11)

Psalm 128:1-4

Blessed *is* every one that feareth the Lord; that walketh in his ways.

For thou shalt eat the labour of thine hands: happy *shalt* thou *be*, and *it* shall *be* well with thee.

Thy wife *shall be* as a fruitful vine by the sides of thine house: thy children
like olive plants round about thy table.

Behold, that thus shall the man be blessed that feareth the Lord.

~ *PRAYER* ~

Father, I have chosen to trust You and walk in Your ways. I live by Your precepts and make myself to be a doer of Your Word. Everything that I set my
hand to do prospers just as You have promised. I eat the labor of my hands.
Joy and happiness flood my day. It goes well with me and with my children
after me. My wife is as a fruitful vine by the sides of my house. My children
are like olive plants round about my table. Father, You cause blessings to
flood my life. You have my deepest gratitude and genuine praise.

──── DECLARATION OF FAITH ────

*I walk in the ways of almighty God as a good son/daughter and disciple.
I mimic His ways. In every way possible, I live like God lives.*

*I eat the fruit of my labor and live my life in happiness, peace, divine
favor, and good fortune of every kind.*

*My wife/husband is fruitful and productive within my house, and my
children are anointed and blessed at my table.*

My life is a pleasure to live.

(Ephesians 5:1; John 10:10; Ecclesiastes 2:24; 3:22; Psalm 52:8; 144:12; 127:3-5;
Proverbs 31:10-31; 1 Peter 3:10,11)

PSALM 147:10-15

He delighteth not in the strength of the horse: he taketh not pleasure in the
legs of a man.

The Lord taketh pleasure in them that fear him, in those that hope in his mercy.

Praise the Lord, O Jerusalem; praise thy God, O Zion.

For he hath strengthened the bars of thy gates; he hath blessed thy children
within thee.

He maketh peace *in* thy borders, *and* filleth thee with the finest of the wheat. He sendeth forth his commandment *upon* earth: his word runneth very swiftly.

~ *PRAYER* ~

Father, You are my God and there is no other. I do not trust or glory in the strength of my arm or the power of others to provide for me. I do not trust in money or the economy. I trust in You and You alone. I hope in Your mercy and rest in Your grace. You have strengthened the bars of my gates and have blessed my children with me. You make peace in my borders and fill my storage places with the best that the earth has to offer. Your Word has gone forth to bless me. You have commanded that I be blessed. That Word runs swiftly in my life, and it is fulfilled without breach or deviation. I am Your covenant child, and I am blessed in this earth!

———— DECLARATION OF FAITH ————

Reports of shortages do not cause me to worry. The things of this world are not worthy of my allegiance. My trust is in God alone. He is the strength by which I live and the power that brings forth my prosperity.

I bring my Father great joy just because I'm me. I rest in His mercy.

I am a wielder of the Word of God. It is my sword and a mighty weapon in my arsenal. When I hurl it into the battle, the enemy is routed.

(Titus 3:4,5; Ephesians 1:4,5; 2:1-10; 6:17; John 17; Luke 12:32; Hebrews 4:12; 2 Corinthians 10:3-6; Psalm 107:20; Job 37:10)

CHAPTER SEVENTEEN

PROVERBS

PROVERBS 3:1-10

My son, forget not my law; but let thine heart keep my commandments: For length of days, and long life, and peace, shall they add to thee. Let not mercy and truth forsake thee: bind them about thy neck; write them upon the table of thine heart: So shalt thou find favour and good understanding in the sight of God and man. Trust in the Lord with all thine heart; and lean not unto thine own understanding. In all thy ways acknowledge him, and he shall direct thy paths.

Be not wise in thine own eyes: fear the Lord, and depart from evil. It shall be health to thy navel, and marrow to thy bones.

Honour the Lord with thy substance, and with the firstfruits of all thine increase: So shall thy barns be filled with plenty, and thy presses shall burst out with new wine.

~ PRAYER ~

Father, I purpose in my heart to never forget Your law. Your precepts and promises are life to me in abundance. Through them, length of days, long life, and peace are added unto me. Teach me to walk in them, Father. Help me to be the person You have created me to be.

I will not let mercy and truth depart from me. I bind them about my neck and write them on the tablet of my heart. I know by the authority of Your Word that when I cling to mercy and truth, I win favor from You and all of mankind.

Father, I choose to trust in You with all of my heart. I do not lean on what my eyes see or what my ears hear. My trust is in You alone. I choose to believe in Your promises. I will not be guided by circumstances. I am guided by Your Word. By it, all of my paths are made straight and my success is guaranteed.

I reject human wisdom and cling to the spiritual understanding You have given me. I do not consider myself to be wise because of the things that I see. I maintain a deep and reverential respect for You, Father, and I depart from the evil ways of the world system. This is health to my flesh and strength to my bones.

I will not take Your Word lightly, Father. I know that I would have nothing if it weren't for You. Therefore, I will honor You by giving You the firstfruits of all of my increase. In this, I declare that You are in charge of all that I possess. I know today that power is set in motion on my behalf. You cause my income to multiply exponentially. My storage places are anointed for prosperity. My accounts shall be filled with plenty, and my vats shall burst forth with new wine.

—— *DECLARATION OF FAITH* ——

I do not forget the benefits of living wisely.

I understand the rules that I must follow to be a success in life, and I submit to them willingly. Because of this, my life is prolonged by many years and my prosperity overflows like a geyser in a desert land.

I will never fail to let love and faithfulness fill me. I bind them about my neck and write them on the tablet of my heart. By them, favor prevails in my life, and I obtain a good and honorable name in the sight of God and men.

I give my whole heart to trust in the Lord. I will not be the fool who balances his life on the brace of human understanding. I am God-inside minded at all times and never cease to acknowledge His presence to guide me in all that I do. He sees what I cannot see and knows what I do not know. With Him at the point, all of my paths are made straight. Therefore, I will never put my own wisdom before the Lords.

I shun all evil and look to God for my provision. This brings health and vitality to my body and strength to all of my bones.

I would have nothing if it weren't for my heavenly Father. Therefore, I will honor Him with my wealth and the best part of all of my increase. I am a tither and a giver. Because of this, everything that I set my hand to do is blessed and brings forth an abundant harvest. My storage places are filled to overflowing and my vats brim over with new wine.

(Psalm 1:1-3; 37:3-5; 91:16; 103:1-5; Joshua 1:8; Deuteronomy 6:5-7; 28:1-14; Genesis 12:1-3; 39:2-5; Isaiah 46:4; Jeremiah 9:23,24; Romans 8:11; 12:16; John 16:13; 1 Corinthians 3:16; 10:26; Philippians 4:19; Malachi 3:6-12)

PROVERBS 3:13-17

Happy *is* the man *that* findeth wisdom, and the man *that* getteth understanding. For the merchandise of it *is* better than the merchandise of silver, and the gain thereof than fine gold. She *is* more precious than rubies: and all the things thou canst desire are not to be compared unto her. Length of days *is* in her right hand; *and* in her left hand riches and honour. Her ways *are* ways of pleasantness, and all her paths *are* peace.

~ *PRAYER* ~

Father, Your wisdom is precious to me. What a joy it is to be filled with the knowledge of God. The harvest of Your wisdom is better than any harvest of money or material things. To know You and to be known by You is my most coveted prize. With You, Father, I enjoy length of days worth living. I enjoy riches and honor. In the wisdom of Your precepts I have learned peace and contentment. I choose the ways of Your wisdom, Father, and I enjoy the abundant life that You have called me to live.

———— *DECLARATION OF FAITH* ————

My Father instructs me according to His Word.

He enjoys my companionship and gives me the ability to function in every circumstance.

I am a happy and prosperous man/woman, full of wisdom and understanding.

I know the profits and returns of knowledge. I pursue her with a whole heart. It is a great joy to me when I find her. She is more precious to me than any treasure on the face of the earth. Long life is in her right hand and in her left are riches and honor. I have determined to embrace her like a lover. My union with her brings me happiness, prosperity, and health.

I shall enjoy the pleasantries of life, follow the paths of peace, and end my days an old, vibrant, and happy man/woman.

(Psalm 119:34-38,65-68; 1 John 1:3; 2:27; 1 Corinthians 2:6-16; Job 28:13; Matthew 11:29; 13:44; 1 Timothy 4:8)

PROVERBS 3:27,28

Withhold not good from them to whom it is due, when it is in the power of thine hand to do *it*. Say not unto thy neighbour, Go, and come again, and to morrow I will give; when thou hast it by thee.

~ *PRAYER* ~

Father, I thank You for the wisdom that You have given me to be a blessing to others. When it is in my hand to bless, I will not hesitate. It is what You have called me to be and to do. When good is due someone and You have put the blessing in my hand, I will not hold it for myself. I am blessed to be a blessing.

———— DECLARATION OF FAITH ————

I give honor to whom honor is due. I do not hold back good things from those who have a right to them. When good things are placed within my power, I distribute them with justice and equity. I do not put off giving when the gift is within my hand.

(Romans 2:5-10; Luke 6:38; Psalm 84:11)

PROVERBS 6:1-5

My son, if thou be surety for thy friend, *if* thou hast stricken thy hand with a stranger, thou art snared with the words of thy mouth, thou art taken with the words of thy mouth. Do this now, my son, and deliver thyself, when thou art come into the hand of thy friend; go, humble thyself, and make sure thy friend. Give not sleep to thine eyes, nor slumber to thine eyelids. Deliver thyself as a roe from the hand *of the hunter,* and as a bird from the hand of the fowler.

~ *PRAYER* ~

Father, I thank You for giving me balanced wisdom. You have not placed me here to be taken advantage of. My name is important to me, and I will not risk dishonoring it just to be security for another. I will not be one to co-sign and then find my name muddied due to lack of payment.

———— *DECLARATION OF FAITH* ————

My name is too important to me to give it to another. A true friend would not ask me to risk my name just so they can have something they haven't yet earned. I am too wise to let that happen.

I know that my word is the caretaker of my reputation. When I give it, I intend to keep it. Therefore, I will not give it hastily. I will not be snared by the words of my mouth, nor will I allow them to place me in bondage.

(Proverbs 18:20,21; Matthew 12:36,37)

PROVERBS 6:6-11

Go to the ant, thou sluggard; consider her ways, and be wise: Which having no guide, overseer, or ruler, provideth her meat in the summer, *and* gathereth her food in the harvest. How long wilt thou sleep, O sluggard? when wilt thou arise out of thy sleep? *Yet* a little sleep, a little slumber, a little folding of the hands to sleep: So shall thy poverty come as one that travelleth, and thy want as an armed man.

~ *PRAYER* ~

Father, I purpose in my heart never to be lazy. I will not allow myself to be without a vision and purpose for my life. I set my goals and work hard to attain them. I am a provider and a gatherer. Poverty shall have no place in my life. I rise early and meet the day as a warrior. I diligently set my hand to the plow, and I do not return until the work is done.

—————— *DECLARATION OF FAITH* ——————

I am wise in my undertakings. I consider the ways of the ant who—having no guide, overseer, or ruler—provides her meat in the summer and gathers food in the harvest. I do not need to be ruled over or told what to do. I clearly see what needs to be done, and I do it. I sow my seed and work hard for my harvest. I do not allow myself to be a lover of sleep, nor can I be found resting when there is no need for rest. By my hard work and diligence, I repel poverty in my life.

(Proverbs 10:4-6; 19:15; 20:13; 2 Timothy 2:15)

PROVERBS 6:30,31

Men do not despise a thief, if he steal to satisfy his soul when he is hungry; But *if* he be found, he shall restore sevenfold; he shall give all the substance of his house.

~ *PRAYER* ~

Father, I have arrested the thief. Satan has stolen my harvest and has devoured what was rightfully mine. I now say, according to Your Word, that he must restore to me sevenfold that which he has stolen. All that he has taken control of, he must relinquish. He must now gather together all of the substance of his house and refill my treasuries with seven times as much as he took.

—————— *DECLARATION OF FAITH* ——————

Whatever Satan has stolen from me, he must restore to me sevenfold.

(Psalm 85:1-3; Joel 2:25; John 10:10)

PROVERBS 8:10,11

Receive my instruction, and not silver; and knowledge rather than choice gold. For wisdom *is* better than rubies; and all the things that may be desired are not to be compared to it.

~ PRAYER ~

Father, I choose to keep my priorities in order. Though I desire rubies, gold, and material things, they pale in comparison to my desire to know wisdom. Enlighten the eyes of my understanding, Father. Teach me wisdom and instruct me in the ways of Your Word.

———— DECLARATION OF FAITH ————

I choose the Lord's insight and understanding over choice riches. There is not a material thing in existence that can draw me away from His wisdom. He is the first and most vital necessity of my life. I covet His wise counsel in every contract that I make and every endeavor that I undertake. Nothing will ever change that.

(2 Chronicles 1:10-12; Proverbs 3:13-15)

PROVERBS 8:12

I wisdom dwell with prudence, and find out knowledge of witty inventions.

~ PRAYER ~

Father, teach me discretion and good sense. Make me wise in the ways of the world. Show me the ways of Your knowledge that I may discover new and more efficient ways of doing things. Make me to be the resourceful and inventive person You have created me to be.

———— DECLARATION OF FAITH ————

I am uniquely and wonderfully made. No one is able to do what I am called to do as well as I can. Knowledge and creativity come to me as easily as breathing. When I walk in my purpose, I walk in the wisdom of God.

(Psalm 139:13-17; Exodus 35:35; 1 Kings 7:14)

PROVERBS 8:18-21

Riches and honour *are* with me; *yea*, durable riches and righteousness. My fruit *is* better than gold, yea, than fine gold; and my revenue than choice silver. I lead in the way of righteousness, in the midst of the paths of judgment: That I may cause those that love me to inherit substance; and I will fill their treasures.

~ *PRAYER* ~

Father, I know that Jesus has been made unto me wisdom, righteousness, sanctification, and redemption. Teach me to walk in these, Father. Teach me to walk in godly wisdom. Lead me in the way of righteousness, in the midst of the paths of judgment. Show me how to inherit substance that my treasuries may be filled.

———— *DECLARATION OF FAITH* ————

I walk in the ways of righteousness and remain fixed on the paths of justice.
I have been anointed to become an affluent and wealthy man/woman. It is God's perfect will that all of my treasuries be full to the brim.

(Psalm 112:1-3; Proverbs 3:16,19; Genesis 13:2; 2 Corinthians 8:9; 9:5-11)

PROVERBS 8:32-35

Now therefore hearken unto me, O ye children: for blessed *are they that* keep my ways. Hear instruction, and be wise, and refuse it not. Blessed *is* the man that heareth me, watching daily at my gates, waiting at the posts of my doors. For whoso findeth me findeth life, and shall obtain favour of the Lord.

~ *PRAYER* ~

Father, I choose to walk in the ways of wisdom. I feed on the instruction of wise and godly teachers. I welcome correction and never refuse it. I watch daily at wisdom's gates and wait at the posts of her doors. Jesus has become my wisdom and my life. By Him, I have obtained Your unfailing favor, Father. Through Him, all of Your promises concerning wisdom have become my own.

I am a wise man/woman who heeds the counsel that God has placed in my life. I listen carefully to instruction and do not refuse it. I seek out wisdom as the choicest of treasures. My love for wisdom brings me energy, spunk, vitality, and God's own favor. Through wisdom I walk this life fully expecting God's blessings to come my way.

(Proverbs 3:3-6; John 17:3; Isaiah 61:1-3; Ephesians 1:3)

PROVERBS 10:3-5

The Lord will not suffer the soul of the righteous to famish: but he casteth away the substance of the wicked.

He becometh poor that dealeth *with* a slack hand: but the hand of the diligent maketh rich.

He that gathereth in summer *is* a wise son: *but* he that sleepeth in harvest *is* a son that causeth shame.

~ PRAYER ~

Father, I thank You for diligently caring for me. You are my steady provider. In You, I never suffer hunger or lack.

Teach me the ways of diligence. Set me on a persistent path toward abundant riches.

I set my hand firmly to the plow, Father. I am determined to maintain a reputation as a hard worker who gathers in summer and never sleeps through his harvest.

I am a born-again son/daughter of the living God. I am under His constant and unfailing protection. I am always well fed and never have to go hungry. My Father provides me with all that I need and more.

My hands have been given skill over and above that of all worldly people, and I am clever and discerning in the art of obtaining wealth. I am wise enough to know that wealth does not come to me as I sit and wait for it. I must create it. I must go out and get it. Therefore, I will work hard for my harvest and live my life in the realm of God's abundance.

(Deuteronomy 8:18; Proverbs 12:24; 13:4; 21:5)

PROVERBS 10:14,15

Wise *men* lay up knowledge: but the mouth of the foolish *is* near destruction. The rich man's wealth *is* his strong city: the destruction of the poor *is* their poverty.

~ PRAYER ~

Father, I thank You for prospering and anointing what I set my hand to do. I am wise enough to understand that riches provide strength, whereas poverty can bring one to ruin. But I am not one to suffer ruin, for I fully understand that Jesus was made to be poor so that I might be made rich.

──── DECLARATION OF FAITH ────

I am a man/woman of wise words who stores up knowledge as a precious commodity.

My wealth surrounds me like a fortified city.

(Psalm 112:1-3; 2 Timothy 2:15)

PROVERBS 10:22

The blessing of the Lord, it maketh rich, and he addeth no sorrow with it.

~ PRAYER ~

Thank You for Your blessing, Father. It causes me to acquire riches free of all turmoil and sorrow.

──── DECLARATION OF FAITH ────

My Father has blessed me with an abundance of wealth and eternal riches free of all of the troubles that the wealthy of the world must endure.

(Psalm 112:1-3; 145:19; Genesis 24:35; Daniel 1:17,20; John 16:13)

PROVERBS 11:1

A false balance *is* abomination to the Lord: but a just weight *is* his delight. *When* pride cometh, then cometh shame: but with the lowly *is* wisdom. The integrity of the upright shall guide them: but the perverseness of transgressors shall destroy them. Riches profit not in the day of wrath: but righteousness delivereth from death. The righteousness of the perfect shall direct his way: but the wicked shall fall by his own wickedness. The righteousness of the upright shall deliver them: but transgressors shall be taken in *their own* naughtiness.

~ PRAYER ~

Father, I choose to honor You by being a fair and honest man/woman. I will deal justly with others and never cheat them for dishonest gain. I reject arrogant pride and cling to honor and humility. Teach me the ways of integrity, Father. Lead me on paths of justice and righteousness. For riches will not profit me in the day of wrath, but righteousness will deliver me from death.

——— DECLARATION OF FAITH ———

I am a fair and just man/woman and never allow myself to cheat others. When arrogant pride tries to enter my heart, I stand strong against it. I always remain humble and aware of who I am. My integrity guides me, and my trust is properly directed. My riches are but a tool. I know that they will not profit me in the day of wrath, but my righteousness will deliver me from death. Therefore, I let righteousness and purity direct me in my way. When trouble comes, righteousness shall deliver me.

(2 Corinthians 5:21; Romans 4; Colossians 2:18; 1 Peter 5:5-7)

PROVERBS 11:11

By the blessing of the upright the city is exalted: but it is overthrown by the mouth of the wicked.

~ *PRAYER* ~

Father, You have not raised me to be a fool. I know that a city is made up of people, not buildings and dirt. Therefore, I shall bless my city; and by my blessing, it shall be exalted. I will only speak good of her and never speak against her as the heathen do.

──── *DECLARATION OF FAITH* ────

I will not allow the words of my mouth to shower seeds of destruction on my city. I declare that my city is blessed; and by my blessing, it is exalted!

(Proverbs 14:34; 18:20,21; Genesis 12:1-3; Mark 11:22-25)

PROVERBS 11:16

A gracious woman retaineth honour: and strong *men* retain riches.

~ *PRAYER* ~

Father, You have blessed all of my accounts and have filled my treasuries. Teach me to save and invest well that I may show myself to be a man/woman of power.

──── *DECLARATION OF FAITH* ────

I am gracious and generous in all that I do. I am strong in the Lord and in the power of His might. Through His wisdom I fill my savings accounts with an abundance of riches.

(Genesis 13:2; Proverbs 10:4,15; 11:25; Nehemiah 8:10)

PROVERBS 11:23-28

The desire of the righteous *is* only good: *but* the expectation of the wicked *is* wrath. There is that scattereth, and yet increaseth; and *there is* that withholdeth more than is meet, but *it tendeth* to poverty.

The liberal soul shall be made fat: and he that watereth shall be watered also himself.

He that withholdeth corn, the people shall curse him: but blessing *shall be* upon the head of him that selleth *it*. He that diligently seeketh good procureth favour: but he that seeketh mischief, it shall come unto him. He that trusteth in his riches shall fall: but the righteous shall flourish as a branch.

~ PRAYER ~

Father, I purpose in my heart to gain a reputation as a generous and honest man/woman. I look for ways to strategically give so that my substance increases continually. I will not withhold more that what is right. I sow bountifully, and I reap bountifully. I give and it is given unto me good measure, pressed down, shaken together, and running over. I choose to be a cheerful giver, and I rejoice in the abundance of my harvest.

Father, I know that as I seek the good of others, I shall procure favor. People will go out of their way to bless me because of the anointing You have placed on my life.

I know that riches are a fragile form of security. I do not trust in them or set my heart on them. My trust and allegiance are in You and You alone, Father. In You, I find steadfast security and flourish as a well nourished branch of the Vine.

DECLARATION OF FAITH

All of my desires are for good things.

I give freely, without restraint, and yet gain even more. My generosity causes a tremendous abundance of good things to pour forth into my life. When I refresh others, I also am refreshed. When my hand is ready to give and do good, my head is crowned with the blessings of God.

I seek what is good and find goodwill. By my actions, I show that my trust is not in riches, but in the prosperity that only God can provide. By Him, I have abundance and thrive like a green leaf.

(Malachi 3:10; 2 Corinthians 9:7,8; Psalm 1:1-3; 112:9; Job 31:24)

PROVERBS 12:9

He that is despised, and hath a servant, *is* better than he that honoureth himself, and lacketh bread.

~ PRAYER ~

Father, I know that being in a position of leadership often births unwarranted enemies. I will not let them bring me down. I am called to be the head and not the tail, above only and not beneath. Murmurers and backbiters might as well get used to it.

———— DECLARATION OF FAITH ————

I will not allow myself to be influenced by those who do not know the truth. I would rather be despised and have a servant, than to be caught up in false humility and struggle to make ends meet.

(Psalm 112; Proverbs 10:6; 22:7-10)

PROVERBS 12:11

He that tilleth his land shall be satisfied with bread: but he that followeth vain *persons is* void of understanding.

~ PRAYER ~

Father, I am not so foolish as to follow after get rich quick schemes. I will not listen to vain persons who try to get me to join their wealth building systems—telling me how easy and effortless it is. I am wise enough to know that riches and laziness are contrary to each other. You prosper what I set my hand to do, not what I sit back and expect to be blessed with.

———— DECLARATION OF FAITH ————

I do not chase after fantasies or "get rich quick" schemes that require no work on my behalf. It is the diligence of my hands that brings me abundant wealth. What I have, I have earned through hard work and keeping the precepts of the Lord my God.

(Proverbs 28:19; 20:13; Romans 12:11)

PROVERBS 12:14-16

A man shall be satisfied with good by the fruit of *his* mouth: and the recompense of a man's hands shall be rendered unto him. The way of a fool *is* right in his own eyes: but he that hearkeneth unto counsel *is* wise.

A fool's wrath is presently known: but a prudent *man* covereth shame.

~ *PRAYER* ~

Father, You have taught me the power of my words, and I am determined that Your teaching will not be in vain. I shall speak good words that produce good things. By the good words of my mouth and the recompense of my hands, I will work Your anointing to produce an abundance of good things in my life.

Father, my sincere prayer is that Your will be done on earth as it is in heaven. I am not going to be like the fool who tries to reason his way out of Your blessings. You say that You take pleasure in my prosperity. Therefore, I will pursue prosperity with all of my heart. I choose to be a profitable servant who pleases You in every way.

—— *DECLARATION OF FAITH* ——

I understand the laws of the spirit regarding the power of the tongue. By the fruit of my lips, my life is filled to overflowing with good things just as surely as the work of my hands rewards me.

I listen to sound advice and find good, honorable role models to help guide me in my prosperity.

Furthermore, it does not bother me when people have a problem with my pursuit of prosperity. Let them hurl their insults all they want. I will still choose to go forward in the ways of my Father.

(Proverbs 13:2; 18:20,21; Mark 11:22-25; 2 Corinthians 4:13; Psalm 35:27)

PROVERBS 12:24

The hand of the diligent shall bear rule: but the slothful shall be under tribute.

~ PRAYER ~

Father, I thank You for making me a lender and not a borrower. You bless the work of my hands so that I may prosper and be promoted to positions of leadership and authority. I refuse to forfeit my blessings because of laziness and thereby find myself under the boot of the creditors.

———— DECLARATION OF FAITH ————

I am a hardworking, industrious, and creative man/woman.
I am destined for leadership.

(1 Thessalonians 4:11; Genesis 39:2-5; Deuteronomy 28:12,13)

PROVERBS 12:27

The slothful *man* roasteth not that which he took in hunting: but the substance of a diligent man *is* precious.

~ PRAYER ~

Father, all that You give me I consider to be precious. I purpose in my heart to be a good steward of Your riches. I am determined to be a man/woman who works hard for his/her substance. I will take good care of what I have and diligently reinvest in Your kingdom.

———— DECLARATION OF FAITH ————

I diligently attend to that which the Lord has given me. The substance
that I have is precious in my sight.

(Proverbs 13:4; 21:17; 1 Thessalonians 4:10-12)

PROVERBS 13:2-4

A man shall eat good by the fruit of *his* mouth: but the soul of the transgressors *shall eat* violence. He that keepeth his mouth keepeth his life: *but* he that openeth wide his lips shall have destruction. The soul of the sluggard desireth, and *hath* nothing: but the soul of the diligent shall be made fat.

~ PRAYER ~

Father, teach me to train my tongue to speak good things. I am not going to allow my words to be an invitation for violence and destruction. My words shall bring goodness, health, and an abundance of riches into my life.

Father, I know that the desires of my heart are fully met when I focus on Your kingdom and do things the way You have taught me to do them. I only prosper under Your anointing when I diligently set my hand to fulfill the calling that You have placed on my life.

———— DECLARATION OF FAITH ————

By the words of my mouth, I obtain and enjoy all good things. I am careful not to speak those things that would strip me of my blessings. My words produce health, joy, love, peace, prosperity, and power in my life. My mouth is stubborn and inflexible. My words are good ones, and coupled with my diligence and hard work, all of my desires are fully satisfied.

(Mark 11:22-25; Proverbs 18:20,21; Deuteronomy 28:12)

PROVERBS 13:7,8

There is that maketh himself rich, yet *hath* nothing: *there is* that maketh himself poor, yet *hath* great riches.

The ransom of a man's life *are* his riches: but the poor heareth not rebuke.

~ PRAYER ~

Father, I will not allow riches to cause me to become prideful and arrogant. I am blessed to be a blessing, not a pitiful miser. My deep desire is to have a good name and to be known to all as a generous and honest man/woman.

———— *DECLARATION OF FAITH* ————

I will not pursue riches while forgetting the One who gives them to me. Without the Lord, I am nothing. I choose to give up all that I am in order to have all that He is. My life is God's and I will live it in whatever way He wants me to.

(Proverbs 11:24; Philippians 3:7-11)

PROVERBS 13:11

Wealth *gotten* by vanity shall be diminished: but he that gathereth by labour shall increase.

~ *PRAYER* ~

Father, I know that ill-gotten treasures are fleeting. They are like grasping at oil and soon they diminish. Therefore, I commit myself to work hard with my own hands, for that is the channel that causes the flow of Your anointing to pour through my life. I am one who gathers by labor, and my increase never fails.

———— *DECLARATION OF FAITH* ————

I do not seek after "get rich quick" schemes or money gained illegally or dishonestly. My wealth comes to me through hard work and the application of the principles laid out for me in the Word. By these, I make my wealth grow until all of my storage places overflow and every "get rich quick" scheme becomes the laughing stock of my household.

(Proverbs 10:2; 20:21; Psalm 112:1-3; Malachi 3:10)

PROVERBS 13:18

Poverty and shame *shall be to* him that refuseth instruction: but he that regardeth reproof shall be honoured.

~ *PRAYER* ~

Father, I thank You for the godly counsel You have placed in my life. I follow their instruction and gain honor by doing what they teach me to do.

───── *DECLARATION OF FAITH* ─────

I am wise enough to listen to counsel and instruction. I do not disdain correction, but embrace it thankfully so that I may stay on the path of the abundant life. By this, I obtain a place of honor among my peers.

(John 16:13; Proverbs 15:5,22,31,32)

PROVERBS 13:21,22

Evil pursueth sinners: but to the righteous good shall be repayed.

A good *man* leaveth an inheritance to his children's children: and the wealth of the sinner *is* laid up for the just.

~ *PRAYER* ~

Father, I am a good man/woman; and by Your Word, I shall leave an inheritance for my children and my children's children. You have commanded blessings on my storehouses. The wealth of the sinner is laid up for me, and I will use it to be a blessing.

───── *DECLARATION OF FAITH* ─────

I walk in my integrity as an honorable son/daughter of my heavenly Father, and my reward in this life is exceedingly great.

I am wise in the ways of prosperity. Both my children and my grandchildren shall be blessed with a tremendous inheritance.

(Romans 5:17; Ephesians 5:1,2; Deuteronomy 8:18; Job 27:16,17; Ecclesiastes 2:26)

PROVERBS 14:4

Where no oxen *are*, the crib *is* clean: but much increase *is* by the strength of the ox.

~ PRAYER ~

Father, teach me to yoke the strength of others that I may abound in Your prosperity. I pledge that I will not be judgmental and complain about their shortcomings. I know that without them I would have much less to tolerate, but with them my prosperity increases exponentially. Therefore, I will consider all who assist me to be a wonderful blessing, and I will treat them as such.

———— DECLARATION OF FAITH ————

I know that much increase comes with much sweat and that an abundant increase comes with an abundance of help. As I enlist the help of others, my prosperity increases immeasurably.

(Leviticus 25:35; Joshua 1:13-15; Philemon 1:24)

PROVERBS 14:20-24

The poor is hated even of his own neighbour: but the rich *hath* many friends. He that despiseth his neighbour sinneth: but he that hath mercy on the poor, happy *is* he.

Do they not err that devise evil? but mercy and truth *shall be* to them that devise good. In all labour there is profit: but the talk of the lips *tendeth* only to penury. The crown of the wise *is* their riches: *but* the foolishness of fools *is* folly.

~ PRAYER ~

Father, Your system of prosperity is awesome. What a joy it is to give and be a blessing! When I give under Your anointing, I experience tremendous increase and gain friends for myself in the process.

Father, I refuse to be all talk and no action. I do not shy away from hard work. I willingly set my hand to the plow; and under Your anointing, I gain profit from all of my endeavors.

I choose to walk in Your wisdom, and I wear riches as a crown of honor for a job well done.

─────── *DECLARATION OF FAITH* ───────

I show myself to be concerned and compassionate toward the needy.

All of the plans that I pursue are for the good of my fellow man as well as myself.

I work hard to bring forth profit in my life. I understand the joy of diligence and the reward of persistence.

Wisdom, love, faithfulness, and perseverance are engrafted into my spirit.

I wear abundance of wealth as a crown of blessing from God Himself.

(Psalm 112:1-3,9; Deuteronomy 28:12; Proverbs 19:17)

PROVERBS 14:31

He that oppresseth the poor reproacheth his Maker: but he that honoureth him hath mercy on the poor.

~ *PRAYER* ~

Father, in all that I do, I want to honor You. I refuse to think of myself as being above anyone simply because of income level. I know that You see us all as equals and that You love one just as much as You love another. Therefore, I ask that You love the poor through me, Father. Make me to be Your hand that blesses them.

─────── *DECLARATION OF FAITH* ───────

I am kind and generous to those who are in need, thereby giving great honor to my heavenly Father.

(2 Corinthians 8:3-5; James 2:2-6; Romans 2:11)

PROVERBS 15:6

In the house of the righteous *is* much treasure: but in the revenues of the wicked is trouble.

~ *PRAYER* ~

Father, in You I have riches without anxiety. I have abundant treasure in my house, and I am at peace.

——— *DECLARATION OF FAITH* ———

My house contains an abundance of godly treasures. It is a storehouse of all good things.

(Psalm 112:1-3; Romans 8:32; Malachi 3:10)

PROVERBS 15:16,17

Better is little with the fear of the Lord than great treasure and trouble therewith. Better is a dinner of herbs where love is, than a stalled ox and hatred therewith.

~ *PRAYER* ~

Father, I respect You with all of my life. I maintain a deep and unwavering sense of accountability toward You. I know that in You there is peace and contentment, and that hatred is contrary to all that You desire. I will not allow strife to rob me of Your blessings. I would rather have nothing and be at peace than to have all the great treasure of the world and have to live under the curse of strife.

——— *DECLARATION OF FAITH* ———

I understand what true riches are. No matter how much I have, it is nothing if I live in strife and bitterness. Therefore, I will do everything in my power to expel strife and bitterness from my life.

(Proverbs 13:10; 17:1; 22:10; 1 Corinthians 3:3)

PROVERBS 15:19

The way of the slothful *man is* as an hedge of thorns: but the way of the righteous *is* made plain.

~ PRAYER ~

Father, thank You for revealing to me the folly of laziness. I know that if I am slothful, I will suffer many trials and be brought under the yoke of poverty. Therefore, I choose diligence. I am a wise and industrious man/woman, and my way is made plain before me.

——— *DECLARATION OF FAITH* ———

I am wise enough to know that hard work does not make a hard life. Life is hard when there is no provision. Therefore, I will cast aside all laziness and bring in God's abundance through perseverance and hard work.

(Deuteronomy 33:11; Psalm 62:12; 1 Thessalonians 4:11)

PROVERBS 15:27

He that is greedy of gain troubleth his own house; but he that hateth gifts shall live.

~ PRAYER ~

Father, I am not greedy of gain. Riches can receive no allegiance here. My first thought in all matters of increase is to advance Your kingdom and Your righteousness. Though I respect money, I do not revere it. My reverence belongs to You and You alone, Father. You alone cause me to prosper. Therefore, You alone do I honor. I hate all bribes and dishonest gain, for such gain is dishonorable and brings reproach to the name that I love.

——— *DECLARATION OF FAITH* ———

I am not greedy for gain and I despise all bribes. My riches are gained through diligence under the companionship and leadership of Almighty God.

(Genesis 13:2; Proverbs 10:22)

PROVERBS 16:8

Better *is* a little with righteousness than great revenues without right.

~ *PRAYER* ~

Father, thank You for revealing to me the folly of gaining riches illegally and immorally. I would rather be poor than have great riches with no honor.

——— *DECLARATION OF FAITH* ———

Great riches are not worth the sacrificing of my good name. Therefore, in everything that I do, I will keep my integrity.

(Psalm 110:3; Proverbs 10:9)

PROVERBS 16:11

A just weight and balance *are* the Lord's: all the weights of the bag *are* his work.

~ *PRAYER* ~

Father, You are a God of justice and fairness. Therefore, in all of my business ventures I will seek the benefit of all concerned. I will not be unfair and try to keep all the profits for myself. My goals prosper under Your mighty hand, and the result is gain for all parties concerned.

——— *DECLARATION OF FAITH* ———

I will maintain fairness and honesty in all of my business dealings. I am determined that nothing I do will be considered crooked or unjust.

(Psalm 7:9,10; Isaiah 26:7,8)

PROVERBS 16:16-19

How much better *is it* to get wisdom than gold! and to get understanding rather to be chosen than silver! The highway of the upright *is* to depart from evil: he that keepeth his way preserveth his soul. Pride *goeth* before destruction, and an haughty spirit before a fall. Better *it is to be* of an humble spirit with the lowly, than to divide the spoil with the proud.

~ PRAYER ~

Father, I know that Jesus has become for me wisdom, righteousness, sanctification, and redemption. Therefore, open the eyes of my understanding above all things. Make me wise in my pursuit of prosperity so that I may honor you in all that I do. Help me to maintain my focus on the path You have placed before me.

Father, I choose to have a humble spirit. I choose to be a lover of justice and righteousness. I will not gain riches by dishonest or violent means. I know that pride goes before destruction. Therefore, I will be a companion of the humble, not the proud and arrogant.

——— DECLARATION OF FAITH ———

With me, wisdom is so much better than gold. I cherish understanding infinitely more than fine silver. Riches are fleeting, but wisdom always remains.

My path in this life is completely separate from evil things. I keep my way pure and in so doing I preserve my soul. I do not allow arrogance to enter my heart and cause me to fall. No, my spirit always remains humble and in true submission to God. I would much rather hang out with the homeless than to divide riches with the proud and arrogant.

(2 Chronicles 1:7-12; Proverbs 2:6-8; 1 Corinthians 1:18-31)

PROVERBS 17:5

Whoso mocketh the poor reproacheth his Maker: *and* he that is glad at calamities shall not be unpunished.

~ PRAYER ~

Father, I keep my eyes focused on those things that bring joy to Your heart. I know that You see everyone on equal terms. You do not see the rich as being any better than the poor. All carry the dignity of being made in Your image and likeness. Therefore, I will not mock or scoff at another's misfortune.

———— *DECLARATION OF FAITH* ————

I never mock the poor. They are made in the image and likeness of God and are not deserving of mockery. I never enjoy watching others suffer. When suffering comes, the compassion within me rises to bring healing to the situation.

(James 3:8-10; Matthew 9:36-38; 14:14)

PROVERBS 17:8

A gift *is as* a precious stone in the eyes of him that hath it: whithersoever it turneth, it prospereth.

~ *PRAYER* ~

Father, thank You so much for this unfailing system of seedtime and harvest You have set in the earth. I see my every gift as a precious stone. I know that my seed is my miracle. When I release it into Your kingdom, it prospers in every direction.

———— *DECLARATION OF FAITH* ————

I am a carrier of good seed. My gift is precious to me. When I sow it into good ground it shall become as a tree of life branching out in every direction.

(Genesis 8:22; Ecclesiastes 11:1-6)

PROVERBS 17:18

A man void of understanding striketh hands, and becometh surety in the presence of his friend.

~ *PRAYER* ~

Father, You don't have to tell me twice. I am wise enough to listen and obey. I will not be surety for another. I make it my rule in life to not be a co-signer of things that do not belong to me.

——— DECLARATION OF FAITH ———

I live my life in wisdom and understanding. I will not sacrifice my good name by signing it over to another. Let others build a name and reputation for themselves. I am not so foolish as to give them mine.

(Proverbs 22:1; Ecclesiastes 7:1)

PROVERBS 18:9

He also that is slothful in his work is brother to him that is a great waster.

~ PRAYER ~

Father, I am resolved to never be lazy nor wasteful of that which You have given me. My companions are industrious laborers of Your kingdom, not slothful wasters of Your blessings.

——— DECLARATION OF FAITH ———

I am determined to be diligent in all that I do. I am a companion of the wise, not fools and wasters of God's precious gifts.

(Proverbs 6:6-11; Psalm 119:63)

PROVERBS 18:16

A man's gift maketh room for him, and bringeth him before great men.

~ PRAYER ~

Father, I thank You for always opening the way for me to give. I know that my giving is precious and powerful. It makes a way for me when there is no way, and it brings me into companionship with great men.

——— DECLARATION OF FAITH ———

I am clever and wise in my giving. I choose the right place and the right time to give, and thereby, I am given access to the great men and women in the earth.

(Matthew 13:9; Proverbs 2:10; 22:29; Ecclesiastes 11:1,2)

Proverbs 18:20,21

A man's belly shall be satisfied with the fruit of his mouth; *and* with the increase of his lips shall he be filled. Death and life *are* in the power of the tongue: and they that love it shall eat the fruit thereof.

~ PRAYER ~

Father, enlighten the eyes of my understanding so that I may know the power of my words. Satisfy me with the fruit of my mouth and fill me with the increase of my lips. I know that the things of life and the things of death yield themselves to the power of my tongue. Therefore, teach me to train my tongue to speak good things that bring a shower of blessings in my life.

———— DECLARATION OF FAITH ————

My words produce the fruit that fills my stomach, and my lips produce the harvest by which I am satisfied. The elements of life and death yield themselves to the power of my tongue. My words are seeds of life and prosperity to the kingdom of God but death and destruction to the kingdom of the enemy. I sow my words wisely and reap a harvest that makes my Father proud.

(Proverbs 12:14; 13:2; Mark 11:22-25; Galatians 6:7-9)

Proverbs 19:6

Many will entreat the favour of the prince: and every man *is* a friend to him that giveth gifts.

~ PRAYER ~

Father, I know that You have made me to be a blessing in this earth. You have elevated me to the position of a prince in Your kingdom. As I give, my influence is felt strongly in my community; and I gain favor with those I come into contact.

——— DECLARATION OF FAITH ———

I hold the position of royalty in the kingdom of God, and many are they who entreat my favor. They see my generosity and long to take part in what I am doing.

(Revelation 1:5,6; 1 Peter 2:9; Proverbs 18:16)

PROVERBS 19:15

Slothfulness casteth into a deep sleep; and an idle soul shall suffer hunger.

~ PRAYER ~

Father, I know that if I suffer hunger and find myself under the boot of poverty it is my own doing. You faithfully prosper what I set my hand to do. Therefore, I refuse to be a lover of sleep. I keep my mind and my energy focused on the work that is set before me; and under the power of Your anointing, I complete it without fail.

——— DECLARATION OF FAITH ———

I am not an idle soul. I am diligent and industrious. I will not be found sleeping on the job.

(Proverbs 6:4-11; 27:23,24; 2 Timothy 2:15)

PROVERBS 19:17

He that hath pity upon the poor lendeth unto the Lord; and that which he hath given will he pay him again.

~ PRAYER ~

Father, it is such a privilege to give for the advancement of Your kingdom. When I give to those in need, it is like lending You my money. Who is more faithful to repay than You? There is no greater investment. Of all the investments in the world, Yours is the most secure and reliable. I always receive back from You good measure, pressed down, shaken together, and running over!

—— *DECLARATION OF FAITH* ——

My kindness and generosity to the poor is like lending to the Lord. He will repay everything that I have given, while adding His own compound interest as my reward.

(Deuteronomy 15:7,8; Ecclesiastes 11:1; Matthew 10:42; 2 Corinthians 9:6-9)

PROVERBS 20:4

The sluggard will not plow by reason of the cold; *therefore* shall he beg in harvest, and *have* nothing.

~ *PRAYER* ~

Father, I am not a man/woman who looks for the perfect time to do my work. I work in season and out of season. The discomforts of life do not guide my hand. I am wise enough to know that a harvest comes from tilling, planting, and tending. Therefore, no matter what the circumstances are, I shall continue to work hard and find a way to profit.

—— *DECLARATION OF FAITH* ——

I am not a sluggard who refuses to work until the conditions are perfect. My production is continual and God prospers what I set my hand to do.

Furthermore, I do not allow circumstances to direct my giving. I sow in good times and bad, and my harvest never fails.

(Proverbs 6:6-11; Ecclesiastes 11:1-6)

PROVERBS 20:10

Divers weights, *and* divers measures, both of them *are* alike abomination to the Lord.

~ PRAYER ~

Father, You are a God of fairness, and I am a son/daughter of fairness. I do not cheat my way to prosperity. I choose integrity over dishonesty, reliability over untrustworthiness, and freedom over prison.

——— DECLARATION OF FAITH ———

I am fair and just in all of my business dealings. I do not cheat my associates and try to get ahead through deception.

(Proverbs 16:11; 20:23; Leviticus 19:13)

PROVERBS 20:13

Love not sleep, lest thou come to poverty; open thine eyes, *and* thou shalt be satisfied with bread.

~ PRAYER ~

Father, I will not let the love of sleep rob me of my provision. I choose to remain disciplined with my sleeping habits. When the alarm goes off I arise quickly—refreshed and ready to bring in the day's harvest.

——— DECLARATION OF FAITH ———

I refuse to allow my flesh to lead me on the path of poverty by loving to sleep. I sleep only as long as it takes to refresh my body, then I awake and focus on prospering another day.

(Proverbs 6:6-11; Psalm 119:147,148; Joshua 1:8)

PROVERBS 20:14,15

It is naught, *it is* naught, saith the buyer: but when he is gone his way, then he boasteth. There is gold, and a multitude of rubies: but the lips of knowledge are a precious jewel.

~ *PRAYER* ~

Father, Your wisdom is greater than precious stones. Your understanding far exceeds material wealth. Through it I gain understanding of the ways of business. No buyer can gain advantage over me, and no seller can cheat me out of my fair share of the profits.

─────── *DECLARATION OF FAITH* ───────

I cannot be deceived by a wicked negotiator. I know what is just and right, and that is what I do. When I pledge myself to a deal, both parties benefit.

(Leviticus 19:13; Colossians 2:8)

PROVERBS 20:16

Take his garment that is surety *for* a stranger: and take a pledge of him for a strange woman.

~ *PRAYER* ~

Father, I choose the ways of wisdom and shun the folly of giving a stranger the use of my name. I shall never sign my name for a stranger nor pledge my will to a cause that does not concern me.

─────── *DECLARATION OF FAITH* ───────

I am wise and discerning in the ways of profit. I do not involve myself in things that do not concern me, and I will not pledge my name to a cause that I am not part of.

(Proverbs 6:1,2; 11:15; 22:26,27)

PROVERBS 20:25

It is a snare to the man *who* devoureth *that which is* holy, and after vows to make enquiry.

~ *PRAYER* ~

Father, You have decreed that the tithe of all my income is holy. I shall not devour it but honor You by giving it willingly and cheerfully. I will not give second thought to my pledge, nor will I make a vow and then find an excuse not to pay it.

──────── DECLARATION OF FAITH ────────

I am not quick to commit myself to anything. I think through my every vow carefully, for when my word is given, I intend to keep it.

(Proverbs 14:29; 20:21; 21:5; 25:8; 29:20; Isaiah 55:11)

PROVERBS 21:5

The thoughts of the diligent *tend* only to plenteousness; but of every one *that is* hasty only to want.

~ *PRAYER* ~

Father, You establish my thoughts and guide me on the path of prosperity. I am diligent in all of my ways, and my thoughts tend only to plenteousness. I do not hastily make decisions, nor do I spend my substance on poorly planned ventures. I have consideration for my every step and will only move forward in the counsel of Your will.

──────── DECLARATION OF FAITH ────────

My plans in life are carefully laid out before me. I have considered them from every angle, making certain that they are in line with the precepts of God, and my diligence to fulfill them absolutely ensures an abundance of profits for my storehouses.

(Proverbs 10:4; 15:22; Joshua 1:8; Psalm 1:1-3; 112:1-3)

PROVERBS 21:6

The getting of treasures by a lying tongue *is* a vanity tossed to and fro of them that seek death.

~ PRAYER ~

Father, I choose to be a man/woman of integrity and good character. I will not try to lie and cheat my way into prosperity. All of my resources are gained honestly through diligence and hard work.

———— DECLARATION OF FAITH ————

I maintain my integrity in all of my business dealings. I do not use lies and deceit to gain my treasures. Such foolishness is a vanity tossed to and fro of them that seek death, and I will not be a part of it.

(Proverbs 8:7-21; 13:11; Revelation 18:19)

PROVERBS 21:13

Whoso stoppeth his ears at the cry of the poor, he also shall cry himself, but shall not be heard.

~ PRAYER ~

Father, I pledge that as I increase, I will not stop my ears to the cry of the poor. Those in need shall find me to be a blessing in their lives.

———— DECLARATION OF FAITH ————

I am a champion to the poor and needy. In me, they find the provision that helps them back on their feet.

(Leviticus 19:10; Proverbs 19:17)

PROVERBS 21:17

He that loveth pleasure *shall be* a poor man: he that loveth wine and oil shall not be rich.

~ *PRAYER* ~

Father, keep me wise in the ways of pleasure. I will not give an inordinate amount of time to leisure, nor will I swallow my time with revelry. Though I enjoy the finer things in life, I will not be consumed by them. I keep my heart fixed on that which glorifies You, Father. My greatest pleasure is to know You and to honor You.

—— *DECLARATION OF FAITH* ——

I am not given to wine and strong drink, nor do I spend my substance on the pleasures that the world indulges in. My fulfillment in life is found in God alone, not in worldly lusts.

(1 Thessalonians 5:7,8; Proverbs 31:4)

PROVERBS 21:20

There is treasure to be desired and oil in the dwelling of the wise; but a foolish man spendeth it up.

~ *PRAYER* ~

Father, keep me from a heart of greed. Make me to know the proper balance between saving and spending. Fill my home with Your choice treasures and fill my heart with the wisdom to maintain it.

—— *DECLARATION OF FAITH* ——

I am a wise man/woman whose house is filled with an abundance of provisions. I do not eat my seed or spend all that I earn. I am wise to set aside what is the Lord's, give generously for the advancement of His kingdom, and invest a substantial amount for myself and those in my circle of influence.

(Psalm 112:1-3; Malachi 3:6-12; Proverbs 8:21)

PROVERBS 21:25,26

The desire of the slothful killeth him; for his hands refuse to labour. He coveteth greedily all the day long: but the righteous giveth and spareth not.

~ *PRAYER* ~

Thank You, Father, for prospering all the work of my hands. Thank You for the promotions and raises that provide me with the resources to give without sparing. I choose to be a cheerful and bountiful giver, not an indolent and greedy person who is always expecting something for nothing. I will not choose the ways of death due to laziness. My ways are the ways of life.

—— *DECLARATION OF FAITH* ——

I am not as the lazy man who never has his desires satisfied. I am one who gives without sparing, and my life is satisfied with all good things. Through hard work and the application of God's laws of increase, I have all that I desire and more.

(2 Corinthians 9:5-11; Romans 8:32; Proverbs 22:9; Ephesians 4:28)

PROVERBS 22:1

A *good* name *is* rather to be chosen than great riches, *and* loving favour rather than silver and gold.

~ *PRAYER* ~

Father, thank You for giving me a balanced perspective. Great riches, without honor, have no appeal to me. Therefore, in all of my dealings, I choose to maintain a good name and procure favor with You and all of my associates.

—— *DECLARATION OF FAITH* ——

My name is more important to me than all of the riches of the world.

(Genesis 12:1-3; Proverbs 3:3,4; 10:7; Ecclesiastes 7:1)

PROVERBS 22:4

By humility *and* the fear of the Lord *are* riches, and honour, and life.

~ *PRAYER* ~

Father, with all of my heart, I maintain a deep and reverential respect for You and Your Word. I humble myself under Your mighty hand that You may exalt me according to Your perfect timing. With You are riches, honor, and life. I will not forfeit these by doing things my own way because of pride and arrogance.

―――― *DECLARATION OF FAITH* ――――

I humble myself with a deep and solemn trust in my heavenly Father, and He brings me wealth, honor, and a good life in return.

(1 Peter 5:5-7; James 4:6-10; John 10:10; Psalm 112:1-3)

PROVERBS 22:7

The rich ruleth over the poor, and the borrower *is* servant to the lender.

~ *PRAYER* ~

Father, You have made me to be a lender and not a borrower. I am the head and not the tail, above only and not beneath. You made me a leader in this earth and a blessing to the poor.

―――― *DECLARATION OF FAITH* ――――

I am a lender and not a borrower. I am the head and not the tail, above only and not beneath. My service is unto God, not the bank. I will not be the servant of a lender.

(Deuteronomy 28:12,13; Luke 16:13)

PROVERBS 22:9

He that hath a bountiful eye shall be blessed; for he giveth of his bread to the poor.

~ PRAYER ~

Father, I am a man/woman with a bountiful eye. I give freely and never hold back more than what is due. I am Your covenant child—blessed to be a blessing to others.

——— DECLARATION OF FAITH ———

I am a generous man/woman who shares his/her abundance with those in need. By this, I receive blessings from every direction.

(2 Corinthians 9:5-11; Proverbs 19:17; Ecclesiastes 11:1,2)

PROVERBS 22:13

The slothful *man* saith, *There is* a lion without, I shall be slain in the streets.

~ PRAYER ~

Father, I will not make excuses to get out of work, nor will I be afraid of the challenges that are set before me. I move forward with courage and boldness and remain diligent in the face of all circumstances.

——— DECLARATION OF FAITH ———

Fear does not guide my financial decisions. I know the One in whom I have put my trust. He blesses all the work of my hands and sees to it that I prosper under any and every circumstance.

(Isaiah 41:10-13; Deuteronomy 28:8)

PROVERBS 22:16

He that oppresseth the poor to increase his *riches, and* he that giveth to the rich, *shall* surely *come* to want.

~ PRAYER ~

Father, thank You for making me a blessing to the poor. I shall never oppress them or give them cause to hate me. I give to meet needs, not to try to impress or gain the favor of the rich. As with all things, my purpose is to advance Your kingdom and Your righteousness.

———— *DECLARATION OF FAITH* ————

I am an advocate for the poor, not an oppressor of the poor. I purpose in my heart to see them as God sees them: as people of value, worthy of the blood of Jesus.

I do not give in order to gain favors and rub elbows with the rich. I am not out to please men but God, to whom I must give account. In all of my giving, I maintain my focus on the advancement of His kingdom.

(Luke 6:35-38; Matthew 6:19-33; Galatians 1:10)

PROVERBS 22:22,23

Rob not the poor, because he *is* poor: neither oppress the afflicted in the gate: For the Lord will plead their cause, and spoil the soul of those that spoiled them.

~ *PRAYER* ~

Father, I know that You are a shield for the poor. Therefore, I imitate You as a good son/daughter. Through me, the poor and afflicted have a warrior advocate who will meet their needs and plead their cause.

———— *DECLARATION OF FAITH* ————

My pursuit of prosperity does not include taking riches from the poor. I plead the cause of the poor right alongside the Lord. Together we are working to end their poverty.

(Proverbs 14:21,31; Isaiah 61:1-3)

PROVERBS 22:26,27

Be not thou *one* of them that strike hands, *or* of them that are sureties for debts. If thou hast nothing to pay, why should he take away thy bed from under thee?

~ *PRAYER* ~

Father, thank You for giving me the wisdom not to be a co-signer. I will not pledge my substance as collateral for another and run the risk of losing what I have as a result.

—— *DECLARATION OF FAITH* ——

I do not offer my name lightly. If I have no part in the matter I will not sign. Let others use their own name to get what they need. I will not give them mine and risk losing what the Lord and I have gained for His kingdom.

(Proverbs 6:1,2; 11:15; 17:18; 20:16; 27:13)

PROVERBS 22:29

Seest thou a man diligent in his business? he shall stand before kings; he shall not stand before mean *men.*

~ *PRAYER* ~

Father, Your Word is true and is working in my life. I have proven myself to be diligent on the job and in my business dealings. Set me up as the peer of nobles and kings, and keep me from obscure individuals who have no passion for Your kingdom.

—— *DECLARATION OF FAITH* ——

I am diligent in my business. I am a hard worker who constantly finds ways to make things better. In my diligence, I have earned the right to stand in the presence of kings. Mediocre men will find no peer in me.

(Proverbs 10:4; 12:24; 30:28; Psalm 119:146)

PROVERBS 23:4,5

Labour not to be rich: cease from thine own wisdom. Wilt thou set thine eyes upon that which is not? for *riches* certainly make themselves wings; they fly away as an eagle toward heaven.

~ PRAYER ~

Father, I purpose in my heart to keep greed far from me. My focus in life and in all of my business dealings is not to hoard riches for myself but to advance Your kingdom and build Your church. In You, I am already rich. I have all that I need and more. Therefore, I do not look to what my eyes see or what my human understanding tells me. I look to You, Father. It is You who give me the unfailing power to create wealth. Gaining riches by worldly means is like grasping at oil. But in You, Father, I have riches without turmoil. In You and You alone, I have unfailing provision and security on every side.

——— DECLARATION OF FAITH ———

I do not wear myself out trying to get rich. I am already God's heir; therefore, I will walk in wisdom and show restraint.

I clearly understand that riches make themselves wings and fly away toward heaven. Therefore, I shall keep a careful accounting and not spend my money on foolish things.

(Romans 8:17,32; 12:16; Proverbs 28:20; Matthew 6:19)

PROVERBS 23:20,21

Be not among winebibbers; among riotous eaters of flesh: For the drunkard and the glutton shall come to poverty: and drowsiness shall clothe *a man* with rags.

~ PRAYER ~

Father, I am not a fool who spends his/her time in riotous living. I am not given to revelry, drunkenness, or gluttony. I shall not waste my living on such things and find myself clothed in rags. To the contrary, I am a man/woman of honor who remains sober and diligent in all that I do.

──── DECLARATION OF FAITH ────

I am not a companion of drinkers or gluttons. I am a sober and temperate man/woman. I will not be influenced by the destructive ways of those who choose to live outside of the will of God.

(Ephesians 5:1-18; 1 Corinthians 2:6-16; Proverbs 23:29-35; Isaiah 28:7; Hosea 4:11)

PROVERBS 23:22,23

Hearken unto thy father that begat thee, and despise not thy mother when she is old. Buy the truth, and sell *it* not; *also* wisdom, and instruction, and understanding.

~ PRAYER ~

Father, I listen to my mother and father and freely give them the honor they deserve. I set wisdom and instruction as a top priority in my life. I continually use my resources to get wisdom and understanding. I acquire books, tapes, references, and the like that I may be wise and do well in life.

──── DECLARATION OF FAITH ────

I am always open to wise counsel. I regularly and consistently seek the wisdom and counsel of others who are experienced in financial matters. I fill my library with books, tapes, CD's and videos that teach me the ways of godly prosperity.

(Proverbs 11:14; 12:15; 15:22; 19:20,21; 20:5,18; 24:6)

PROVERBS 24:3,4

Through wisdom is an house builded; and by understanding it is established: And by knowledge shall the chambers be filled with all precious and pleasant riches.

~ PRAYER ~

Father, You have said that wisdom is the principal thing. Therefore, I make it a top priority to gather knowledge to myself. Open the eyes of my understanding that I may know how to deal rightly with the knowledge I gain. Give me the insight to build and establish my house. Teach me how to fill my chambers with all precious and pleasant riches.

——— DECLARATION OF FAITH ———

The foundations of my household are carefully planned and well established. Through extensive knowledge it is built, and all of its rooms are filled with rare and costly treasures.

(Matthew 7:24,25; Psalm 112:1-3; Deuteronomy 8:6-18)

PROVERBS 24:27

Prepare thy work without, and make it fit for thyself in the field; and afterwards build thine house.

~ PRAYER ~

Father, teach me wise planning. Show me how to prepare my work so that I may have the means to build my house. I will not put the cart before the horse. I know that it is foolish to start a project if the means are not available to finish it. Therefore, fill me with Your wisdom, Father, and teach me the ways of wise planning so that I may glorify You with a house worthy of a child of God.

——— DECLARATION OF FAITH ———

I plan ahead and prepare the provision before I set my hand to build. In all things I keep a proper focus and through understanding I build my house.

(Psalm 127:1; Ecclesiastes 3:3; Luke 14:28)

Proverbs 24:30-34

I went by the field of the slothful, and by the vineyard of the man void of understanding; And, lo, it was all grown over with thorns, *and* nettles had covered the face thereof, and the stone wall thereof was broken down. Then I saw, *and* considered *it* well: I looked upon *it, and* received instruction. *Yet* a little sleep, a little slumber, a little folding of the hands to sleep: So shall thy poverty come *as* one that travelleth; and thy want as an armed man.

~ PRAYER ~

Father, I choose to honor You in all of my ways. I will not allow myself to become lazy. I am not a lover of sleep who does not tend to that which he has been given. I will not allow myself to be seized by the spirit of poverty because of my own foolishness. I shall remain a diligent and industrious man/woman who gives You honor and glory in all that I do.

—— DECLARATION OF FAITH ——

I keep careful watch over all that the Lord has given me. I am not as one who is lazy and unfruitful. I work hard at my job and produce an abundance for God's glory. Poverty cannot gain a foothold in my life, for the Lord prospers what I set my hand to do.

(Proverbs 6:6-11; Deuteronomy 28:8)

Proverbs 25:21,22

If thine enemy be hungry, give him bread to eat; and if he be thirsty, give him water to drink: For thou shalt heap coals of fire upon his head, and the Lord shall reward thee.

~ PRAYER ~

Father, I am wise enough to understand that there are those in the world who will make themselves my enemies. Teach me how to bless them. Show me how to expose the folly of their ways and turn them from the ways of wickedness to the ways of justice and righteousness.

——— *DECLARATION OF FAITH* ———

I do not lash out against those who make themselves to be my enemies. To the contrary, if they are hungry, I give them food. If they are thirsty, I give them something to drink. This is a burning source of frustration for them and confounds their every act and plan against me.

When all is said and done, I have a great reward coming from the Lord for my persistent patience and perfect self-control.

(Exodus 23:4,5; Matthew 5:4; 6:4-6; Romans 12:20)

PROVERBS 27:23,24

Be thou diligent to know the state of thy flocks, *and* look well to thy herds. For riches *are* not for ever: and doth the crown *endure* to every generation?

~ *PRAYER* ~

Father, teach me accounting skills. Open my eyes that I may properly oversee what You have given me. Teach me how to invest and manage my holdings wisely so that my riches do not take wing.

——— *DECLARATION OF FAITH* ———

I am diligent to know the exact state of my financial affairs. I keep a careful accounting and know where every penny goes. I know every element of my business so that I can guard against those things that would rob me of my substance.

(Luke 14:28-31; 1 Chronicles 28:1; Malachi 3:6-12)

PROVERBS 28:6

Better *is* the poor that walketh in his uprightness, than *he that is* perverse *in his* ways, though he *be* rich.

~ PRAYER ~

Father, I choose the ways of holiness. I will not walk in the perverse ways of society. I would rather be poor and have honor, than be rich and be known as a perverse man/woman.

——— DECLARATION OF FAITH ———

I would rather be poor and walk in honesty and integrity, than be filthy rich and have a perverse and deceitful heart.

(Psalm 119:118,119; Proverbs 16:19; 20:17)

PROVERBS 28:8

He that by usury and unjust gain increaseth his substance, he shall gather it for him that will pity the poor.

~ PRAYER ~

Father, I know that Your justice cannot be thwarted. If I choose to get rich at the expense and extortion of others, I will only sow the seeds of my own downfall. It is not in my heart to be that kind of person. My desire is to see Your blessings rain down upon everyone in my circle of influence. I am blessed to be a blessing, and that's just what I intend to be.

——— DECLARATION OF FAITH ———

Those who gain wealth dishonestly and unfairly are merely gathering it all together to place it into my bank account. My Father knows my heart. I am blessed to be a blessing. I will take the wealth of the ungodly and be a blessing to those in need.

(Proverbs 13:22; Genesis 12:1-3)

PROVERBS 28:13

He that covereth his sins shall not prosper: but whoso confesseth and forsaketh *them* shall have mercy.

~ *PRAYER* ~

Father, reveal to me any sin that would hinder my prosperity. I know that I receive from You by grace through faith and not because of my own right-eousness, but I also know that seedtime and harvest is in the earth and that I will reap what I sow. Therefore, Father, help me to see any hindrance that stands in my way so that I may cast it from my life and move forward in the ways of prosperity and abundance.

——— *DECLARATION OF FAITH* ———

I do not prohibit the flow of prosperity in my life by harboring uncon-fessed sin. It is my continuous prayer that the Holy Spirit reveal to me any-thing in my life that does not glorify Him, and I am reliable to renounce and turn away from all sin no matter how menial it may seem.

(Psalm 32:3-5; 1 John 1:8-10; James 4:1-10)

PROVERBS 28:19,20

He that tilleth his land shall have plenty of bread: but he that followeth after vain *persons* shall have poverty enough.

A faithful man shall abound with blessings: but he that maketh haste to be rich shall not be innocent.

~ *PRAYER* ~

Father, thank You for teaching me to live honorably and patiently. I do not pursue get rich quick schemes or follow vain persons who continually go from one system to another in their pursuit of easy prosperity. I find what works and then I work it. I set my hand to the plow and keep it there. I am a diligent and faithful man/woman, and in accordance with Your Word, I shall abound with blessings!

——— *DECLARATION OF FAITH* ———

I am a faithful and industrious man/woman, and God blesses and pros-pers all that I set my hand to do.

Unlike the one who chases after riches to gain them at any cost, I remain focused upon the Lord, doing those things that are good and proper in His sight. By this, I have made my prosperity certain, for I know that God alone has provided all that I have. He alone is my source of supply, and He has promised to bless me abundantly.

(Matthew 6:33; Deuteronomy 28:8; Proverbs 10:22; John 10:10)

PROVERBS 28:22

He that hasteth to be rich *hath* an evil eye, and considereth not that poverty shall come upon him.

~ PRAYER ~

Father, open the eyes of my understanding. Teach me patience and make me to see things justly and righteously. Build me from the ground up. Make me a wealth creator that will glorify You in every way.

——— DECLARATION OF FAITH ———

I do not focus on a greedy pursuit of riches. I refuse to have an evil eye that searches for ways to get rich in spite of the moral consequences. I know that such a person leads a life of destruction and will one day lose everything.

(Proverbs 13:11,22; Job 15:20-29)

PROVERBS 28:25-27

He that is of a proud heart stirreth up strife: but he that putteth his trust in the Lord shall be made fat.

He that trusteth in his own heart is a fool: but whoso walketh wisely, he shall be delivered. He that giveth unto the poor shall not lack: but he that hideth his eyes shall have many a curse.

~ *PRAYER* ~

Father, I trust in You with all of my heart. I put strife far from me and commit myself to kindness and self-control. I will not allow anger and contentions to rob me of the riches You have prepared for me.

Father, I know that poverty saddens Your heart. Teach me to war against it. Bless me so that I may be a blessing to the poor. Make me to be Your powerful fist that destroys the spirit of poverty by openly pouring showers of blessings on those in need.

———— DECLARATION OF FAITH ————

I trust in the Lord with all of my heart, and my prosperity is as certain as seedtime and harvest.

I walk in wisdom and am kept safe.

I give to the poor and lack no good thing in my life.

(Genesis 8:22; Proverbs 3:5,6; 19:17; 22:9; 29:25; Deuteronomy 15:7)

PROVERBS 29:3

Whoso loveth wisdom rejoiceth his father: but he that keepeth company with harlots spendeth *his* substance.

~ *PRAYER* ~

Father, I truly do love wisdom. It is indeed the principal thing. You will not find me keeping company with those who despise the truth. To the contrary, I am a companion of the wise, and I spend my substance sensibly so that through me You may receive the honor and glory that You deserve.

———— DECLARATION OF FAITH ————

I am not a fool who spends his substance on revelry and harlots. What I have is the gift of the Lord. I will not dishonor Him with lustful living.

(James 4:2,3; Proverbs 23:20,21)

Proverbs 30:8,9

Remove far from me vanity and lies: give me neither poverty nor riches; feed me with food convenient for me: Lest I be full, and deny *thee*, and say, Who *is* the Lord? or lest I be poor, and steal, and take the name of my God *in vain*.

~ *PRAYER* ~

Father, riches are not the object of my desire. My one desire is to honor You. My pursuit of prosperity is not for greed but for love. If riches were to draw me from You, I would be the most wretched of men/women. My first thought in all things is to work Your system in order to advance Your kingdom and Your righteousness, and in this I do abound with blessings; but the greatest blessing of all is just to be Your child.

———— *DECLARATION OF FAITH* ————

I keep falsehood and lies far from me. I am not overly anxious for poverty or riches. My focus is always on the Lord. He will provide my daily bread—the portion of my inheritance as a child of the King. Therefore, I will remain content in whatever state I find myself in.

(Matthew 6:11,19-33; 1 Peter 3:10,11; 1 Timothy 6:9; Hebrews 13:5,6; Philippians 4:9-13)

CHAPTER EIGHTEEN
ECCLESIASTES

ECCLESIASTES 5:3a

For a dream cometh through the multitude of business;

~ *PRAYER* ~

Father, You have placed a dream within my heart. Open it up to me that I may understand it and run with it. Give me a vision and a goal. Strengthen my hands as I actively fulfill Your call on my life.

———— *DECLARATION OF FAITH* ————

The Lord has placed a dream within my spirit. It is a blueprint of what He wants me to do to advance His kingdom in this earth. I dedicate my life to the fulfillment of that dream.

(James 1:21-25; 4:6-10; Hosea 6:6; Proverbs 10:19; 18:20,21; 20:25)

ECCLESIASTES 5:4-6

When thou vowest a vow unto God, defer not to pay it; for *he hath* no pleasure in fools: pay that which thou hast vowed. Better *is it* that thou shouldest not vow, than that thou shouldest vow and not pay. Suffer not thy mouth to cause thy flesh to sin; neither say thou before the angel, that it *was* an error: wherefore should God be angry at thy voice, and destroy the work of thine hands?

~ *PRAYER* ~

Father, I will not be double-minded. I choose to be a man/woman of my word. Set a guard over my mouth and teach me the folly of rashness. Help me not to give my word hastily. Build in me character that exudes trust, confidence, and self-control. Help me to be the person I am created to be.

―――― *DECLARATION OF FAITH* ――――

I will not allow my mouth to cause my flesh to sin. I do not make vows without considering the cost. My word is important to me. It is the wellspring of my reputation. Therefore, I consider my word carefully before I give it, because when it is given, it is going to be kept.

(Psalm 65:1; Deuteronomy 23:21; James 3:2-6)

ECCLESIASTES 5:9-11

Moreover the profit of the earth is for all: the king *himself* is served by the field. He that loveth silver shall not be satisfied with silver; nor he that loveth abundance with increase: this *is* also vanity. When goods increase, they are increased that eat them: and what good *is there* to the owners thereof, saving the beholding *of them* with their eyes?

~ *PRAYER* ~

Father, I refuse to give my allegiance to material things. I shall not serve money or find my satisfaction in the abundance of my wealth. I love and serve You and You alone. You are my strength and my portion forever.

I will not forget that the profit of the earth is for all. There is plenty to go around. Therefore, there is no need to be covetous and miserly.

My increase does not dwindle when I give but increases all the more. I give and it is given unto me: good measure, pressed down, shaken together, and running over. I love Your system, Father. I choose the way of the giver!

―――― *DECLARATION OF FAITH* ――――

I am content with what I have in the Lord. I do not love and serve money. I love and serve my heavenly Father. All that I have is His gift to me so that I may have joy, satisfaction, and fulfillment in this life. I will not be covetous and hold back all of my surplus for myself. As my finances increase, my ability to give increases. Therefore, I will not fail to give as I am able.

(Matthew 6:24-33; Hebrews 13:5,6; 1 Corinthians 10:26; 1 Timothy 6:17)

ECCLESIASTES 5:12,13

The sleep of a labouring man *is* sweet, whether he eat little or much: but the abundance of the rich will not suffer him to sleep. There is a sore evil *which* I have seen under the sun, *namely*, riches kept for the owners thereof to their hurt.

~ *PRAYER* ~

Father, thank You for Your Word and Your wisdom that teaches me to be industrious and work with my own hands. I know that You prosper what I set my hand to do. Therefore, circumstances cannot cause me to be afraid. I am perfectly content no matter what is going on around me. I sleep soundly at night and wake up refreshed every day.

—— DECLARATION OF FAITH ——

I will not keep riches to my hurt. I trust in the Lord and not uncertain riches. What He has given me is good and He adds no sorrow to it. Therefore, I will lie down and sleep in perfect peace, knowing the Lord is watching over my finances. No matter what is going on, or what the evil report has declared, I rest in the arms of my God.

(Psalm 4:8; Isaiah 26:3; Proverbs 10:22)

ECCLESIASTES 5:18,19

Behold *that* which I have seen: *it is* good and comely *for one* to eat and to drink, and to enjoy the good of all his labour that he taketh under the sun all the days of his life, which God giveth him: for it *is* his portion. Every man also to whom God hath given riches and wealth, and hath given him power to eat thereof, and to take his portion, and to rejoice in his labour; this *is* the gift of God.

~ PRAYER ~

Thank You, Father, for all that You have given me. You have filled my treasuries and given me an abundance to enjoy. It is good that I take my part and my portion of this great bounty. It is Your gift to me, and I deeply appreciate it. I rejoice in how You have prospered what I set my hand to do. You are wonderful, Father, and I am honored to serve You.

—— DECLARATION OF FAITH ——

As a child of God, it is my right to have tremendous satisfaction on the job and to be able to thoroughly enjoy the fruit of my labor. God has given me great wealth and many possessions, and He enables me to enjoy them.

I lay claim to my right to have a job that brings me happiness and fulfillment. This is God's gift to me, and I receive it with thanksgiving.

I do not waste time worrying about riches or other things—I am too occupied with my heavenly Father and the gladness that He brings me.

(Deuteronomy 8:18; Proverbs 21:20,21; Matthew 6:24-33; Hebrews 13:5,6; Ecclesiastes 2:24-26; 3:12,13,22; 8:15; 9:9)

ECCLESIASTES 6:1,2

There is an evil which I have seen under the sun, and it *is* common among men: A man to whom God hath given riches, wealth, and honour, so that he wanteth nothing for his soul of all that he desireth, yet God giveth him not power to eat thereof, but a stranger eateth it: this *is* vanity, and it *is* an evil disease.

~ PRAYER ~

Father, I know that You are good and all that You do is good. Your hand is opened wide to me. All I need to do is ask, and You shower me with riches, wealth, and honor. I sow my seed and reap an abundant harvest. Teach me to guard what You have given, Father. Make me a wise steward who glorifies You in all that I do.

──── *DECLARATION OF FAITH* ────

I will not allow my wealth to go unprotected. I see to it that the first and best part of my increase is given to the Lord. I honor Him with my wealth and He rebukes the devourer for my sake. I will not allow strangers to consume my substance, nor will I be bound to a creditor. As I obey the laws of increase, I remain free, secure, and in want of nothing.

(Proverbs 3:9,10; 22:7; Malachi 3:10-12; Psalm 23)

ECCLESIASTES 7:11-14

Wisdom *is* good with an inheritance: and *by it there is* profit to them that see the sun. For wisdom *is* a defence, *and* money *is* a defence: but the excellency of knowledge *is, that* wisdom giveth life to them that have it. Consider the work of God: for who can make *that* straight, which he hath made crooked? In the day of prosperity be joyful, but in the day of adversity consider: God also hath set the one over against the other, to the end that man should find nothing after him.

~ *PRAYER* ~

Father, teach me to walk in the wisdom I have been given. Teach me to avoid foolish and wasteful living. I know that in You I have wisdom and blessings in abundance. Your wisdom gives me life and secures me in times of trouble. I rejoice in Your prosperity, and I ever acknowledge that You alone are my provider. I do not look to circumstances as the final word, nor do I question Your ways. I trust in You with all of my heart and rest securely in Your powerful embrace.

──── *DECLARATION OF FAITH* ────

I do not spend all of the inheritance I am given. By it, I see the opportunity for profit. I use wisdom and restraint in all of my spending and investing.

I am sheltered by my wisdom as well as the wealth that God has provided for me. I store up an abundance of knowledge and my wisdom preserves my life.

I know that without my Father, riches will bring me stress and anxiety. Only through the Lord am I granted both riches and a worry-free life.

(1 Corinthians 1:30; 2:6-16; Ecclesiastes 9:18; Proverbs 3:18)

ECCLESIASTES 9:10,11

Whatsoever thy hand findeth to do, do *it* with thy might; for *there is* no work, nor device, nor knowledge, nor wisdom, in the grave, whither thou goest.

I returned, and saw under the sun, that the race *is* not to the swift, nor the battle to the strong, neither yet bread to the wise, nor yet riches to men of understanding, nor yet favour to men of skill; but time and chance happeneth to them all.

~ *PRAYER* ~

Father, You alone are my God. I do not trust in my own abilities to bring in my harvest. I remain ever aware of Your anointing. You have anointed my hands to create wealth. The anointing of favor, wisdom, and prosperity are Your gifts to me. It is Your power within me that brings my prosperity and not my own abilities. Therefore, I will work Your anointing with all of my might. I cannot be stopped, hindered, or held back. I will set my hand to the task and accomplish that which You have called me to do.

──── DECLARATION OF FAITH ────

I eat and drink with gladness and a joyful heart, for God has given me His favor and has accepted me as His own. I am clothed in His righteousness, and my mind is saturated with His anointing.

My wife/husband is an absolute joy and a blessing to me.

My employment brings me tremendous happiness and satisfaction.

All of this is my lot in life. God has laid it all before me and has given me the right to receive it.

Whatever I set my hand to accomplish, I do it with all of my might. I am filled with an abundance of knowledge and wisdom, and I plan great things for the glory of God.

(Ecclesiastes 2:24-26; 3:12,13,22; 5:18-20; 8:15; 1 Timothy 6:17; 1 John 2:27; Proverbs 5:18; Galatians 4:5,6; Deuteronomy 28:12; Colossians 3:17,23,24)

ECCLESIASTES 9:16

Then said I, Wisdom *is* better than strength: nevertheless the poor man's wisdom *is* despised, and his words are not heard.

~ PRAYER ~

Father, I know that the money You have provided me gives me a voice. I am wise enough to know that people respect riches. Fill me with abundance, Lord, and I will speak those things that glorify Your name.

——— DECLARATION OF FAITH ———

I know that wisdom is better than strength, but I also know that money answers all things. The world does not listen to the poor man. Therefore, I shall be a rich man and be heard. Through the abundance of my wealth, the gospel shall be preached throughout the earth!

(Luke 16:9; Ecclesiastes 7:12; 10:19)

ECCLESIASTES 10:18

By much slothfulness the building decayeth; and through idleness of the hands the house droppeth through.

~ PRAYER ~

Father, I will not let my substance dwindle because of laziness. I am not meant to live an idle, unproductive life. I take good care of that which You have given me, and I work hard to maintain my momentum as I advance Your kingdom.

─────── *DECLARATION OF FAITH* ───────

I am a hard working and industrious man/woman, and I take good care of that which I have been given. I am determined to be a good steward of God's riches in this earth.

(Proverbs 6:6-11; Luke 12:42-44)

ECCLESIASTES 10:19

A feast is made for laughter, and wine maketh merry: but money answereth all *things.*

~ *PRAYER* ~

Father, You have made me to be a man/woman of influence. I am wise enough to know that riches open doors and provide the way to make changes in this world. Money answers all things; therefore, I will use it for Your glory.

─────── *DECLARATION OF FAITH* ───────

I know that the Lord's desire is for me to be a person of influence in this earth. Since money answers all things, I will do my best to get money in order to be the person of influence I am created to be.

(Psalm 35:27; Luke 16:9)

ECCLESIASTES 11:1-6

Cast thy bread upon the waters: for thou shalt find it after many days. Give a portion to seven, and also to eight; for thou knowest not what evil shall be upon the earth. If the clouds be full of rain, they empty *themselves* upon the earth: and if the tree fall toward the south, or toward the north, in the place where the tree falleth, there it shall be. He that observeth the wind shall not sow; and he that regardeth the clouds shall not reap. As thou knowest not what *is* the way of the spirit, *nor* how the bones *do grow* in the womb of her that is with child: even so thou knowest not the works of God who maketh all. In the morning sow thy seed, and in the evening withhold not thine hand: for thou knowest not whether shall prosper, either this or that, or whether they both *shall be* alike good.

~ *PRAYER* ~

Father, I acknowledge that You alone are my provider. You have given me seed to sow and bread to eat. You have set the system of seedtime and harvest into the earth. When I cast my bread upon the waters, I receive the same in return.

Show me where to sow, Father. Show me ministries of good ground that I may sow and receive an abundant harvest.

I declare that my giving has no limits. I give to seven and also to eight. Increase my substance, Father. Make me a blessing to many, in Jesus' name!

Father, I refuse to give in to circumstances. I know that You are above all and that there is no situation or circumstance that can hinder Your blessing in my life. I sow my seed in the morning, and in the evening I do not withhold my hand. I trust You, Father. I know that my seed shall prosper and bring forth fruit to Your glory.

──── DECLARATION OF FAITH ────

I cast my bread upon the waters, and it comes back to me after many days. I give portions of my abundance to several different ministries, thereby securing my harvest in the day of disaster.

Circumstances do not control my giving. I plant my seed regardless of life's storms and reap my harvest in the midst of adversity. God alone is my provider, and I am focused on the precepts of His Word. I sow my seed in the morning and work with my hands until evening, for I have His Word that He will prosper what I set my hand to do and that I will reap an abundant harvest from what I have sown.

(Luke 6:38; 2 Corinthians 9:5-11; Galatians 6:9,10; Hebrews 6:10; 11:1; 1 Timothy 6:17-19; Genesis 39:23, Psalm 1:1-3, Hebrews 11:1; Deuteronomy 28:12,13)

CHAPTER NINETEEN

ISAIAH

Isaiah 1:19,20

If ye be willing and obedient, ye shall eat the good of the land: But if ye refuse and rebel, ye shall be devoured with the sword: for the mouth of the Lord hath spoken *it*.

~ PRAYER ~

Father, I am willing and obedient. Your Word rings true in my life. I shall eat the good of the land!

——— DECLARATION OF FAITH ———

I am willing to do what the Word commands, and I am obedient to all of God's precepts. Because of this, I am ensured a harvest of abundance. I can fully expect God's best in my life.

(Job 29:12-17; James 1:27; Deuteronomy 28:1-14)

Isaiah 32:17-20

And the work of righteousness shall be peace; and the effect of righteousness quietness and assurance for ever. And my people shall dwell in a peaceable habitation, and in sure dwellings, and in quiet resting places; When it shall hail, coming down on the forest; and the city shall be low in a low place. Blessed *are* ye that sow beside all waters, that send forth *thither* the feet of the ox and the ass.

~ PRAYER ~

Father, I rest in the comfort of Your embrace. You bring me peace, quietness, and perfect assurance. I dwell in a peaceful habitation, and my dwelling is made secure under Your relentless hand of protection. Circumstances do not cause me to become fearful. When the storms of life come, I continue to work Your system. I sow beside all waters and produce an abundance despite what is going on around me.

———— DECLARATION OF FAITH ————

The fruit of my righteousness brings me peace, and the effect of my righteousness brings me quietness and confidence forever.

I live in a peaceful dwelling, a safe and secure home, and in undisturbed places of rest.

Although adversity rises and rains destruction on all sides, even if those around me are completely annihilated, I remain secure and blessed, sowing my seed by every stream and enjoying God's abundant increase in my life.

(Psalm 91:7; Proverbs 12:7; Genesis 8:22; 2 Corinthians 9:6-11; Ecclesiastes 11:1,2)

ISAIAH 51:2,3

Look unto Abraham your father, and unto Sarah *that* bare you: for I called him alone, and blessed him, and increased him. For the Lord shall comfort Zion: he will comfort all her waste places; and he will make her wilderness like Eden, and her desert like the garden of the Lord; joy and gladness shall be found therein, thanksgiving, and the voice of melody.

~ PRAYER ~

Father, I look unto Abraham, my father in the faith. I see the way that You blessed him and know that I have the same blessing upon my life. You bless me and increase me continually. You comfort me and cause all of my waste places to become fruitful gardens. You make my desert places like Eden. Joy and gladness are found in my life and songs of thanksgiving never fail to pour forth from my lips.

DECLARATION OF FAITH

I will enjoy the wealth that I am given. I live in comfort and happiness. The voice of melody is in my house and thanksgiving pours forth from my lips continually. My purpose is to be the man/woman that I am created to be. I refuse to be led astray by false humility. I choose wisdom and understanding over religious opinions. The Lord has given me power to create wealth. It is a good gift and one He intends for me to use. Therefore, I will wholeheartedly pursue riches and prosperity, and advance His kingdom like a good son/daughter should.

(Colossians 2:18,19; Deuteronomy 8:18; Matthew 6:33; 15:3-6)

ISAIAH 55:8-13

For my thoughts *are* not your thoughts, neither *are* your ways my ways, saith the Lord. For *as* the heavens are higher than the earth, so are my ways higher than your ways, and my thoughts than your thoughts. For as the rain cometh down, and the snow from heaven, and returneth not thither, but watereth the earth, and maketh it bring forth and bud, that it may give seed to the sower, and bread to the eater: So shall my word be that goeth forth out of my mouth: it shall not return unto me void, but it shall accomplish that which I please, and it shall prosper *in the thing* whereto I sent it. For ye shall go out with joy, and be led forth with peace: the mountains and the hills shall break forth before you into singing, and all the trees of the field shall clap *their* hands. Instead of the thorn shall come up the fir tree, and instead of the brier shall come up the myrtle tree: and it shall be to the Lord for a name, for an everlasting sign *that* shall not be cut off.

~ PRAYER ~

Father, I acknowledge that You know more than I do. I am not such a fool as to think that I can do things better. Your ways are higher than my ways. Therefore, I make my ways Your ways. I will trust You completely and do things the way You have commanded. I will not look to the circumstances as the final authority, but to Your Word. It is a seed that produces fruit in my life. I sow it without fail and always reap an abundant harvest. I go out with joy and am led forth in peace. The mountains and the hills break forth in singing before me. Instead of thorns and briers, I have unfettered abundance!

—— *DECLARATION OF FAITH* ——

As rain and snow fall from heaven to water the earth and make it bring forth seed for the sower and bread for the eater, so it is with God's Word. He has sent it to me for a purpose, and it will accomplish that purpose in my life. It is continually on my lips as a seed, and it brings me a perpetual harvest of good things. What a joy it is to be led forth in such peace and assurance! The mountains and the hills burst forth into song before me, and I enjoy the good-will of all who see God's favor in my life.

(Mark 4:14-20; Psalm 119:138-140; Proverbs 3:3,4; 2 Corinthians 9:10,11)

CHAPTER TWENTY

JEREMIAH

JEREMIAH 4:3

For thus saith the Lord to the men of Judah and Jerusalem, Break up your fallow ground, and sow not among thorns.

~ PRAYER ~

Father, warn me when I need to withhold my hand. Show me the good ground. Keep me from faithless ministries that do not believe in the power of Your Word.

—— DECLARATION OF FAITH ——

I take special care as to where I sow my seed. I will not give it to unplowed soil (a dormant church without a vision), nor will I sow it among thorns (a place where doubt and unbelief prevails).

(Ecclesiastes 11:1,2; 2 Corinthians 9:5-11; Matthew 7:6; 13:7)

JEREMIAH 9:23,24

Thus saith the Lord, Let not the wise *man* glory in his wisdom, neither let the mighty *man* glory in his might, let not the rich *man* glory in his riches: But let him that glorieth glory in this, that he understandeth and knoweth me, that I *am* the Lord which exercise lovingkindness, judgment, and right-eousness, in the earth: for in these *things* I delight, saith the Lord.

~ PRAYER ~

Father, I love You. You have my allegiance far above all others. You are my one source of wisdom, strength, and prosperity. Your loving-kindness is better than life. Your grace and mercy are precious treasures that I do not take for granted. The simplicity of Your companionship far exceeds any desire that I have for riches or honor. I glory in this alone: that You love me, Father, and have made me an heir to Your kingdom.

──────── *DECLARATION OF FAITH* ────────

I do not boast in my worldly wisdom and abilities, nor in the strength of my own arm or the abundance of my riches. All of my boasting is in the Lord. It is He who has made me who I am; and without Him, I am of no great significance.

In this I will boast: that I both know and understand that the Lord is God, the Creator of all things, and that He has become my Father. I boast in His kindness and mercy towards me and in His righteousness and justice that are displayed throughout the earth.

(Romans 3:27; Ecclesiastes 9:11; Psalm 33:16-18)

JEREMIAH 17:5-8

Thus saith the Lord; Cursed *be* the man that trusteth in man, and maketh flesh his arm, and whose heart departeth from the Lord. For he shall be like the heath in the desert, and shall not see when good cometh; but shall inhabit the parched places in the wilderness, *in* a salt land and not inhabited. Blessed *is* the man that trusteth in the Lord, and whose hope the Lord is. For he shall be as a tree planted by the waters, and *that* spreadeth out her roots by the river, and shall not see when heat cometh, but her leaf shall be green; and shall not be careful in the year of drought, neither shall cease from yielding fruit.

~ *PRAYER* ~

Father, neither man nor circumstances can turn me from trusting in You. You are the almighty Creator of the heavens and the earth. I will not be so foolish as to trust in the might of men to make my life secure. I do not surf the waves of the economy. I live above all market fluctuations. Through recession or depression, I remain secure. I am like a tree that is planted by fresh water springs. My roots reach to the river and find satisfaction for all of my thirst. In You I remain unaffected by economic instability. My leaf remains green even in drought, and I never cease to yield fruit.

——— *DECLARATION OF FAITH* ———

I do not put my trust in the ways of man, nor do I rely on the strength of others to sustain me. My trust is in the Lord—my provider. He alone is the strength of my life. I maintain a bold confidence in His Word. It is the final authority in all that I do.

I am like a tree planted beside pure spring water that sends out its roots to the edges of the stream. I do not fear when heat comes, for my leaves will always remain green. You won't find me stressed out and anxiety-ridden in time of drought, for the Lord is my mainstay, and I never fail to bear fruit.

(Isaiah 30:1,2; Proverbs 3:3-10; Ephesians 6:10; Psalm 1:1-3; Joshua 1:5-9; John 15:1-8)

JEREMIAH 29:11

For I know the thoughts that I think toward you, saith the Lord, thoughts of peace, and not of evil, to give you an expected end.

~ *PRAYER* ~

Father, Your love overwhelms me. It is awesome to know that You are always thinking of me. You see past my shortcomings. You choose to see the end from the beginning. Your intention for my life is to prosper me and not to harm me. You give me hope and a wonderful future. The things I presently endure are nothing compared to the glory that awaits me.

——— *DECLARATION OF FAITH* ———

All of God's thoughts for me are for good and never evil. His plan for my life is to make me prosperous, give me hope, and provide for me a glorious future. He has handpicked everything that is best for me in life and presents it to me with great joy. His desire for me is to live in His abundance.

(Deuteronomy 4:29; Colossians 1:13; 2:15; Romans 8:32; Psalm 50:15; 1 John 1:3)

JEREMIAH 33:7-9

And I will cause the captivity of Judah and the captivity of Israel to return, and will build them, as at the first. And I will cleanse them from all their iniquity, whereby they have sinned against me; and I will pardon all their iniquities, whereby they have sinned, and whereby they have transgressed against me. And it shall be to me a name of joy, a praise and an honour before all the nations of the earth, which shall hear all the good that I do unto them: and they shall fear and tremble for all the goodness and for all the prosperity that I procure unto it.

~ *PRAYER* ~

Thank You, Father, for making me Your covenant child. I am no longer Satan's captive. Jesus broke my bonds and set me free. All of my sins have been erased from the first to last. They were all nailed to the cross 2,000 years ago. You now think of me with joy, praise, and honor. The world shall see and hear of Your love for me and stand in awe. They shall fear and tremble at the goodness and prosperity that You pour into my life.

——— *DECLARATION OF FAITH* ———

I am cleansed of all sin and forgiven of all of my rebellion against God. At this very moment, I stand in His presence as holy as Jesus Himself. This puts a smile on God's face and frees Him to do what He has wanted to do all along: be a Father to me and bless me with my portion of His inheritance.

It gives my Father tremendous joy to bless me with all good things. Not only this, but He also receives praise, honor, and great renown among those who hear of what He has done for me. Their mouths gape in astonishment at the abundant prosperity and peace that He provides for His children.

(Hebrews 10:14-17; 2 Corinthians 5:17-21; 1 John 4:17; Romans 8:14-17; Galatians 4:5,6; Deuteronomy 28:1-14)

CHAPTER TWENTY-ONE

EZEKIEL

———————— ✠ ————————

EZEKIEL 44:30

And the first of all the firstfruits of all *things*, and every oblation of all, of every *sort* of your oblations, shall be the priest's: ye shall also give unto the priest the first of your dough, that he may cause the blessing to rest in thine house.

~ PRAYER ~

Father, I give my tithe willingly and not grudgingly. When it is released from my hand, it becomes the property of the pastor in whom I have placed my trust. I know that when I give my tithe willingly, I release my pastor's anointing to speak the blessing over my life. Through my faithful giving, my pastor's blessing rests on my house.

——— DECLARATION OF FAITH ———

I understand the system that God has set in place. My tithe is for a purpose. When I give it, the anointing is released through my pastor to speak the blessing over my household. This causes more and more of God's abundance to be poured into my life. In the Lord, I can do a lot more with 90% than I can with 100%, for when I release the 10%, the blessing I receive in return is more than my world can contain.

(Malachi 3:6-12; Proverbs 3:9,10; 2 Corinthians 9:8)

CHAPTER TWENTY-TWO

JOEL

JOEL 2:12-14a

Therefore also now, saith the Lord, turn ye *even* to me with all your heart, and with fasting, and with weeping, and with mourning: And rend your heart, and not your garments, and turn unto the Lord your God: for he *is* gracious and merciful, slow to anger, and of great kindness, and repenteth him of the evil. Who knoweth *if* he will return and repent, and leave a blessing behind him;

~ PRAYER ~

Father, I am Your child, and I know Your heart. Your desire is to bless me and not curse me. You are ever gracious and loving. You do not look at my sins as reason not to bless me. My sins have been erased in full. I now live in the security of Your grace and mercy. The windows of heaven are opened unto me, and my provision never fails.

—— DECLARATION OF FAITH ——

I have repented of my sins and turned to the Lord. Mine is not a repentance of the mind, simply because I know it is the right thing to do; but it is a repentance of the heart, because I want more than anything in the world to have a close relationship with God.

God has responded to my repentance with great mercy and compassion. He has turned all of His fierce anger from me and has determined to do nothing but good by me. Not only has He forgiven me and made me His own child, but He has also blessed me with every blessing that heaven has to offer.

(Ephesians 1:3; Acts 2:37-39; Psalm 103:10-12; Galatians 4:5,6; Romans 8:38,39)

JOEL 2:18-27

Then will the Lord be jealous for his land, and pity his people. Yea, the Lord will answer and say unto his people, Behold, I will send you corn, and wine, and oil, and ye shall be satisfied therewith: and I will no more make you a reproach among the heathen: But I will remove far off from you the northern *army*, and will drive him into a land barren and desolate, with his face toward the east sea, and his hinder part toward the utmost sea, and his stink shall come up, and his ill savour shall come up, because he hath done great things. Fear not, O land; be glad and rejoice: for the Lord will do great things. Be not afraid, ye beasts of the field: for the pastures of the wilderness do spring, for the tree beareth her fruit, the fig tree and the vine do yield their strength. Be glad then, ye children of Zion, and rejoice in the Lord your God: for he hath given you the former rain moderately, and he will cause to come down for you the rain, the former rain, and the latter rain in the first *month*. And the floors shall be full of wheat, and the fats shall overflow with wine and oil. And I will restore to you the years that the locust hath eaten, the cankerworm, and the caterpillar, and the palmerworm, my great army which I sent among you. And ye shall eat in plenty, and be satisfied, and praise the name of the Lord your God, that hath dealt wondrously with you: and my people shall never be ashamed. And ye shall know that I *am* in the midst of Israel, and *that* I *am* the Lord your God, and none else: and my people shall never be ashamed.

~ *PRAYER* ~

Father, what a wonder it is to know that You are jealous for me. You want me for Yourself and are not willing to share me with other gods. Your love for me is as strong as life, and Your protection of me is as unyielding as the grave. You send me wave after wave of provision from Your great storehouse to satisfy all of my needs and desires. You have defeated all of my enemies and have bid me to walk in Your victory. Oh, the glory of it, Father. I rejoice and exalt Your holy name! I have no need to ever fear again. You are with me at all times and in every circumstance. I am excited as I anticipate Your next move. I know that You are doing great things in my life.

Your anointing has been lavishly poured out upon me. You give me the former and latter rain in the same month. My accounts are filled with plenty, and my vats pour forth with new wine. You are restoring all of the substance that the locust and cankerworm have eaten. You are filling my life with good things of every kind. You deal wondrously with me. My faith is not in vain, and I never have cause to be ashamed. I am proud to call You my Father, and I praise Your name before all the world!

──────── *DECLARATION OF FAITH* ────────

My Father sends me all the provision I need to be satisfied in life and do what He has called me to do. I carry with me the anointing—an ability to function successfully in every area of my life.

As God's son/daughter, I will rejoice and be glad continually, for He has given me a teacher and a guide. He rains blessings down upon me like an autumn rain and causes me to gather a harvest even as I am sowing my seed.

The Lord, my Father, repays me for all of the years that Satan restrained my harvest. I now have all that I need and enjoy daily the fullness of God's way of living. I give all the praise, honor, and glory to my heavenly Father who has done all of these mighty things on my behalf.

I am very proud of my God. He is faithful to His Word.

God, the One and only, dwells within me. He is on my side. So what do I care what the world thinks? Should I be ashamed because I do what is right? Should I be ashamed because I choose to seek the will of God instead of the will of men? I think not!

(Psalm 85:1-3; 89:20,21; Philippians 4:19; Acts 1:8; 2:14-21; 1 John 2:20,27; Amos 9:13; John 16:7,13-15; 2 Corinthians 9:6-12; Proverbs 6:30,31; Jeremiah 30:17,18; Matthew 6:11,19-33; Romans 1:16; 8:31; 10:11; Luke 12:32; Ephesians 2:10)

CHAPTER TWENTY-THREE

AMOS

✛

AMOS 9:13

Behold, the days come, saith the Lord, that the plowman shall overtake the reaper, and the treader of grapes him that soweth seed; and the mountains shall drop sweet wine, and all the hills shall melt.

~ PRAYER ~

Father God, I recognize the times in which I live. I know that Your anointing is accelerating on my behalf. I am living in the days when the plowman overtakes the reaper. I reap an abundant harvest even as I sow my seed. I recognize what You are doing, Father. Make me a vessel that provides for Your kingdom in these last days.

——— DECLARATION OF FAITH ———

I am living in the day of God's inconceivable blessings. His abundance is accelerating on my behalf. My harvest springs up all around me even as I am sowing my seed. The mountains around me drip with new wine and the hills pour out God's blessings, making my harvest one of matchless quality and value.

(Ephesians 3:20; 2 Corinthians 9:6; Leviticus 26:5; Joel 3:18; Proverbs 3:9,10)

CHAPTER TWENTY-FOUR

MICAH

MICAH 4:11-13

Now also many nations are gathered against thee, that say, Let her be defiled, and let our eye look upon Zion. But they know not the thoughts of the Lord, neither understand they his counsel: for he shall gather them as the sheaves into the floor. Arise and thresh, O daughter of Zion: for I will make thine horn iron, and I will make thy hoofs brass: and thou shalt beat in pieces many people: and I will consecrate their gain unto the Lord, and their substance unto the Lord of the whole earth.

~ PRAYER ~

Father, I know the love that You have for me. I know how You care for me and watch over me with a relentless eye. I have no fear, for I know that You are with me. When enemies rise against me, You bring them to nothing in my presence. All that I have is set apart unto You. You are my partner and my friend. I will trust in You and never be afraid.

—— DECLARATION OF FAITH ——

I have no fear when enemies or competitors take counsel against me to destroy me. They know not the God who dwells in my heart. His strength brings me victory in every situation. I cannot be defeated and I will not be overrun. He has gathered them like sheaves into the threshing floor. Therefore, I shall arise and thresh — armed with the Lord's own power and miraculous ability.

(Romans 8:31; Isaiah 41:10-13; Psalm 23)

CHAPTER TWENTY-FIVE

ZECHARIAH

＋

ZECHARIAH 8:12,13

For the seed *shall be* prosperous; the vine shall give her fruit, and the ground shall give her increase, and the heavens shall give their dew; and I will cause the remnant of this people to possess all these *things*. And it shall come to pass, *that* as ye were a curse among the heathen, O house of Judah, and house of Israel; so will I save you, and ye shall be a blessing: fear not, *but* let your hands be strong.

~ PRAYER ~

Father, You are so good to me. Your blessing is upon me and will never leave me. I take my place among the redeemed. My seed is prosperous. My vine gives her fruit and my ground produces abundant increase. The heavens give me their dew, and You cause me to possess all of the blessings of Your kingdom. Your anointing is upon me; therefore, I will let my hands be strong. I will never fear, for You are within me to strengthen me, shield me, and prosper everything that I set my hand to do.

———— DECLARATION OF FAITH ————

My seed grows well, and my vine yields its fruit. My ground produces crops in abundance, and the heavens drop their dew down upon me to ensure my prosperity. This is my inheritance as God's son/daughter and covenant partner. All of this has become a present fact in my life.

I no longer need to bow my head against mockery. I stand firm in my covenant and walk in the riches of my inheritance.

I am known to be a blessing.

I am not afraid of what the world thinks.
I am strong in the Lord and in the power of His might.

(2 Corinthians 9:5-11; Genesis 8:22; 12:1-3; Joel 2:22; Psalm 3:3; 67:6; Haggai 1:10; Romans 8:17; Philippians 4:11-19; Ephesians 6:10)

CHAPTER TWENTY-SIX

MALACHI

MALACHI 3:8-12

Will a man rob God? Yet ye have robbed me. But ye say, Wherein have we robbed thee? In tithes and offerings. Ye *are* cursed with a curse: for ye have robbed me, *even* this whole nation. Bring ye all the tithes into the store-house, that there may be meat in mine house, and prove me now herewith, saith the Lord of hosts, if I will not open you the windows of heaven, and pour you out a blessing, that *there shall* not *be room* enough *to receive it.* And I will rebuke the devourer for your sakes, and he shall not destroy the fruits of your ground; neither shall your vine cast her fruit before the time in the field, saith the Lord of hosts. And all nations shall call you blessed: for ye shall be a delightsome land, saith the Lord of hosts.

~ PRAYER ~

Father, I give my tithe freely. I do not need convincing. I give it because I love You, and I want to honor You in all that I do. All that I have is Yours to begin with. I truly cannot initiate this giving. I can only give back that which is already Yours. Such knowledge, Father, makes this promise even more marvelous. When I give, You give back to me with compound interest. The very windows of heaven are right now opened to me, and You have poured out upon me such a blessing that there is not room enough to receive it. You have even rebuked the devourer for my sake. He cannot destroy the fruit of my ground or cause my increase to fail in any way. I have become a delight-some man/woman, and those who know of me call me blessed.

—— DECLARATION OF FAITH ——

I keep the decrees of my heavenly Father and follow them with all of my heart.

I draw close to Him in perfect fellowship, and He draws close to me in return.

I will not rob Him by holding back my tithes and offerings. The tithe is the Lord's. It is not for me to dictate what is done with it but to simply pay it in the place where I receive my spiritual sustenance.

I fully understand that by paying my tithes and giving my offerings, I am warding off the attacks of the enemy.

Therefore, I bring the whole tithe, along with my offerings, into the church (the place where I fellowship and am fed the Word of God) so that there is provision for the advancement of the kingdom. Because of this, God has thrown open the windows of heaven (the very floodgates of His blessings) and poured out on me so much provision that I do not have room enough to receive it all.

Furthermore, when I paid my tithe and gave my offering, God rebuked the devourer for my sake. Satan cannot get to my stuff because God's hedge of protection surrounds it. My harvest is now made certain, and I shall lose no part of what my Father wants me to have.

(Deuteronomy 28:1-14; James 4:7-10; Proverbs 3:9,10; Job 1:8-10; Luke 6:38; Matthew 6:24-33; 2 Corinthians 9:6-15)

CHAPTER TWENTY-SEVEN

MATTHEW

MATTHEW 6:19-34

Lay not up for yourselves treasures upon earth, where moth and rust doth corrupt, and where thieves break through and steal: But lay up for yourselves treasures in heaven, where neither moth nor rust doth corrupt, and where thieves do not break through nor steal: For where your treasure is, there will your heart be also. The light of the body is the eye: if therefore thine eye be single, thy whole body shall be full of light. But if thine eye be evil, thy whole body shall be full of darkness. If therefore the light that is in thee be darkness, how great *is* that darkness! No man can serve two masters: for either he will hate the one, and love the other; or else he will hold to the one, and despise the other. Ye cannot serve God and mammon.

Therefore I say unto you, Take no thought for your life, what ye shall eat, or what ye shall drink; nor yet for your body, what ye shall put on. Is not the life more than meat, and the body than raiment? Behold the fowls of the air: for they sow not, neither do they reap, nor gather into barns; yet your heavenly Father feedeth them. Are ye not much better than they? Which of you by taking thought can add one cubit unto his stature? And why take ye thought for raiment? Consider the lilies of the field, how they grow; they toil not, neither do they spin: And yet I say unto you, That even Solomon in all his glory was not arrayed like one of these. Wherefore, if God so clothe the grass of the field, which to day is, and to morrow is cast into the oven, *shall he* not much more *clothe* you, O ye of little faith? Therefore take no thought, saying, What shall we eat? or, What shall we drink? or, Wherewithal shall we be clothed? (For after all these things do the Gentiles seek:) for your heavenly Father knoweth that ye have need of all these things. But seek ye first the kingdom of God, and his righteousness; and all these things shall be added unto you. Take therefore no thought for the morrow: for the morrow shall take thought for the things of itself. Sufficient unto the day *is* the evil thereof.

~ *PRAYER* ~

Father, I thank You for Your wisdom. I know the bigger picture and see clearly what is at stake. I am not focused on a greedy pursuit of riches. I do not seek prosperity in order to horde it for myself, nor do I trust in riches as a source of security in my life. My trust is in You and You alone. My heart is with You; and therefore, all of my riches are with You. I do not serve two masters. You alone are my refuge and source of supply. I am not concerned or fearful of reports that say the money is not coming in. I have not placed my trust in money. My trust is in You. The fowls of the air neither sow nor reap and yet You feed them daily. How much more will You feed me? You clothe the lilies of the field in tremendous beauty. How much more lavishly will You clothe me? I have no need to concern myself with such things. You prosper everything I set my hand to do. I sow and reap an abundant harvest every time. You have never once failed to meet my needs. Therefore, I shall not allow worry to come into my life. I drive stress far from my presence and set my one goal before me: to seek first Your kingdom and Your righteousness. In this, I know that all of my needs shall be met, and I will live the way that You have called me to live. I'm not worried about tomorrow for my Lord is with me today.

──── *DECLARATION OF FAITH* ────

I do not center my attention on heaping up earthly treasures like a pitiful miser. My attention is on the treasures of heaven, where God stamps His seal of protection and neither moth, nor rust, nor worm can consume and destroy it, and thieves cannot break in and steal it.

My eyes are the lamp of my body. Therefore, I will be careful what I let them take in. I keep them fixed on the prize that God has set before me. I fully intend to win this race and receive my crown of victory!

I do not serve two masters. I have only one Lord and He is Jesus. He is my strength and my provider. I trust in Him and none other to sustain my existence.

Money is but a tool to achieve a purpose. It is my provision, not my provider. I do not trust in it, nor do I need it. Money can pass from the earth; and I will still prosper, for my hope is in the right place.

I will trust in the Lord and Him only will I serve.

I refuse to be worried about provision for my life. I know that I will have plenty to eat and drink and plenty of clothes to wear.

My Father considers my life precious in His sight and will not force me to go without the things that I need. He is ever ready to be my provider.

When anxiety over the circumstances comes against me, I will look to the birds of the air. They neither sow nor reap, and they don't even have a bank account. Yet, my Father feeds them continually.

When I see the wonderful provision of these birds, I can look back to myself. I do sow and reap, and I gather in a great harvest. I am considered far more important in my Father's eyes than the birds. Therefore, I can look to them and know with certainty that my provision is signed, sealed, and will be delivered without fail.

I know that worrying is useful only for my destruction. It does not add anything good to my life, add a single cubit to my stature, or give me anything that I need. Therefore, I cast worry far from me and live in God's peace and security.

When anxiety comes against me concerning the clothes that I have to wear, I look to the flowers of the field. They neither toil nor spin, but are arrayed in such beauty that even Solomon in all of his glory did not compare to them.

When I see the wonderful clothing of the flowers, I can look back to myself. My Father blesses all of the work of my hands. He considers me to be far more important than the flowers. Therefore, if He clothes flowers—which are here today and gone tomorrow—in such beauty, He will clothe me—His eternal son/daughter—in the finest of apparel.

In light of all of this, I absolutely refuse to worry. I will have plenty to eat, plenty to drink, and plenty to wear. I do not crave these things selfishly and focus my attention on obtaining them, while neglecting God's kingdom. I simply rejoice in the present fact of my Father's provision.

My first thought in all things is the advancement of the kingdom and God's way of being and doing things. With this mindset and spiritual stronghold, all of my physical and material needs will shower into my life in a flood of abundance.

I refuse to worry about tomorrow. This is ridiculous and does me no good at all. I serve the great I AM who is ever in the present. Therefore, as a good and loyal son/daughter, I will focus my attention on what I can do in the present to magnify my heavenly Father and bring glory to His name.

(Psalm 103:13,14; 112:1-3; Deuteronomy 8:6-18; 28:1-14; Proverbs 23:4; Matthew 19:21; 1 Corinthians 9:24-27; Luke 11:34,35; 12:22-24; 16:9-13; Philippians 4:19; Galatians 1:10; 1 Timothy 4:8; 6:9-19; 1 Peter 5:5-7; Zechariah 3:4; James 4:1-10; Exodus 3:14; John 14:13,14)

MATTHEW 7:7-11

Ask, and it shall be given you; seek, and ye shall find; knock, and it shall be opened unto you: For every one that asketh receiveth; and he that seeketh findeth; and to him that knocketh it shall be opened. Or what man is there of you, whom if his son ask bread, will he give him a stone? Or if he ask a fish, will he give him a serpent? If ye then, being evil, know how to give good gifts unto your children, how much more shall your Father which is in heaven give good things to them that ask him?

~ *PRAYER* ~

Father, I know that when I ask I receive, when I seek I find, and when I knock the door is opened unto me. I know Your heart, Father. I'm not afraid to speak to You and ask You for things. You have given me these promises, and You want them fulfilled in my life. Therefore, Father, I am asking You right now to fulfill them in me. Make me prosperous according to Your Word. Make me to be the child You have called me to be.

——— *DECLARATION OF FAITH* ———

I will ask and keep on asking until I have received what I am asking for.

I will seek and keep on seeking until I have found what I am looking for.

I will knock and keep on knocking until the door is opened to me.

I know with certainty that when I ask, I will receive; when I seek, I will find; and when I knock, the door will be opened to me.

My heavenly Father loves me and is always good to me. If I ask Him for a loaf of bread, He does not offer me a stone instead. If I ask Him for a fish, He does not give me a snake. To the contrary, He is more than willing to give me specifically what I persistently ask for. When He sees that my heart is set on it, He makes sure that I have it.

(Mark 11:22-24; Proverbs 8:17; Deuteronomy 4:29; 1 John 5:14,15; Jeremiah 24:6; 29:11; John 14:13,14; 15:7; 16:23,24)

MATTHEW 12:25-29 (MARK 3:27)

And Jesus knew their thoughts, and said unto them, Every kingdom divided against itself is brought to desolation; and every city or house divided against itself shall not stand: And if Satan cast out Satan, he is divided against himself; how shall then his kingdom stand? And if I by Beelzebub cast out devils, by whom do your children cast *them* out? therefore they shall be your judges. But if I cast out devils by the Spirit of God, then the kingdom of God is come unto you. Or else how can one enter into a strong man's house, and spoil his goods, except he first bind the strong man? and then he will spoil his house.

~ *PRAYER* ~

Father, I know that Your kingdom is with me. I have authority over all of the authority of the enemy and nothing shall by any means harm me. I have authority to bind the strongman and spoil his house. Therefore, I bind him now in the name of Jesus.

Satan, I take my authority over you now. You who have hindered my prosperity and caused grief to my family and friends, I bind you now in the name of Jesus. I cast you off of my finances and from every area of my life. I command you to return all of the substance you have stolen from me. Your foothold in my life has ended. Never again will I let you get in the way of my prosperity.

―――― *DECLARATION OF FAITH* ――――

The Spirit of God has come upon me and has taken up residence within me; and by His power, I can drive out any demon. By the Spirit of the living God within me, I have the power to bind the devil and plunder his house, taking back all that he has stolen.

(Isaiah 61:1-3; John 14:12; 1 Corinthians 3:16; Mark 3:27; 16:17-20; Luke 10:18,19; Proverbs 6:30,31; Joel 2:25; Matthew 16:9; 18:18)

MATTHEW 13:11,12

He answered and said unto them, Because it is given unto you to know the mysteries of the kingdom of heaven, but to them it is not given. For whosoever hath, to him shall be given, and he shall have more abundance: but whosoever hath not, from him shall be taken away even that he hath.

~ *PRAYER* ~

Father, thank You for Your wisdom. Enlighten the eyes of my understanding that I may know the mysteries of the kingdom of heaven. Increase my wisdom more and more that I may understand the ways of abundance. This I ask in Jesus' name.

―――― *DECLARATION OF FAITH* ――――

God has given me the ability to know secrets and mysteries of the kingdom of heaven. I have been given a vast supply of wisdom and knowledge, and

God is continually pouring more and more into my life so that I can be furnished richly and live in the fullness of His laws of abundance.

(Luke 8:10; 1 Corinthians 2:6-16; Daniel 1:4,17,20; 2:22,23; John 10:10; Matthew 25:29)

MATTHEW 17:19-21

Then came the disciples to Jesus apart, and said, Why could not we cast him out? And Jesus said unto them, Because of your unbelief: for verily I say unto you, If ye have faith as a grain of mustard seed, ye shall say unto this mountain, Remove hence to yonder place; and it shall remove; and nothing shall be impossible unto you. Howbeit this kind goeth not out but by prayer and fasting.

~ *PRAYER* ~

Father, I purpose in my heart to maintain a regular and steady prayer life. I know that You are with me at all times and that nothing is impossible for me to accomplish. I choose to believe in the abilities that You have given me. I know that Your power works in me mightily and that I can accomplish the task no matter how difficult it seems.

DECLARATION OF FAITH

My faith is a spiritual force that is alive within me. When I use it, it is like a seed planted at the root of the problem. As I cultivate it (continually believing and speaking the answer), it overtakes and uproots whatever is standing in my way.

Even a mountain poses no difficulty for me when I remain stubborn and persistent in my faith. When I tell it to move, it moves. When I tell demons to leave, they leave.

When I command an infirmity to come out of a body, it comes out. With the faith that God has given me, nothing is impossible for me.

(2 Corinthians 4:13; John 6:63; Mark 11:22-24; Hebrews 11:1)

MATTHEW 19:21

Jesus said unto him, If thou wilt be perfect, go *and* sell that thou hast, and give to the poor, and thou shalt have treasure in heaven: and come *and* follow me.

~ PRAYER ~

Father, with all of my heart I am maintaining my focus on You alone as my provider. I give willingly and without restraint. I choose riches in heaven above all earthly possessions. I choose Your system above the system of the world. I know that with You are riches of every kind. Yours are perfect riches, free of all stress and anxiety. Therefore, I choose to follow You and do things Your way.

———— DECLARATION OF FAITH ————

Through my generosity, self-sacrifice, and willingness to give, I maintain a level of honor and spiritual maturity that captures the heart of heaven.

Every time I give, I make a deposit in my heavenly account that I can draw upon in time of need.

In giving, I show myself to be a true disciple of the Lord.

(2 Corinthians 8:12-16; 9:5-11; Philippians 4:10-20; Acts 2:45; 4:34,35)

MATTHEW 24:45-47

Who then is a faithful and wise servant, whom his lord hath made ruler over his household, to give them meat in due season? Blessed *is* that servant, whom his lord when he cometh shall find so doing. Verily I say unto you, That he shall make him ruler over all his goods.

~ PRAYER ~

Father, open the eyes of my understanding that I may be a good steward of Your riches in this earth. Give me my harvest in due season and not before. I commit myself to be the faithful and wise ruler of all of Your goods.

―――――― *DECLARATION OF FAITH* ――――――

I am a faithful and wise servant of the Lord. He has made me a steward of His riches in this earth. Therefore, I shall work hard to see that those riches increase immeasurably and that the borders of His kingdom continue to expand.

(Matthew 25:14-30; Deuteronomy 8:18; Malachi 3:6-12)

MATTHEW 25:14-30

For *the kingdom of heaven is* as a man travelling into a far country, *who* called his own servants, and delivered unto them his goods. And unto one he gave five talents, to another two, and to another one; to every man according to his several ability; and straightway took his journey. Then he that had received the five talents went and traded with the same, and made *them* other five talents. And likewise he that *had received* two, he also gained other two. But he that had received one went and digged in the earth, and hid his lord's money. After a long time the lord of those servants cometh, and reckoneth with them. And so he that had received five talents came and brought other five talents, saying, Lord, thou deliveredst unto me five talents: behold, I have gained beside them five talents more. His lord said unto him, Well done, *thou* good and faithful servant: thou hast been faithful over a few things, I will make thee ruler over many things: enter thou into the joy of thy lord. He also that had received two talents came and said, Lord, thou deliveredst unto me two talents: behold, I have gained two other talents beside them. His lord said unto him, Well done, good and faithful servant; thou hast been faithful over a few things, I will make thee ruler over many things: enter thou into the joy of thy lord. Then he which had received the one talent came and said, Lord, I knew thee that thou art an hard man, reaping where thou hast not sown, and gathering where thou hast not strawed: And I was afraid, and went and hid thy talent in the earth: lo, *there* thou hast *that is* thine. His lord answered and said unto him, *Thou* wicked and slothful servant, thou knewest that I reap where I sowed not, and gather where I have not strawed: Thou oughtest therefore to have put my money to the exchangers, and *then* at my coming I should have received mine own with usury. Take therefore the talent from him, and give *it* unto him which hath ten talents. For unto every one that hath shall be given, and he shall have abundance: but from him that hath not shall be taken away even that which he hath. And cast ye the unprofitable servant into outer darkness: there shall be weeping and gnashing of teeth.

~ PRAYER ~

Father, I will not allow fear to rob me of my blessing. I will not be afraid to do that which You have called me to do. I will not be afraid to seek profit and produce an abundance for Your kingdom. I will not be fearful and lazy. I choose to be the good and faithful servant whom You make ruler over much. I will set my hand to the plow and produce an abundance for Your glory. I know that when I seek profit to advance Your kingdom, I enter into the joy of my Lord!

DECLARATION OF FAITH

I understand the laws of sowing and reaping and that my God is a God of increase. Therefore, I take what I have been given, sow it into the kingdom, and reap an abundant harvest. In this, I am counted as faithful and honorable in the eyes of the Lord, and I enter into His joy and blessings.

When I am faithful and operate in the laws of kingdom living persistently and without fail, I shall reap even the seed that was given to the faithless. More and more will be given to me so that I am furnished richly and have an abundance.

My God is a God of increase, and He takes great pleasure in my prosperity.

(2 Corinthians 9:5-11; Malachi 3:6-12; Psalm 35:27; 115:14; Deuteronomy 14:22)

CHAPTER TWENTY-EIGHT

MARK

MARK 4:14-20

The sower soweth the word. And these are they by the way side, where the word is sown; but when they have heard, Satan cometh immediately, and taketh away the word that was sown in their hearts. And these are they likewise which are sown on stony ground; who, when they have heard the word, immediately receive it with gladness; And have no root in themselves, and so endure but for a time: afterward, when affliction or persecution ariseth for the word's sake, immediately they are offended. And these are they which are sown among thorns; such as hear the word, And the cares of this world, and the deceitfulness of riches, and the lusts of other things entering in, choke the word, and it becometh unfruitful. And these are they which are sown on good ground; such as hear the word, and receive *it*, and bring forth fruit, some thirtyfold, some sixty, and some an hundred.

~ *PRAYER* ~

Father, I am a sower of the Word. This book that I hold in my hand is my precious seed. I have sown it and will continue to sow it. I will guard it with all that I am. Satan cannot steal this Word from my heart. I will not allow persecution and affliction to cause me to turn from the Word. I am not easily offended or easily distracted. The cares of this world, the deceitfulness of riches, and the lust of other things cannot cause me to turn from Your promises, Father. I make myself to be good ground for Your Word. I hear it, receive it, sow it, and bring forth an abundant harvest for Your glory!

——— *DECLARATION OF FAITH* ———

The Word to me is as seed sown into good ground.

Satan has been unable to pluck it out of me. It has taken root deep within me; and when the winds of trouble and persecution arise, I remain secure and steadfast.

All of the cares and worries in the world cannot cause the seed of the Word within me to perish.

I do not allow distractions such as fame, the deceitfulness of riches, or the lusts of the flesh to choke the Word and make it unfruitful in my life.

To the contrary, I am good ground. I receive the Word with an open heart and understand the principles of seedtime and harvest that are contained within it. As I operate these principles, I reap a harvest even one hundred times as much as what I have sown.

(Matthew 13:18-23; Luke 21:34; 1 Timothy 6:9-17; 2 Corinthians 9:5-11; Romans 7:4; John 15:1-8)

MARK 11:22-25

And Jesus answering saith unto them, Have faith in God. For verily I say unto you, That whosoever shall say unto this mountain, Be thou removed, and be thou cast into the sea; and shall not doubt in his heart, but shall believe that those things which he saith shall come to pass; he shall have whatsoever he saith. Therefore I say unto you, What things soever ye desire, when ye pray, believe that ye receive *them*, and ye shall have *them*. And when ye stand praying, forgive, if ye have ought against any: that your Father also which is in heaven may forgive you your trespasses.

~ PRAYER ~

Father, I stand boldly before You and make my requests. I know that You are my loving Father and that I am welcome at Your throne. Therefore, I do not hesitate to ask for those things that I both need and desire. I know that You are more than willing to grant my requests if I will but ask. I also know that You have put your faith within me that I may speak to the formidable circumstances in life and command them to come in line with Your will. When I speak Your words of faith, I will not doubt in my heart. I believe that what

I say will come to pass, because it is not my power that causes it to happen but the power You have placed within me. I choose to be a man/woman of faith words, and I shall have the things that I say.

———— *DECLARATION OF FAITH* ————

I am constantly functioning in God-like faith.

God has created me as a faith being. My words bring into existence whatever I am believing for.

If I command a mountain (a formidable circumstance or barrier) to be removed and cast into the sea and have no doubt that it will happen, it will happen.

Everything that I believe with my heart and speak from my mouth, within the boundaries of God's Word, becomes reality for me. Whatever I ask for in prayer, if I believe I have received it, I will have it.

I understand that unforgiveness and strife bring cancellation to what I am praying for. Therefore, I refuse to harbor them in my life. I continually remember my own frame, all that God has forgiven me of, and that I have no right to withhold grace from others when I myself walk in it so freely.

(2 Corinthians 4:13; 5:7; Romans 5:1,2; 10:8-10; Hebrews 11:1,6; Matthew 6:14; 8:13; 17:20; 18:23-35; 21:21,22; Proverbs 18:20,21; Luke 11:9; John 14:13,14; 15:7; 16:23,24; James 1:6-8; Ephesians 4:32; Colossians 3:13)

MARK 12:41-44

And Jesus sat over against the treasury, and beheld how the people cast money into the treasury: and many that were rich cast in much. And there came a certain poor widow, and she threw in two mites, which make a farthing. And he called *unto him* his disciples, and saith unto them, Verily I say unto you, That this poor widow hath cast more in, than all they which have cast into the treasury: For all *they* did cast in of their abundance; but she of her want did cast in all that she had, *even* all her living.

~ *PRAYER* ~

Father, I know that You are watching over all of my giving. Nothing I have placed into Your kingdom has been in vain. You see the importance I place on giving. Through my giving, I have proven that my faith is not in money or in the things which I possess. My faith is in You, Father. I know that no matter what my circumstance may be, I can give my way out of it, because You see all and will bless me in return.

——— DECLARATION OF FAITH ———

I keep my faith out on the edge. I know that the quality of my seed is not in the amount, but in the sacrifice. I do not give the Lord leftovers and extras. I give Him my best and He gives me His best in return.

(2 Samuel 24:24; Luke 6:38; 2 Corinthians 9:8)

CHAPTER TWENTY-NINE

LUKE

LUKE 1:45

And blessed *is* she that believed: for there shall be a performance of those things which were told her from the Lord.

~ *PRAYER* ~

Father, I choose to believe in spite of all pomp and circumstance. You are faithful. You will perform those things You have promised me in Your Word.

——— *DECLARATION OF FAITH* ———

I am blessed (happy, joyful, and to be envied) because I believe that I am who God says I am, and I can do what He says I can do.

(Isaiah 55:11; Psalm 119:38; John 14:12)

LUKE 6:20

And he lifted up his eyes on his disciples, and said, Blessed *be ye* poor: for yours is the kingdom of God.

~ *PRAYER* ~

Father, no matter what my situation is, I know that I am blessed. Mine is the kingdom of God. I have wealth and provision from the very throne of heaven!

——— *DECLARATION OF FAITH* ———

I am blessed, satisfied, and filled with the joy and favor of almighty God regardless of my outward condition.

I have been made a prince/princess in God's royal house and have inherited the kingdom of heaven.

All poverty and affliction must step aside as I enter into my rights as God's son/daughter and heir to the covenants of promise.

(Revelation 1:5,6; Nehemiah 8:10; Galatians 4:5,6; Luke 12:32; 2 Corinthians 8:9)

LUKE 6:27-38

But I say unto you which hear, Love your enemies, do good to them which hate you, Bless them that curse you, and pray for them which despitefully use you. And unto him that smiteth thee on the *one* cheek offer also the other; and him that taketh away thy cloak forbid not *to take thy* coat also. Give to every man that asketh of thee; and of him that taketh away thy goods ask *them* not again. And as ye would that men should do to you, do ye also to them likewise. For if ye love them which love you, what thank have ye? for sinners also love those that love them. And if ye do good to them which do good to you, what thank have ye? for sinners also do even the same. And if ye lend *to them* of whom ye hope to receive, what thank have ye? for sinners also lend to sinners, to receive as much again. But love ye your enemies, and do good, and lend, hoping for nothing again; and your reward shall be great, and ye shall be the children of the Highest: for he is kind unto the unthankful and *to* the evil. Be ye therefore merciful, as your Father also is merciful.

Judge not, and ye shall not be judged: condemn not, and ye shall not be condemned: forgive, and ye shall be forgiven: Give, and it shall be given unto you; good measure, pressed down, and shaken together, and running over, shall men give into your bosom. For with the same measure that ye mete withal it shall be measured to you again.

~ PRAYER ~

Father, I thank You for making me a blessing in this earth. I am blessed so that I may be a blessing to others. I am not a revenge seeker. To the contrary, I look for ways to fix problems and bring peace to the situation. I love my earthly enemies and seek the greater good for everyone in my circle of influence. I give without holding back, and I bless without demanding payment in return. I purpose in my heart to remain a forgiving and merciful man/woman. I refrain from harsh judgment and despise condemnation. I choose the path of blessing. I give and it is given unto me: good measure, pressed down, shaken together, and running over. I sow bountifully and I reap bountifully. I recognize You in all of my giving, Father, for I know that You always add Your own compound interest in my return.

DECLARATION OF FAITH

I am completely focused and attentive on the Word of the Lord, not just to learn it but also to live it.

I make it a practice to love my enemies. Those who detest me and are continually looking for ways to hurt me find only love from me in return. I never retaliate in anger. Instead, I show myself to be a child of nobility who finds creative ways to do good by them. I fully understand that all of their curses upon me do not have the power to harm me in any way. Therefore, I look for ways to bless them, showing them God's love and mercy, as well as my own.

I never forget that I am a born-again child of God. I do not stand idle and allow myself to be beaten upon, but I retaliate in the spirit of love and goodness under the direction of the Holy Spirit.

The children of the devil do not fully understand what they are doing when they try to harm me. Therefore, instead of repaying evil for evil, I do what is best for them and demonstrate the blessings of God. Nothing that they can take from me can harm me or cause me to fail to prosper. When they take, I give, and yet increase all the more. And I give freely to all, both the good and the evil, in order that I may demonstrate God's love and mercy and display His true nature to all who see.

I treat others exactly the way I would want to be treated if I were in their situation. I make it a point in my life to see the world through other people's eyes.

All of my actions toward my fellow man are rooted in love. I am even kind and good to my enemies, finding ways to help them and make their lives easier to live. I am not moved by how they respond to me, nor do I hold back my blessings when they try to harm me.

Even if they do not readily receive what I have for them, I know that my Father takes notice. In Him, I find recompense and a rich, abundant reward.

In all of these things, my Father sees that I am living as a good son/daughter, showing myself to be just like He is, for He is kind and charitable to both the good and the evil. Even the selfish and ungrateful ones enjoy His blessings. Therefore, I shall walk in the spirit of mercy and compassion just as He does.

I do not seek judgment and condemnation on people, nor do I harbor strife and resentment toward anyone. I always remember how far God has brought me, how patient He has been towards me, and how much He has forgiven me of. Being an imitator of my Father, I am resolved to be just as patient and forgiving as He is.

I live my life in a spirit of generosity. I am always looking for ways to give to others. I am not a parasite that looks for something to take and lives my life by what others can give me. I find God's way, the way of giving, to be much more satisfying.

When I give, God causes men to give the same back to me. He takes the measure that I have given, presses it down, adds a little more, shakes it all together, adds some more, jumps up and down on it, adds some more, gets the angels to fill in all the little nooks and crannies, then pours as much as He can on the top until the measure that I get back is overflowing with His abundance!

What a blessing it is to be a giver in the family of God!

(Romans 8:31; 12:14-20; 13:10; Hebrews 13:16; Matthew 5:46-48; 7:1-5,12; 18:21-35; Mark 11:25; Proverbs 19:17; 28:27; Psalm 79:12; Genesis 12:1-3; James 1:22-25; 2:13; Galatians 4:5,6; 6:6-10; Acts 7:60; 1 Corinthians 6:7; 13:4-6; Deuteronomy 15:7,8; 1 Peter 3:13)

LUKE 10:18-20

And he said unto them, I beheld Satan as lightning fall from heaven. Behold, I give unto you power to tread on serpents and scorpions, and over all the power of the enemy: and nothing shall by any means hurt you.

Notwithstanding in this rejoice not, that the spirits are subject unto you; but rather rejoice, because your names are written in heaven.

~ PRAYER ~

Father, I have no fear of the things I face in this life. You are my own loving Father, and You are greater than all. With You on my side, no enemy can succeed against me. I know that in Jesus I have been given tremendous power and authority. I have power to tread upon serpents and scorpions and over all the power of the enemy, and nothing shall by any means harm me! Therefore, I take authority over every evil force that is hindering my prosperity. I command every spirit of poverty to leave me now, in Jesus' name!

Father, even though I have this authority, it is not what matters most. What is most important is that I am Your son/daughter. My name is written in heaven. I am a child in covenant partnership with You. In this I truly rejoice.

———— DECLARATION OF FAITH ————

All wicked spirits are subject to my authority in Jesus' name.

I have all of the authority that I need to trample down serpents and scorpions; and I have mental, physical, and spiritual strength over and above all that the enemy possesses. There is nothing that Satan can do to harm me in any way.

For me, Satan and his demons are little more than harmless, pesky bugs.

Nevertheless, I do not find great joy in my ability to cast out demons or the fact that they are subject to my authority, but I rejoice that my name has been written in heaven and that I am honored as a son/daughter of the living God.

(Mark 16:17,18; Luke 9:1,2; Psalm 91:13; Ephesians 1:17-23; Philippians 4:3)

LUKE 11:5-13

And he said unto them, Which of you shall have a friend, and shall go unto him at midnight, and say unto him, Friend, lend me three loaves; For a friend of mine in his journey is come to me, and I have nothing to set before him? And he from within shall answer and say, Trouble me not: the door is now shut, and my children are with me in bed; I cannot rise and give thee. I say unto you, Though he will not rise and give him, because he is his friend, yet because of his importunity he will rise and give him as many as he needeth. And I say unto you, Ask, and it shall be given you; seek, and ye shall find; knock, and it shall be opened unto you. For every one that asketh receiveth; and he that seeketh findeth; and to him that knocketh it shall be opened.

If a son shall ask bread of any of you that is a father, will he give him a stone? or if *he ask* a fish, will he for a fish give him a serpent? Or if he shall ask an egg, will he offer him a scorpion? If ye then, being evil, know how to give good gifts unto your children: how much more shall *your* heavenly Father give the Holy Spirit to them that ask him?

~ *PRAYER* ~

Father, I am one importune dude/dudette! I am fervent and persistent. I know that when I ask, You give. When I seek, You cause me to find. When I knock, You open the door wide unto me. I am a receiver and a finder who regularly walks through open doors. I know that You are more than willing to give me what I ask for; therefore, I will not give in until I have it.

Father, I recall those times when people wanted something from Jesus. He did not just give it to them. He asked them what it was that they wanted. He asked for specifics, and when they made their requests, He granted them. Therefore, Father, I will be specific as well. I will ask according to Your Word and stand confident that I receive what I am asking for.

———— *DECLARATION OF FAITH* ————

I am a man/woman who is persistent in prayer. I relentlessly call on my Father to fill my every need and the needs of those in my circle of influence.

God is honored by my insistence and gladly provides me with all of the necessities of life.

When I speak one of God's promises into my life, I know that I must continually believe and speak it until what I have called for is manifested in this natural world.

Whenever I am seeking anything, I remember that I have a guide within me. Therefore, I will not give up until I have found what I am looking for.

When I have come to a door of promised blessing that is shut, I will knock at that door until it opens to me and my life is showered with all of the benefits of that promise.

When I persistently ask, I receive all that I am praying for and more. When I persistently seek, I find what I am looking for and more. When I persistently knock, the door eventually opens to me, and I walk in the fullness of God's blessings in my life.

I am careful to ask for specific things. God does not operate in vague generalities, nor does He respond to my prayers with something other than what I am asking for.

Even I, as a good father/mother, know how to give good gifts to my children. I give them specifically what they are asking for so that their joy may be full. If my children ask me for something that is not good for them, I simply do not give it.

The same goes for my heavenly Father. It brings Him great pleasure to give me those specific desires of my heart. I am granted anything I desire that is in line with His perfect will as is revealed in His Word. He gives me anything that I ask for that is beneficial to me and will work to my advantage. If I faithfully ask Him for the Holy Spirit, I can fully trust that He will give me the Holy Spirit and not some devil full of counterfeit gifts.

(Matthew 7:7-9; Isaiah 55:6; Philippians 4:19; James 1:5-8,17; 4:3,4; 1 John 5:14,15; John 14:13,14; 16:13,23,24; Mark 11:22-25; 2 Corinthians 1:20; Psalm 37:4)

LUKE 11:17-26

But he, knowing their thoughts, said unto them, Every kingdom divided against itself is brought to desolation; and a house *divided* against a house falleth. If Satan also be divided against himself, how shall his kingdom stand? because ye say that I cast out devils through Beelzebub. And if I by Beelzebub cast out devils, by whom do your sons cast *them* out? therefore shall they be your judges. But if I with the finger of God cast out devils, no doubt the kingdom of God is come upon you. When a strong man armed keepeth his palace, his goods are in peace: But when a stronger than he shall come upon him, and overcome him, he taketh from him all his armour wherein he trusted, and divideth his spoils. He that is not with me is against me: and he that gathereth not with me scattereth. When the unclean spirit is gone out of a man, he walketh through dry places, seeking rest; and finding none, he saith, I will return unto my house whence I came out. And when he cometh, he findeth *it* swept and garnished. Then goeth he, and taketh *to him* seven other spirits more wicked than himself; and they enter in, and dwell there: and the last *state* of that man is worse than the first.

~ PRAYER ~

Father, I thank You for Your wisdom and guidance. I clearly see the folly of strife and will not allow it to remain in my presence. Neither my house nor my business shall be divided against itself. I take my authority and cast the spirit of strife from my presence for good. Never again will I allow strife and ungodly practices to become a part of my life. I take up arms against them. I have the strength of almighty God, and my goods are in peace. This is not a faltering decision, Father. I will not allow myself to waver and then find myself in a situation seven times worse than when the problem started. My house and business shall remain safe and secure under the power of Your anointing.

——— DECLARATION OF FAITH ———

I will not allow Satan to bring strife and bitterness into my life. I stand strong against spirits of division and confusion. My home and my finances are secure because I remain in partnership with God through tithing and taking my authority over evil forces.

I carry the kingdom within me and drive out demons by the very finger of God.

Demons may overpower many in the world, holding them captive to their every whim, but I have been sent into the world to set the captives free!

Jesus attacked and conquered the forces of Satan, stripping them of all of their power and authority over the believer, and He has given me my portion of the spoils of war.

I have taken my stand at His side, with total and complete authority over all demonic forces.

I have taken His yoke upon me and hold His interests as my very own.

(Luke 9:1,2; 10:19; Isaiah 61:1-3; Matthew 28:18-20; Colossians 2:15; Ephesians 1:17-23; John 14:12)

LUKE 12:13-15

And one of the company said unto him, Master, speak to my brother, that he divide the inheritance with me. And he said unto him, Man, who made me a judge or a divider over you? And he said unto them, Take heed, and beware of covetousness: for a man's life consisteth not in the abundance of the things which he possesseth.

~ PRAYER ~

Father, keep me from a heart of covetousness. I have no desire to take what belongs to my brother. What he has received is his, and I rejoice with him that he has it. I know that my life is not about riches. It is about You, Father. It is about living under Your care and protection. It is about living the kingdom way and not the way of the world. It is not about selfishness or wanting a portion of what others have.

——— DECLARATION OF FAITH ———

I am careful not to be greedy in my new abundant life. I remain free of all covetousness, for I fully understand that my life does not consist of, nor is it sustained by, the amount of wealth and possessions that I have. I remain focused on the whole kingdom and not just the wealth therein.

(1 Timothy 6:5-20; Matthew 4:1-11; 6:25-34)

LUKE 12:16-31

And he spake a parable unto them, saying, The ground of a certain rich man brought forth plentifully: And he thought within himself, saying, What shall I do, because I have no room where to bestow my fruits? And he said, This will I do: I will pull down my barns, and build greater; and there will I bestow all my fruits and my goods. And I will say to my soul, Soul, thou hast much goods laid up for many years; take thine ease, eat, drink, *and* be merry. But God said unto him, *Thou* fool, this night thy soul shall be required of thee: then whose shall those things be, which thou hast provided? So *is* he that layeth up treasure for himself, and is not rich toward God. And he said unto his disciples, Therefore I say unto you, Take no thought for your life, what ye shall eat; neither for the body, what ye shall put on. The life is more than meat, and the body *is more* than raiment. Consider the ravens: for they neither sow nor reap; which neither have storehouse nor barn; and God feedeth them: how much more are ye better than the fowls? And which of you with taking thought can add to his stature one cubit? If ye then be not able to do that thing which is least, why take ye thought for the rest? Consider the lilies how they grow: they toil not, they spin not; and yet I say unto you, that Solomon in all his glory was not arrayed like one of these. If then God so clothe the grass, which is to day in the field, and to morrow is cast into the oven; how much more *will he clothe* you, O ye of little faith? And seek not ye what ye shall eat, or what ye shall drink, neither be ye of doubtful mind. For all these things do the nations of the world seek after: and your Father knoweth that ye have need of these things. But rather seek ye the kingdom of God; and all these things shall be added unto you.

~ PRAYER ~

Father, I will not be the fool who trusts in uncertain riches. I do not work to the end that one day I can be lazy and do nothing. My life does not consist of the abundance of things that I possess. I do not lay up treasures for myself and trust them as my security. You alone are the security of my life. My riches are for Your glory and the advancement of Your kingdom. I know that You prosper everything I set my hand to do. Therefore, I will find a way to be productive until the last breath leaves my body.

Father, I know that riches cause great stress and anxiety in the world. But You have bid me to live free of stress and anxiety. Therefore, I will not allow any fear to come upon me. I cast all of my cares upon You, for I know that You care for me diligently. I do not concern myself with credit ratings, stock market analsis, inflation, recession, or depression. My concern is the advancement of Your kingdom and Your righteousness. With You as my Father, I will always have all that I need and more.

——— DECLARATION OF FAITH ———

I will not lay up and hoard treasures, riches, and possessions for myself (in greed, selfishness, or fear of the future) and thereby neglect my relationship with my heavenly Father. He alone is my provider and the sustainer of my life. My contentment is in Him and not in the things that I possess. If men took all that I have and left me with just the clothes on my back, I would take off my shirt, hand it to them, and walk away praising God. He never fails to provide my needs regardless of the circumstances, and neither man, nor devil, can stop His prosperity in my life.

I am not anxious or troubled by the necessities of life—what I will eat, or what I will have to wear—for my life is more than food and my body more than clothing. God has made me His own son/daughter—the highest priority of all of His creation—and He does not neglect my needs.

When I observe, study, and meditate on the life of the raven—how they neither sow nor reap, nor have any storehouses to provide for their future, and yet my Father feeds them and cares for them—I find reason to believe. He makes it His business to care for the raven and never fails as their source of supply. How much more will He care for me, His eternal son/daughter? In my heavenly Father's eyes, I am worth more than many flocks of ravens!

In light of this, fear (worry, stress, and anxiety) becomes ever-increasingly ridiculous. It does absolutely nothing for me. It doesn't add a single minute to my life, never fixes my situation, and its infectious nature only causes everything around me to get worse. In all honesty, fear is an act of total and complete foolishness. It is rooted in either ignorance of, or defiance of, the knowledge of God's love that He has for His children.

When fear raises itself against me, I can look to the lilies of the field and how they grow. They don't wear themselves out trying to survive. Even if they're plowed over, they grow right back and bloom like a smile. Yet, even Solomon in all of his glory was not clothed in such beauty.

If my heavenly Father clothes the grass of the field, which is here today and gone tomorrow, in such beauty, how much more wonderfully shall He clothe me, His eternal son/daughter?

What reason is there to fear when I have such a loving Father watching over me? I refuse to be overly concerned about a single issue of life. My Father knows what I need better than I do, and He never fails to be the source of my supply.

My walk with God is focused around the whole of the kingdom. There is no single issue that overwhelms my attention. I live the kingdom life, and I enjoy all of the benefits therein. I do not allow fear to enter in and steal what I have been given, for I know that it is my Father's good pleasure to give me the kingdom and all of its blessings.

I do not hoard things to myself in fear that I will have nothing in the future. I give to the poor freely, bringing the kingdom into their midst. I understand my source of supply, and I am always willing to give. Through my generosity, I store up an endless, inexhaustible supply of treasure in heaven that no thief can steal and no moth can devour.

This is kingdom-living and the life that I have chosen.

(Philippians 4:10-19; Matthew 5:40-42; 6:19-33; Genesis 22:14; Hebrews 13:5,6; 1 Kings 10:4-7; James 1:22-25; 2:5; 5:1-5; 1 Peter 5:5-7; Joshua 1:5-9; Psalm 103:1-5; 2 Corinthians 9:5-11)

LUKE 12:32-34

Fear not, little flock; for it is your Father's good pleasure to give you the kingdom. Sell that ye have, and give alms; provide yourselves bags which wax not old, a treasure in the heavens that faileth not, where no thief approacheth, neither moth corrupteth. For where your treasure is, there will your heart be also.

~ PRAYER ~

Father, examine my life. Take note of where my treasure is. Through my giving I have proven that my heart is with You. You alone are my provider. I acknowledge that without You I would have nothing. Therefore, I am not afraid to give. I have no fear, because I know it is Your good pleasure to give me the kingdom. When I give, You give back to me in abundance. The riches I receive in return never fail. They cannot be corrupted or stolen. My harvest is always protected by Your anointing, and in You my increase is eternally guaranteed.

—— DECLARATION OF FAITH ——

I have no fear of financial ruin. I do not entertain thoughts of bankruptcy or even ruined credit ratings. I know that it is my Father's good pleasure to give me His kingdom. He enjoys showering me with His blessings. What have I to fear when I have such a loving Father taking care of me? No, I will not fear, but will continue to work His unfailing laws of increase. I give and I'm given back incorruptible riches. My heart is with my Lord and His provision is with me.

(Isaiah 41:10-13; Luke 6:38; Deuteronomy 28:1-14)

LUKE 15:17-24

And when he came to himself, he said, How many hired servants of my father's have bread enough and to spare, and I perish with hunger! I will arise and go to my father, and will say unto him, Father, I have sinned against heaven, and before thee, And am no more worthy to be called thy son: make me as one of thy hired servants. And he arose, and came to his father. But when he was yet a great way off, his father saw him, and had compassion, and ran, and fell on his neck, and kissed him. And the son said unto him, Father, I have sinned against heaven, and in thy sight, and am no more worthy to be called thy son. But the father said to his servants, Bring forth the best robe, and put *it* on him; and put a ring on his hand, and shoes on *his* feet: And bring hither the fatted calf, and kill *it*; and let us eat, and be merry: For this my son was dead, and is alive again; he was lost, and is found. And they began to be merry.

~ PRAYER ~

Father, I never want to be found outside of You. You are the surest source of security in my life. Even Your servants have abundance with plenty to spare. How much more shall You give to me, Your son/daughter? Thank You for making me Your heir. Thank You for placing Your best robe upon me and granting me the royal authority of heaven. I am now called by Your name, and I enjoy all the benefits of sonship.

—— DECLARATION OF FAITH ——

My Father runs to embrace me every time I turn to Him. His love for me is stronger than any sin I can commit.

Whenever I turn to my Father in repentance, He immediately dresses me in the festive robe of honor (the robe of His righteousness). He doesn't just put clothes on me, but adorns me in the finest of apparel.

He then has the signet ring placed upon my finger and reinstates me to my position of authority as His son/daughter.

He has shoes placed upon my feet so that I am well prepared to expand the borders of His kingdom.

He breaks out the fatted calf (that tremendous supply of the new covenant where there is enough to spare and to share) and bids me to take my fill in great joy and gladness.

All of the angels of God come together to rejoice with us, for the power of death has been broken over my life, and I have been reborn into the royal family of almighty God!

(Psalm 103:13; Jeremiah 3:12-14; Matthew 9:36; Acts 2:39; Ephesians 2:1-14,17; Luke 15:10; Galatians 4:5,6; 2 Corinthians 5:17-21; 8:9; Colossians 2:13)

LUKE 16:9-13

And I say unto you, Make to yourselves friends of the mammon of unrighteousness; that, when ye fail, they may receive you into everlasting habitations. He that is faithful in that which is least is faithful also in much: and he that is unjust in the least is unjust also in much. If therefore ye have not been faithful in the unrighteous mammon, who will commit to your trust the true *riches?* And if ye have not been faithful in that which is another man's, who shall give you that which is your own?

No servant can serve two masters: for either he will hate the one, and love the other; or else he will hold to the one, and despise the other. Ye cannot serve God and mammon.

~ PRAYER ~

Father, I recognize that money is a tool that You have given me. I clearly see the purpose of money. It is not a source of provision. It is a tool of provision. Therefore, I will be shrewd with it to the end that I may gain friends for myself who will welcome me into eternal dwellings.

I commit myself to be faithful with the money You have given me. I will not horde it for myself, trusting that the abundance of my riches will keep me supplied. You alone are the source of my supply. Therefore, I am faithful to give freely and without restraint. I know that You reward my faithfulness, Father. I am faithful with that which is little, and I shall be ruler over much. Your blessing is ever upon me, and my accounts fill to overflowing because my heart is in the right place. I do not trust and serve money. I trust and serve You.

By giving for the advancement of the gospel, I gain new friends for myself who will be with me for all of eternity. I may never meet them on this earth, but one day they will welcome me into their mansions and thank me for what I have done.

When I provide for the needs of a soul-winning ministry, I prove myself to be a soul-winner.

I am faithful to do with my money just as God would have me do. It doesn't matter how little I have, or how great my wealth may be, I am a faithful steward. By proving myself faithful with the riches of the world, I earn true, enduring, and incorruptible riches for my heavenly account.

(Philippians 4:14-19; Matthew 25:21; 1 Peter 1:3,4)

LUKE 19:11-26

And as they heard these things, he added and spake a parable, because he was nigh to Jerusalem, and because they thought that the kingdom of God should immediately appear. He said therefore, A certain nobleman went into a far country to receive for himself a kingdom, and to return. And he called his ten servants, and delivered them ten pounds, and said unto them, Occupy till I come. But his citizens hated him, and sent a message after him, saying, We will not have this *man* to reign over us. And it came to pass, that when he was returned, having received the kingdom, then he commanded these servants to be called unto him, to whom he had given the money, that he might know how much every man had gained by trading. Then came the first, saying, Lord, thy pound hath gained ten pounds. And he said unto him, Well, thou good servant: because thou hast been faithful in a very little, have thou authority over ten cities. And the second came, saying, Lord, thy pound hath gained five pounds. And he said likewise to him, Be thou also over five cities. And another came, saying, Lord, behold, *here is* thy pound, which I have kept laid up in a napkin: For I feared thee, because thou art an austere man: thou takest up that thou layedst not down, and reapest that thou didst not sow. And he saith unto him, Out of thine own mouth will I judge thee, *thou* wicked servant. Thou knewest that I was an austere man, taking up that I laid not down, and reaping that I did not sow: Wherefore then gavest not thou my money into the bank, that at my coming I might have required mine own with usury? And he said unto them that stood by, Take from him the pound, and give *it* to him that hath ten pounds. (And they said unto him, Lord, he hath ten pounds.) For I say unto you, That unto every one which hath shall be given; and from him that hath not, even that he hath shall be taken away from him.

~ *PRAYER* ~

Father, You are very clearly a God of abundance. You fully expect me to increase and prosper in my life. Your desire for me is to take that which You have given me and cause it to increase under Your anointing. Therefore, I choose to be a profitable servant. I give and it is given unto me good measure, pressed down, shaken together, and running over. My borders increase and my storehouses are filled with the finest of treasures. I am blessed to be a blessing! I am a supporter of soul-winning ministries who take what I have given and advance Your kingdom with fervency and purpose. I prosper that I may conquer and win this world for Your glory!

—— *DECLARATION OF FAITH* ——

I am in this earth to occupy and control it until Jesus returns. He has given me His own resources as a foundation to build upon. It is His will and purpose that I produce more and more until I have increased beyond measure. I will not be the wicked servant who fears the pursuit of prosperity. To the contrary, I am the profitable servant, and I will honor the Lord by working hard and producing an abundance for His kingdom.

(Genesis 1:28; Psalm 35:27; Jeremiah 29:11; 33:9)

CHAPTER THIRTY

JOHN

JOHN 14:13,14

And whatsoever ye shall ask in my name, that will I do, that the Father may be glorified in the Son. If ye shall ask any thing in my name, I will do *it*.

~ *PRAYER* ~

Father, in Jesus' name I ask You to prosper all that I set my hand to do today. In accordance with Your Word, fill my treasuries to overflowing. Increase my holdings that I may have the means to give in ever-increasing measure. Make me a tool to bless this earth. Use me to feed the hungry, clothe the naked, give comfort to the widow and orphan, and win lost souls. Advance Your kingdom through me, Father, in Jesus' name.

———— *DECLARATION OF FAITH* ————

Whatever I ask for, in Jesus' name, I receive so that the Father may be glorified through the Son. Only through Jesus are my prayers answered. He has given me the very power of attorney to use His name. It is like a legal document proclaiming that all of the power that is in His name is now mine to use. I can freely draw upon all that He is and all that He has. Whatever I have asked for in His name, I can confidently claim as done.

(John 15:7; 16:23,24; 17:20-26; Mark 11:22-25; 16:15-20; Matthew 28:18-20; 2 Corinthians 5:17-21; Acts 1:8; 2:43; 4:23-33; 1 Peter 1:2-4; Colossians 1:29; Ephesians 1:17-23; Hebrews 10:14; 1 John 5:14,15; Philippians 2:10)

JOHN 14:26,27

But the Comforter, *which is* the Holy Ghost, whom the Father will send in my name, he shall teach you all things, and bring all things to your remembrance, whatsoever I have said unto you. Peace I leave with you, my peace I give unto you: not as the world giveth, give I unto you. Let not your heart be troubled, neither let it be afraid.

~ PRAYER ~

Father, thank You for sending me the Holy Spirit to lead and guide me through the affairs of this life. I thank You that He opens the eyes of my understanding so that I may know what to do in any and every situation. He teaches me all things and brings to my remembrance all that You have taught me.

Father, I know that You are with me at all times. I rest in the comfort of Your care. I will not let my heart be troubled, neither will I let it be afraid. My trust is in You and not the situation I am in. I am taught, led, and cared for by the most powerful and faithful God in existence. I am destined to succeed.

──── DECLARATION OF FAITH ────

The Holy Spirit, who is my Comforter, Counselor, and strength, whom the Father has sent to me in Jesus' name, teaches me all things. I can turn to Him at any time and receive all of the wisdom that I need in any given situation. He brings to my remembrance all of those things that Jesus has taught me in His Word. He opens it up to me, giving me revelation knowledge and complete working understanding of all that His Word calls me to do. He sees to it that I know all that I need to know to live this holy life that I have been called to live.

I have, at this moment, the very peace of Jesus within my heart. He has given it to me, not as the world gives, but as He gives. It is mine forever. He will never take it from me.

I will not allow my heart to be troubled or afraid. In Jesus, I have a boldness of faith and confidence that puts me over in every situation.

(John 16:13-15; 1 Corinthians 2:6-16; James 1:5-8; Matthew 13:15,16; Romans 14:17; Philippians 4:7; 2 Timothy 1:7; Mark 11:22-25; Ephesians 2:14; Hebrews 4:16)

JOHN 15:1-8

I am the true vine, and my Father is the husbandman. Every branch in me that beareth not fruit he taketh away: and every *branch* that beareth fruit, he purgeth it, that it may bring forth more fruit. Now ye are clean through the word which I have spoken unto you. Abide in me, and I in you. As the branch cannot bear fruit of itself, except it abide in the vine; no more can ye, except ye abide in me. I am the vine, ye *are* the branches: He that abideth in me, and I in him, the same bringeth forth much fruit: for without me ye can do nothing. If a man abide not in me, he is cast forth as a branch, and is withered; and men gather them, and cast *them* into the fire, and they are burned. If ye abide in me, and my words abide in you, ye shall ask what ye will, and it shall be done unto you. Herein is my Father glorified, that ye bear much fruit; so shall ye be my disciples.

~ *PRAYER* ~

Father, thank You for sculpting me in such a way that I produce much fruit for Your kingdom. I am a productive branch of the Vine. I have been pruned for abundant increase. I abide in Jesus and He abides in me. I do not produce things by my own power, but by the power of almighty God! I am completely dependent upon Jesus as the source of all of my abilities. Miracles do not come to me by my own power but by Your power flowing through me.

Father, I have sown the Word in my heart. It is living and abiding within me. I know that whatever I ask according to Your Word, I shall receive. I purpose in my heart to glorify You, Father. I will bear much fruit and produce in abundance for Your glory.

———— *DECLARATION OF FAITH* ————

Jesus is the true Vine and my Father is the master gardener.

I am a branch of the true Vine. If I am not bearing fruit, my Father will prune away at me (cleansing and training me) until I do. He makes me what I am—joyfully molding and forming me—until I continually increase and bear richer and more excellent fruit.

I am a cleansed, pruned, and well-fed branch of the Vine because of the Word.

I dwell in Jesus and He dwells in me. My life is totally dependent upon Him. Just as a branch cannot live, let alone bear fruit, if it is not in vital union with the Vine, neither can I live and bear fruit unless I remain in vital union with Jesus.

Jesus is the Vine, and I am one of the branches that come forth from Him. I live in and by Him, and I bear an abundance of good fruit. Apart from Him, I can do nothing.

I am in vital union with Jesus, living and remaining in Him continually. His Word remains in me, rooted and grounded within the depths of my heart. Through the Word, I have a complete revelation of the will and purpose of my Father. Therefore, whatever I ask of the Father in Jesus' name, in line with the Word and in incessantly active faith, I am guaranteed to receive.

My Father is honored and glorified when I bear a great variety and abundance of fruit. By this, I show myself to be a true disciple of Jesus.

(Ephesians 2:10; 3:17; Matthew 4:4; 5:16; 13:12,15,16; 1 Corinthians 1:30; 2:6-16; 3:16; Colossians 1:27-29; 2:7; John 14:13,14; 16:23,24; 17:17; James 2:14-26; Luke 8:10; 1 John 5:14,15; Mark 11:22-25)

JOHN 16:23-27

And in that day ye shall ask me nothing. Verily, verily, I say unto you, Whatsoever ye shall ask the Father in my name, he will give *it* you. Hitherto have ye asked nothing in my name: ask, and ye shall receive, that your joy may be full. These things have I spoken unto you in proverbs: but the time cometh, when I shall no more speak unto you in proverbs, but I shall show you plainly of the Father. At that day ye shall ask in my name: and I say not unto you, that I will pray the Father for you: For the Father himself loveth you, because ye have loved me, and have believed that I came out from God.

~ PRAYER ~

Father, it is a glory and a wonder that I have become Your child. It is an awesome thing to me to be welcome at Your throne. I am Your own son/daughter, and Jesus is my elder brother. At this very moment I am an heir to Your kingdom. You love me as much as You love Jesus. Whatever I ask of You in Jesus' name, You give to me so that my joy may be full. You speak to me plainly, and I enjoy sweet fellowship in Your presence. Oh, the wonder of it, Father. I plan on taking full advantage. I will cling to Your garments and find refuge in Your arms. I place You at the front of all that I do. I know that with You at the point, everything I set my hand to do will prosper.

——— DECLARATION OF FAITH ———

My heart rejoices in Jesus, and no one can take my joy from me.

I am now a born-again child of God—the very brother/sister of Jesus Himself.

In His name, I have all that I desire from God. My heavenly Father freely grants me whatever I desire that is in accordance with His will and purpose as established in His Word. What I ask for in Jesus' name is a done deal the moment I ask. Therefore, I will continually ask, receiving all that I desire from God, so that my joy may be made complete.

Jesus has given me a mind to receive the Word with complete understanding. He opens it up to me, making it plain and clear. All that He tells me of the Father, I fully understand.

He has built for me a perfect relationship with the Father. In Jesus' name, I can stand before the Father free of all sense of unworthiness, for I know that it is not my own righteousness that gives me this right, but the righteousness of Jesus Himself.

All that Jesus is and has done has been credited to my account. Through His name, I am identified with everything that He did.

Therefore, I can come boldly into the Father's presence without any sense of guilt or inadequacy. He loves me with all of His heart and is overjoyed that I have taken the name of Jesus as my own and have become His son/daughter.

Because of Jesus, my heavenly Father welcomes me with open arms every time I enter His presence, and He is more than willing to grant my every request.

(Nehemiah 8:10; 1 Peter 1:8; John 3:3; 14:13,14; 15:7,11; 17:13; 2 Corinthians 5:17, 21; Titus 3:5; Hebrews 2:11; 4:15,16; Romans 8:28-30; Matthew 7:7; 13:15,16; 21:22; 1 John 2:20; 5:14,15; 1 Corinthians 1:30; 2:6-16; Galatians 2:20; 4:5,6; Mark 11:22-25)

JOHN 20:29

Jesus saith unto him, Thomas, because thou hast seen me, thou hast believed: blessed *are* they that have not seen, and *yet* have believed.

~ *PRAYER* ~

Father, I do not give honor to circumstances. You are above any situation I find myself in. I do not look to what my eyes can see. I believe Your Word is at work and is producing that which You have sent it forth to do. I believe and therefore I am blessed. Period.

———— DECLARATION OF FAITH ————

I am not filled with doubt and unbelief but with steadfast faith.

Jesus is my Lord, my friend, and my God. Although I have never seen or touched Him (physically), I believe in Him; and I am blessed by, in, and through Him.

The Word has been given to me so that I may believe that Jesus is the Christ. Through my believing, and the confession of my faith, I have received eternal life.

(James 1:6-8; Mark 11:22-25; John 15:15; Romans 10:8-10; 1 John 5:11,12)

CHAPTER THIRTY-ONE

ACTS

ACTS 20:32-35

And now, brethren, I commend you to God, and to the word of his grace, which is able to build you up, and to give you an inheritance among all them which are sanctified. I have coveted no man's silver, or gold, or apparel. Yea, ye yourselves know, that these hands have ministered unto my necessities, and to them that were with me. I have shewed you all things, how that so labouring ye ought to support the weak, and to remember the words of the Lord Jesus, how he said, It is more blessed to give than to receive.

~ PRAYER ~

Father, I thank You for Your Word of grace, which is able to build me up and give me an inheritance among the sanctified. I do not covet that which belongs to another, and I keep myself from a spirit of greed and selfishness. I work with my own hands to produce profit in my life, and I am ever willing to give to those in need. I know that nothing that I give is in vain. My giving is like making a deposit into my heavenly account. I always receive back more than I have provided. I give liberally and yet increase all the more. In You, Father, it is truly more blessed to give than to receive.

—— DECLARATION OF FAITH ——

I am entrusted to God and the Word of His grace. He is well able to build me up, establish me, and fulfill my part of His tremendous inheritance among my brothers and sisters in Christ.

I do not covet another man's silver, or gold, or costly garments, but work with my own hands to provide for myself and those under my authority.

I am ever willing to assist the weak and ever mindful of the words of Jesus, who Himself said that there is more blessing in giving than receiving.

(Hebrews 9:15; 13:5-9; Acts 9:31; 18:3; Romans 8:17; 15:1; Genesis 12:1-3; Deuteronomy 28:9,12; Philippians 4:15-19)

CHAPTER THIRTY-TWO

ROMANS

✠

ROMANS 5:15-17

But not as the offence, so also *is* the free gift. For if through the offence of one many be dead, much more the grace of God, and the gift by grace, *which is* by one man, Jesus Christ, hath abounded unto many. And not as *it was* by one that sinned, *so is* the gift: for the judgment *was* by one to condemnation, but the free gift *is* of many offences unto justification. For if by one man's offence death reigned by one; much more they which receive abundance of grace and of the gift of righteousness shall reign in life by one, Jesus Christ.

~ *PRAYER* ~

Father, I thank You for my salvation. Through Jesus' substitution I have received abundance of grace and the gift of righteousness. I am now identified with all that He did. There is nothing that can hold Your blessings from me. I receive them through Jesus alone. I receive them by grace. I do not earn them. I just thank You for them. Sin is no longer an issue. I now reign in life through Christ Jesus my Lord!

─── *DECLARATION OF FAITH* ───

God has joyfully given me the free gift of grace, justification, and right-eousness. His gift to me has no strings attached, but He gives it to me freely so that I may have continuous fellowship with Him in a legitimate Father and son/daughter relationship.

The gift of God to me is not like the result of Adam's sin; for by Adam's sin, judgment and condemnation fell on me without choice. Freedom and jus-tification, on the other hand, are offered to me as a free gift.

*Though Adam's sin condemned me, God's free gift has brought me justi-
fication; for as Adam's sin brought me death, God's abundant provision of
grace (unmerited, undeserved favor) and free gift of righteousness have made
it so that I can reign in this life as a king.*

(Ephesians 2:4-10; Galatians 4:4-6; 5:1; Titus 3:4-7; Revelation 1:4-6)

ROMANS 8:31,32

What shall we then say to these things? If God *be* for us, who *can be* against
us? He that spared not his own Son, but delivered him up for us all, how
shall he not with him also freely give us all things?

~ *PRAYER* ~

Father, since You did not spare Your own Son, but delivered Him up for me,
I know that You freely give me all things. You have proven Your desire to
bless me. I will not listen to Satan's lies. I will receive Your blessings and live
the abundant life that You have called me to live.

—— *DECLARATION OF FAITH* ——

*What shall I declare about all of this? If God is on my side, where is there
a formidable foe or worthy enemy? God didn't spare His own Son but gave
Him for my salvation. Shall He not freely and graciously give me everything
else as well?*

(Hebrews 7:25; 10:10,14; 13:5,6; 2 Peter 1:3; Numbers 14:9; Isaiah 50:8,9;
2 Corinthians 5:17,21; John 3:16-18; Ephesians 1:17-23; 3:14-21; 1 Corinthians
15:57)

CHAPTER THIRTY-THREE

1 CORINTHIANS

1 CORINTHIANS 9:9-11

For it is written in the law of Moses, Thou shalt not muzzle the mouth of the ox that treadeth out the corn. Doth God take care for oxen? Or saith he *it* altogether for our sakes? For our sakes, no doubt, *this* is written: that he that ploweth should plow in hope; and that he that thresheth in hope should be partaker of his hope. If we have sown unto you spiritual things, *is it* a great thing if we shall reap your carnal things?

~ *PRAYER* ~

Father, I will not listen to religious rhetoric that claims You do not bless Your children materially in this life. You are a God of increase and prosperity. You have promised over and over that You will bless what I set my hand to do. It is a good thing for me to expect an abundant harvest. I know that You are causing Your favor to rain upon me. The angels are working for my increase. Nothing that I have set my hand to do will fail. To the contrary, my borders are increasing and my accounts are overflowing!

—— *DECLARATION OF FAITH* ——

I will not muzzle the ox that treadeth out the corn. I firmly believe that the laborer is worthy of his/her reward. Therefore, I will not hesitate to seek profit for the things that I accomplish. I am worthy of payment for what I do.

I have every right to expect a return on my giving as well. I live in a kingdom where I am blessed to be a blessing. I give, and it is given back to me good measure, pressed down, shaken together, and running over.

I am always worthy to receive a reward for my labor, and it is right and just for me to reap a material harvest from the spiritual seed that I have sown.

(2 Corinthians 9:5-11; Galatians 6:7-9; Romans 15:27)

1 CORINTHIANS 13:1-3

Though I speak with the tongues of men and of angels, and have not charity, I am become *as* sounding brass, or a tinkling cymbal. And though I have *the gift of* prophecy, and understand all mysteries, and all knowledge; and though I have all faith, so that I could remove mountains, and have not charity, I am nothing. And though I bestow all my goods to feed *the poor*, and though I give my body to be burned, and have not charity, it profiteth me nothing.

~ PRAYER ~

Father, I choose to keep my priorities in order. Love is the center of all of my actions. I do not seek profit for selfish gain. I seek profit that I may be a blessing in this earth.

───── DECLARATION OF FAITH ─────

If I speak in the tongues of men or angels but do not walk in love, all of my talk amounts to nothing.

If I have the gift of prophecy and can fathom all mysteries and knowledge, and if I have the kind of faith that can move mountains but do not walk in love, it is all worthless.

(Galatians 5:6; Philippians 1:9; 1 Thessalonians 4:9; 1 John 4:6-21)

1 CORINTHIANS 15:58

Therefore, my beloved brethren, be ye stedfast, unmoveable, always abounding in the work of the Lord, forasmuch as ye know that your labour is not in vain in the Lord.

~ PRAYER ~

Father, I know that You are always involved in what I am doing. I will never allow circumstances to cause me to doubt Your Word. I shall remain steadfast, immovable, and always abounding in Your work. My labor is never in vain. You always prosper what I set my hand to do.

—— DECLARATION OF FAITH ——

I shall let nothing move me to fear. I always give myself fully to the work of the Lord, because I know with certainty that my labor in Him is not in vain. My reward and my destiny are fixed, secured by the blood of Jesus and the seal (guarantee) of the Holy Spirit.

(1 Thessalonians 4:15-17; Hosea 13:14; 2 Timothy 1:6,7; 1 Corinthians 3:8)

CHAPTER THIRTY-FOUR

2 CORINTHIANS

---

2 CORINTHIANS 6:10

As sorrowful, yet alway rejoicing; as poor, yet making many rich; as having nothing, and *yet* possessing all things.

~ PRAYER ~

Father, thank You for opening my spiritual eyes. I know that there is more to my situation than what the natural eye can see. When it looks grim in the natural realm, I know that the circumstance looks awesome in the spiritual realm. I always have all that I need and more.

—— DECLARATION OF FAITH ——

I will not allow my circumstances to ever make me worried or afraid. Even when I feel sorrowful, I still have cause to rejoice. When it looks as though I am poor, I still bring riches to many. And when it looks as though I have nothing, I still have provision in abundance.

(Matthew 6:19-34; 2 Corinthians 5:7; Philippians 4:6-8)

2 CORINTHIANS 8:2-5

How that in a great trial of affliction the abundance of their joy and their deep poverty abounded unto the riches of their liberality. For to *their* power, I bear record, yea, and beyond *their* power *they were* willing of themselves; Praying us with much intreaty that we would receive the gift, and *take upon us* the fellowship of the ministering to the saints. And *this they did*, not as we hoped, but first gave their own selves to the Lord, and unto us by the will of God.

~ PRAYER ~

Father, You are the first and most vital necessity in my life. All that I have is from You. Therefore, I give myself to You fully and unconditionally. I am Yours. I choose to do all of my giving by Your will and not my own feelings. I will not allow circumstances to cause me to hold back my hand. I give passionately and with purpose through good times and bad. I always consider it a joy and a privilege to support the advancement of Your kingdom.

———— DECLARATION OF FAITH ————

No matter what my situation is, it brings me abounding joy to give whatever I can to the work of the Lord. It is my pleasure to give as much as I am able, and even beyond my ability.

This I do entirely on my own and not under compulsion. As a matter of fact, I don't even have to be asked to give. I am always looking for an opportunity to share in the ministry through my financial blessings.

What makes this even more awesome is the fact that I am in partnership with the Lord in my giving. So there is no telling what I might do, because when God and I get together in this, blessings can flow from any direction.

(2 Corinthians 9:7; Philippians 4:14-20; Genesis 12:1-3; Romans 12:1,2)

2 CORINTHIANS 8:7-9

Therefore, as ye abound in every *thing, in* faith, and utterance, and knowledge, and *in* all diligence, and *in* your love to us, *see* that ye abound in this grace also. I speak not by commandment, but by occasion of the forwardness of others, and to prove the sincerity of your love. For ye know the grace of our Lord Jesus Christ, that, though he was rich, yet for your sakes he became poor, that ye through his poverty might be rich.

~ PRAYER ~

Father, I refuse to be a part of the crowd who abounds in everything You ask but holds back their hand when it comes to giving. You have me completely. I know that for my sake Jesus became poor that through His poverty I might be well supplied. I will not dishonor You by refusing to believe this truth. I am a well-supplied man/woman, and I prove my faith and love by giving freely and without restraint.

——— *DECLARATION OF FAITH* ———

In Jesus, I excel in everything that I do—in faith, in teaching, in under-standing (knowledge), in enthusiasm, in my love for my brothers and sisters in Christ—and I see to it that I excel in the grace (God-given ability) of giving as well.

I know the grace of my Lord Jesus, that though He was rich, for my sake He became poor, so that I, through His poverty, could become rich. Because of what Jesus did for me, I can count on being continually and abundantly sup-plied with all good things.

(Deuteronomy 28:12; 2 Corinthians 6:10; 9:5-11; 8:2-5; 9:7,8; Philippians 2:5-13; 4:14-20; 1 Corinthians 1:5; Romans 8:32; 2 Peter 1:3)

2 Corinthians 8:12-14

For if there be first a willing mind, *it is* accepted according to that a man hath, *and* not according to that he hath not. For *I mean* not that other men be eased, and ye burdened: But by an equality, *that* now at this time your abundance *may be a supply* for their want, that their abundance also may be *a supply* for your want: that there may be equality:

~ *PRAYER* ~

Father, I choose to give willingly and not grudgingly. When I have the means to give, I do so. I know that You do not see things by amounts but by per-centages. You are not impressed by the gift but by the heart behind the giving. Therefore, I choose to be a cheerful giver who believes in Your prom-ises. You always supply all that I need. When I give, You cause men to give back to me good measure, pressed down, shaken together, and running over.

─── *DECLARATION OF FAITH* ───

My eagerness to give is matched by my actual giving. I do not allow stumbling blocks to get in the way of my generosity but give as the Lord wills whenever I have the means to do so, for it is my willingness and readiness to give that makes my gifts acceptable in the sight of God; and my gift is weighed in proportion with my ability to give.

I recognize that quality seed produces a quality crop. Therefore, I will give quality seed and plant it into good soil so that I may reap a superior harvest.

(Mark 12:41-43; Luke 6:38; Proverbs 19:17; 28:27; Psalm 79:12; James 2:13)

2 CORINTHIANS 9:6-15

But this *I say*, He which soweth sparingly shall reap also sparingly; and he which soweth bountifully shall reap also bountifully. Every man according as he purposeth in his heart, *so let him give*; not grudgingly, or of necessity: for God loveth a cheerful giver. And God *is* able to make all grace abound toward you; that ye, always having all sufficiency in all *things*, may abound to every good work: (As it is written, He hath dispersed abroad; he hath given to the poor: his righteousness remaineth for ever. Now he that ministereth seed to the sower both minister bread for *your* food, and multiply your seed sown, and increase the fruits of your righteousness;) Being enriched in every thing to all bountifulness, which causeth through us thanksgiving to God. For the administration of this service not only supplieth the want of the saints, but is abundant also by many thanksgivings unto God; Whiles by the experiment of this ministration they glorify God for your professed subjection unto the gospel of Christ, and for *your* liberal distribution unto them, and unto all *men*; And by their prayer for you, which long after you for the exceeding grace of God in you. Thanks *be* unto God for his unspeakable gift.

~ *PRAYER* ~

Father, I thank You for the anointing of prosperity You have placed upon my life. I sow bountifully and I reap bountifully! I love being a blessing to others. When I give, You make all grace abound toward me so that I am always sufficient in all things and can abound to every good work.

I thank You that when I disperse abroad and give to the poor, You take notice of what I have done. You call it righteousness and set it as a memorial for all time. You apply it to my heavenly account, and it is security for me in times of trouble.

You always supply me with seed to sow and bread to eat, and You continually multiply my seed sown and increase the fruits of my righteousness. I am enriched in everything to all bountifulness. Your grace dwells within me richly and causes me to flourish with abundance. I always have all that I need and more. I praise You, exalt You, and magnify Your holy name. The gift of your prosperity is indescribable. I thank You for it with all of my heart!

———— DECLARATION OF FAITH ————

I always give generously with great joy in what I am doing for the advancement of the gospel. I never give grudgingly or with a regretful heart. I fully understand that seedtime and harvest is at work in my giving just as it is in everything else that I do. If I sow sparingly, I will reap a sparing harvest. But if I sow generously, I will reap a generous harvest.

Each time I have opportunity, I pray to determine what I should give so that I will have no regrets. I will never give reluctantly or under compulsion but only with a willing and joy-filled heart, for God loves and blesses the cheerful giver.

Once I have given from my heart (with all joy), God is able to make every favor and earthly blessing abound toward me so that I have all sufficiency in every circumstance and can abound in every good work.

As it is written, "He has scattered abroad his gifts to those in need; his righteousness endures forever." In this, God has made my harvest synonymous with righteousness. Therefore, I will expect His abundant return on my giving.

Now He who supplies me with seed to sow and bread to eat will also supply and increase my store of seed and will enlarge and multiply the harvest of my righteousness. This is my promise of blessing on my savings account. I can absolutely count on my Father to increase my savings as I give to Him in faith.

Through my giving, I am made rich in every way so that I can be generous in every way.

Tremendous thanksgiving to God comes in abundance through the ministries of those I am giving to. My giving not only supplies the needs of the church but overflows in every direction causing many to thank God for what is being done.

Men and women continually praise God because of my obedience in giving. The fruit produced by my generosity touches their hearts and draws them to God. They see what is being done and give Him the glory.

I never give a gift without adding prayer and affirmation to it in order to receive the insurance of the maximum blessing. Furthermore, because of my generous giving, God will inspire the hearts of others, causing them to agree with me in prayer and call down an abundance of blessings upon me because of the surpassing grace that God has given me.

I thank God for this remarkable system of giving that He has established. What a wonder it is!

(Luke 6:38; 2 Corinthians 8:2-5; Philippians 4:15-20; 1 Chronicles 29:1-17; Malachi 3:6-12; Proverbs 3:9,10; 11:24; 22:9; Galatians 6:7-9; Ecclesiastes 11:1-6; Matthew 6:19-33; Romans 12:8; Deuteronomy 15:7-11; 8:6-18; Psalm 112:1-10; Isaiah 55:10,11; Hosea 10:12; James 1:17)

CHAPTER THIRTY-FIVE

GALATIANS

GALATIANS 3:6-9

Even as Abraham believed God, and it was accounted to him for righteousness. Know ye therefore that they which are of faith, the same are the children of Abraham. And the Scripture, foreseeing that God would justify the heathen through faith, preached before the gospel unto Abraham, *saying*, In thee shall all nations be blessed. So then they which be of faith are blessed with faithful Abraham.

~ PRAYER ~

Father, I thank You for making me the spiritual offspring of Abraham through faith. I am a recipient of the same blessings that were bestowed upon him. I receive because I believe. I am man/woman of faith, and I am blessed with faithful Abraham.

——— DECLARATION OF FAITH ———

I consider Abraham a chief role model for my faith. As it is written, "He believed God, and it was credited to him as righteousness." In this respect, as a believer; I am a child of Abraham. The Scripture foresaw that God would justify me through faith, and He announced the gospel to Abraham all those many years ago, saying, "All nations will be blessed through you." Therefore, as a man/woman of faith, I am blessed in the same ways that Abraham was, for he is the father of my faith.

(Genesis 12:1-3,16; 13:2,6; 15:1,6,15; 17:1,2,6-9; 18:27; 20:7; 24:35; 26:3,12-14; Hebrews 11:1,6; Romans 3:21-26; 4:1-4; 8:1-4; 11:6; Deuteronomy 21:23; 27:26; 28:15-68; Leviticus 18:5; Ephesians 1:3,4,7,11,13,14; 2:13-15; 6:10; John 17:6-26; 2 Corinthians 1:20)

GALATIANS 3:13,14

Christ hath redeemed us from the curse of the law, being made a curse for us: for it is written, Cursed *is* every one that hangeth on a tree: That the blessing of Abraham might come on the Gentiles through Jesus Christ; that we might receive the promise of the Spirit through faith.

~ PRAYER ~

Father, I thank You for my redemption. I recognize that I have been bought with a price. Christ has redeemed me from the curse of the Law. The power of poverty has been broken over my life, and I am now free to pursue profit and prosperity. The blessing of Abraham has come upon me through Christ Jesus my Lord, and I have received the promise of the Spirit through faith. You bless me and make my name great, just as You did father Abraham. You shower me with Your abundance and make me to be a blessing in this earth.

DECLARATION OF FAITH

I am redeemed from the curse of the law! I am no longer bound by any of the financial curses that come from breaking the covenant. Jesus was made a curse for me so that I could receive the very blessing of Abraham. I can now receive the promise of the spirit through faith. All of God's financial blessings are now mine. When I believe them with my heart and speak them with my mouth, they become a reality in my life.

(2 Corinthians 1:20; 4:13; Romans 10:8-10; Mark 11:22-24; Genesis 12:1-3; 13:2; Deuteronomy 28:1-68)

GALATIANS 6:4-10

But let every man prove his own work, and then shall he have rejoicing in himself alone, and not in another. For every man shall bear his own burden.

Let him that is taught in the word communicate unto him that teacheth in all good things. Be not deceived; God is not mocked: for whatsoever a man soweth, that shall he also reap. For he that soweth to his flesh shall of the flesh reap corruption; but he that soweth to the Spirit shall of the Spirit reap life everlasting. And let us not be weary in well doing: for in due season we shall reap, if we faint not. As we have therefore opportunity, let us do good unto all *men*, especially unto them who are of the household of faith.

~ PRAYER ~

Father, I know that You have made me to be a productive member of Your family. Therefore, I shall work with my own two hands and faithfully bear the burden You have called me to bear.

I know that the chief purpose of my calling is the advancement of Your kingdom and Your righteousness. Therefore, I will not hesitate to give to my pastors, teachers, and those called to full-time ministry. My gift is as seed sown into good ground, and it is destined to produce an abundant harvest.

In our covenant partnership, You have blessed me so that I can be a blessing to others. Therefore, I will not grow weary in well doing, for I know that in due season I will reap if I faint not. At every opportunity I will do good to all, especially unto them that are of the household of faith.

——— DECLARATION OF FAITH ———

I share all good things (financial blessings, services, etc.) with those who instruct me in the Word.

I cannot be deceived into thinking that I can do whatever I want and still get away with it. God will not be mocked in such a way, for He has established the laws of seedtime and harvest in the earth; and as long as the earth remains, these laws shall remain as well. Therefore, I will reap exactly what I sow. If I sow to please the sinful nature, from that nature I will reap destruction; if I sow to my spirit, through the Holy Spirit, I shall reap the benefits of eternal life.

I purpose in my heart to never become weary in doing good, for at the proper time, I will reap an abundant harvest as long as I do not give up. Therefore, whenever I have an opportunity, I do good to all people, especially to those who are in the family: the household of faith.

(1 Corinthians 9:9-14; 15:58; Deuteronomy 25:4; Romans 2:5-7; 12:9-21; Genesis 8:22; Titus 3:4-7)

CHAPTER THIRTY-SIX

EPHESIANS

EPHESIANS 1:3

Blessed *be* the God and Father of our Lord Jesus Christ, who hath blessed us with all spiritual blessings in heavenly *places* in Christ:

~ *PRAYER* ~

Father, I recognize that You have already blessed me with all spiritual blessings in heavenly places in Christ Jesus my Lord. I receive them by grace through faith, and I will honor You by walking in them every day of my life.

——— *DECLARATION OF FAITH* ———

I give all praise, honor, and glory to my God, the Father of my Lord Jesus, for He has blessed me with every spiritual blessing in Christ.

(Romans 8:17,28-32; 2 Peter 1:3; 1 Peter 1:2-5,13-16; Luke 12:32)

EPHESIANS 4:28

Let him that stole steal no more: but rather let him labour, working with *his* hands the thing which is good, that he may have to give to him that needeth.

~ *PRAYER* ~

Father, I refuse to dishonor You by pilfering my way to prosperity. You prosper what I set my hand to do, not what I take from others. I will perform the good work You have given me and produce profit in abundance so that I may have the means to give to those who are in need. I am blessed to be a blessing, and I intend to be just that.

——— *DECLARATION OF FAITH* ———

I will not steal any longer in any way, even ways that are acceptable to the world. Instead, I will work, doing something useful with my own two hands, for in this God blesses me with His abundance, and I shall have the surplus that I need so that I can share with others.

(Romans 12:1,2,5; 14:17;2 Peter 1:4; 1 Thessalonians 4:11; Deuteronomy 28:12; Galatians 6:1,2)

CHAPTER THIRTY-SEVEN

PHILIPPIANS

✣

PHILIPPIANS 4:10-19

But I rejoiced in the Lord greatly, that now at the last your care of me hath flourished again; wherein ye were also careful, but ye lacked opportunity. Not that I speak in respect of want: for I have learned, in whatsoever state I am, *therewith* to be content. I know both how to be abased, and I know how to abound: every where and in all things I am instructed both to be full and to be hungry, both to abound and to suffer need. I can do all things through Christ which strengtheneth me. Notwithstanding ye have well done, that ye did communicate with my affliction. Now ye Philippians know also, that in the beginning of the gospel, when I departed from Macedonia, no church communicated with me as concerning giving and receiving, but ye only. For even in Thessalonica ye sent once and again unto my necessity. Not because I desire a gift: but I desire fruit that may abound to your account. But I have all, and abound: I am full, having received of Epaphroditus the things *which were sent* from you, an odour of a sweet smell, a sacrifice acceptable, well pleasing to God. But my God shall supply all your need according to his riches in glory by Christ Jesus.

~ PRAYER ~

Father, in You I am always content. You are with me at all times. You see me through every trial that I face. You never leave me nor forsake me. Therefore, I remain confident that my supply will never fail. I realize that what is seen in the natural world is not the complete picture. You are there and Your blessing is with You. When things look grim, I have Christ which strengthens me. I need merely to set my hand to the task, and the anointing will take over. I can overcome any and every situation that I face because the power to overcome is not mine but the power of almighty God.

Father, as You have blessed me, I will not hesitate to bless others. I give freely and without restraint. I choose to see things from a spiritual perspective. I will not hold back my finances because I see that a ministry is already prospering. To the contrary, I see that ministry as good soil that will produce a great harvest. I know that the fruit produced in that ministry will abound to my account. I understand the system of giving and receiving and will not cancel my blessing by holding back the gift when it is in my hands to give it. I trust in Your Word, Father. I am blessed to be a blessing. You are a God who enjoys abundance, and You supply all of my need according to Your riches in glory by Christ Jesus.

DECLARATION OF FAITH

I greatly rejoice in the Lord because of my Father's favor. There are many who are concerned about my well-being.

Not that I am in want, but, to the contrary, I know the secret of being content in any situation I find myself in. I know what to do when I find myself in adverse circumstances, and I know what to do when I am living in God's abundance. I have learned—in any and every circumstance—the secret of facing every situation as a conqueror, whether well fed or hungry, whether having all sufficiency and enough to spare, or not having a dime to my name. The secret is this: I can do all things through the power of Christ that is within me. With His anointing, there isn't a single circumstance that can hold me down! I am self-sufficient in His sufficiency.

I am wise to share in the process of giving and receiving that God has established in the earth. I faithfully support ministries that are advancing the kingdom in the earth, and every gift that I give is a deposit into my heavenly account.

I do all that I can to ensure that the ministries I support are amply supplied and more. It is my heart's desire that, through me and others of the same heart, God's financial blessings will shower over these ministries in so much abundance that they will have no idea what to do with all of the excess. It is my desire to see God's ministers living like true ambassadors of heaven.

When I present my offerings with this heart attitude, they go up before the Lord like a sweet fragrance. This is what makes my offerings acceptable for an abundant return. Because of my persistent and joy-filled generosity, I have God's Word that He will supply all of my needs according to His riches in glory through Christ Jesus. He sees to it that all of my giving returns to me overflowing with His abundance. In this, I give glory to God, my Father, forevermore. Amen.

(Luke 6:38; Matthew 6:19-33; Acts 4:32-37; Hebrews 13:5,6, 16; 2 Corinthians 9:5-15; Romans 8:37; John 14:13,14; 15:5,7; Galatians 6:7-9; 1 Chronicles 29:1-9; Titus 3:14)

CHAPTER THIRTY-EIGHT
COLOSSIANS

COLOSSIANS 1:9-12

For this cause we also, since the day we heard *it,* do not cease to pray for you, and to desire that ye might be filled with the knowledge of his will in all wisdom and spiritual understanding; that ye might walk worthy of the Lord unto all pleasing, being fruitful in every good work, and increasing in the knowledge of God; strengthened with all might, according to his glorious power, unto all patience and longsuffering with joyfulness; giving thanks unto the Father, which hath made us meet to be partakers of the inheritance of the saints in light:

~ PRAYER ~

Father, I thank You that You fill me with the knowledge of Your will in all wisdom and spiritual understanding. Mold my life that it may be pleasing unto You. Prosper me and make me fruitful in every good work. Increase my knowledge of You that we may enjoy ever increasing intimacy. Strengthen me with all might according to Your glorious power, unto all patience and perseverance. Fill me with Your joy as I walk in the inheritance that You have given me.

—— DECLARATION OF FAITH ——

God has filled me with a complete working knowledge of His will. By the wisdom and understanding that He has given me of the things of the spirit, I now have assurance of direction in any given circumstance.

I now can live a life worthy of the Lord, pleasing Him in every way.

I am bearing fruit in every good work to which I am called, continually growing in the knowledge of God, being strengthened with all power according *to the might of His glory, exercising every kind of endurance, and persevering through every trial with patience and joy, giving thanks to my Father who has made me worthy to share in the inheritance of the saints in the kingdom of light, for He rescued me from the kingdom of darkness and has translated me into the kingdom of the Son of His love. In Jesus, I have my redemption and forgiveness for all of my sins.*

(1 Corinthians 1:30; 2:6-16; 1 John 2:20; 5:20; Ephesians 1:3-23; 4:1-3; 5:1-20; 6:10; 1 Thessalonians 4:1; John 15:5; Hebrews 13:21; Galatians 4:4-6; 5:22,23; Colossians 2:13-15; James 1:2-4; 2 Peter 1:11; Titus 3:4-7)

COLOSSIANS 4:1

Masters, give unto *your* servants that which is just and equal; knowing that ye also have a Master in heaven.

~ *PRAYER* ~

Father, make me to be a wise supervisor. I choose to be good to my subordinates and treat everyone, both high and low, with fairness and equality. I know that I have a master in heaven who treats me very well; therefore, I too will treat others in kind.

——— DECLARATION OF FAITH ———

(For employers)

So far as it is in my power, I will provide for my employees what is just and fair, for I know that I myself am employed by God, and He is more than fair with His provision for me.

(Ephesians 6:9; Romans 12:11)

CHAPTER THIRTY-NINE

1 THESSALONIANS

1 THESSALONIANS 4:10-12

And indeed ye do it toward all the brethren which are in all Macedonia: but we beseech you, brethren, that ye increase more and more; and that ye study to be quiet, and to do your own business, and to work with your own hands, as we commanded you; that ye may walk honestly toward them that are without, and *that* ye may have lack of nothing.

~ *PRAYER* ~

Father, fill me with Your knowledge, for in it I find refuge from the stresses of my workload and the confidence to do my work in peace and quietness of spirit. I fully understand that I am created to be a productive member of Your household. It is Your perfect will that I increase more and more. I know that it is good and proper for me to seek profit in my life. Therefore, I will do so with all of my heart. I will manage my own affairs and work with my own hands. I choose to be a man/woman of honesty and integrity, and thus provide a good example for others to follow. I know that You reward my diligence, Father. In You, I lack no good thing in my life.

—— *DECLARATION OF FAITH* ——

I make it my heart's ambition to live a peaceful life, no matter how many devil heads I have to stomp to attain it.

I mind my own business, attend to my own affairs and needs, and work with my own hands to build a foundation for my prosperity.

I am dependent upon no man to meet my needs. I am never found begging for money or support. In this way, my life wins the respect of those who are outside of faith.

(Romans 14:19; Psalm 37:25; 91:13; 112:1-10; Deuteronomy 28:9-13; Philippians 4:19)

CHAPTER FORTY

2 THESSALONIANS

2 THESSALONIANS 1:11,12

Wherefore also we pray always for you, that our God would count you worthy of *this* calling, and fulfil all the good pleasure of *his* goodness, and the work of faith with power: that the name of our Lord Jesus Christ may be glorified in you, and ye in him, according to the grace of our God and the Lord Jesus Christ.

~ PRAYER ~

Father, I recognize that Your power is at work within me. I have it by Your grace and mercy alone and not because I deserve it. You have given it to me to fulfill the good pleasure of Your goodness. It is Your great desire that I work the work of faith, in the power of Your anointing, so that the name of my Lord Jesus Christ may be glorified in me and I in Him.

—— DECLARATION OF FAITH ——

My heavenly Father has counted me worthy of His calling. He has chosen me from among all the people of the earth to be His own son/daughter. By His power, which works so mightily within me, He fulfills every good purpose I have set my hand to perform and every act prompted by my faith.

The name of Jesus is glorified in me, and I in Him, according the grace of my God and Lord, Jesus Christ.

(Romans 8:26-30; 11:29; Ephesians 1:4; Colossians 1:27-29; Philippians 2:13; Deuteronomy 28:12; Isaiah 55:11; John 14:13,14; 17:20-26)

2 THESSALONIANS 2:16,17

Now our Lord Jesus Christ himself, and God, even our Father, which hath loved us, and hath given *us* everlasting consolation and good hope through grace, comfort your hearts, and stablish you in every good word and work.

~ *PRAYER* ~

Father, I thank You that You establish every good work that I set my hand to do. I have peace in my heart because I know that I have received this by Your grace alone. You are my confidence, Lord. I find rest in the wonder of Your mercy.

———— *DECLARATION OF FAITH* ————

Jesus Himself, and God my Father, encourage my heart and strengthen me in every good deed and word. My Father loves me deeply; and by His grace, He gives me eternal encouragement and good hope.

(Romans 8:28-30,38,39; Ephesians 1:4; 1 Peter 1:2,3; John 17:20-26; Galatians 5:1; 2 Chronicles 20:20; Psalm 138:3)

2 THESSALONIANS 3:6-10

Now we command you, brethren, in the name of our Lord Jesus Christ, that ye withdraw yourselves from every brother that walketh disorderly, and not after the tradition which he received of us. For yourselves know how ye ought to follow us: for we behaved not ourselves disorderly among you; neither did we eat any man's bread for nought; but wrought with labour and travail night and day, that we might not be chargeable to any of you: not because we have not power, but to make ourselves an ensample unto you to follow us. For even when we were with you, this we commanded you, that if any would not work, neither should he eat.

~ *PRAYER* ~

Father, I commit myself to walk in an orderly manner. I will not allow laziness to rob me of my blessings. I know that You prosper what I set my hand to do and not what I expect others to provide for me.

———— DECLARATION OF FAITH ————

I will not keep company with fellow believers who are lazy or indifferent to their duties as a child of God and who do not live according to the clear teachings of the Word.

I do not live like a useless drone in the world. I work hard for my sustenance and the provisions of life. I am not as a parasite, living off of others without doing anything to earn my keep. I live according to the rule: "If a man will not work, he shall not eat."

(1 Corinthians 5:1; Romans 16:17; 1 Thessalonians 2:9; 4:1; Deuteronomy 28:12; Proverbs 6:6-11; 20:4)

CHAPTER FORTY-ONE

1 TIMOTHY

1 TIMOTHY 4:14,15

Neglect not the gift that is in thee, which was given thee by prophecy, with the laying on of the hands of the presbytery. Meditate upon these things; give thyself wholly to them; that thy profiting may appear to all.

~ PRAYER ~

Father, I recognize that You have given me a gift and a calling. You intend for me to use my gift to produce increase and profit. Therefore, I will not neglect it. I give myself wholly to that which You have called me to do so that my profiting may be evident to all.

—— DECLARATION OF FAITH ——

I will not neglect my gift, which was given to me by the Holy Spirit for the edification of the church.

I cultivate my distinct abilities for the benefit and well-being of others as well as myself.

I remain diligent, giving myself wholly to the things of God within me, so that my progress will be made known and be beneficial to all.

I watch my life and doctrine closely, persevering in and through them, because in doing so, I obtain deliverance for myself as well as those who hear my message.

(2 Timothy 1:6; Ephesians 4:11-13; Psalm 1:1-3; Joshua 1:8; 2 Corinthians 11:3,4)

1 TIMOTHY 6:6-10

But godliness with contentment is great gain. For we brought nothing into *this* world, *and it is* certain we can carry nothing out. And having food and raiment let us be therewith content. But they that will be rich fall into temptation and a snare, and *into* many foolish and hurtful lusts, which drown men in destruction and perdition. For the love of money is the root of all evil: which while some coveted after, they have erred from the faith, and pierced themselves through with many sorrows.

~ PRAYER ~

Father, I will not forget my provider. I do not look to riches as my source of supply, nor do I give them my devotion. I do not love money. I love You. Money can pass from this earth for all I care. I will not covet after it or give it undue allegiance. You are the only provider that I trust, Father. You alone have my unfailing devotion. I am content in You regardless of how much money I have. My profit is not for greed but for kingdom advancement. I would rather be homeless and penniless than to have all the riches in the world and be without You. I will not seek worldly prosperity. My prosperity is kingdom prosperity, and it never fails and has no end.

——— DECLARATION OF FAITH ———

I will be content in all circumstances, knowing full well that God, my Father and provider, is always with me, and I am never without His provision.

If all that I have in this natural world is food and the clothing on my back, I will remain content and assured of my provision. I will not set my mind on money and riches—forgetting the fact that I have a heavenly Father who loves me and is caring for me—for I know that those who focus on money and riches fall into many temptations and are taken in many traps (get-rich-quick schemes, etc.)—through such focus they enter into many foolish and harmful desires that plunge them into ruin and destruction.

Money isn't worthy of such devotion. The love of it is the root of all kinds of evil. It is a denial of God as our one true provider. Some people, who have *set their focus and attention on gaining it, have wandered from the faith and pierced themselves through with many sorrows. I refuse to go down with them.*

As a man/woman of faith, I will flee from such misplaced allegiance and pursue righteousness, godliness, faith, love, endurance, and gentleness. I fight the good fight of faith, taking hold of the eternal life to which I was called when I made my good confession in the presence of many witnesses.

(Romans 1:20-32; 8:14-17; 16:17-19; 2 Timothy 1:13; 3:5-7; 1 Corinthians 2:6-16; Colossians 1:13; 2:4; Philippians 2:14-16; 3:17-19; 4:15-19; Matthew 6:19-33; 11:12; 18:15-17; Hebrews 11:1; 13:5,6; Deuteronomy 28:1-14; Psalm 24:1; Genesis 22:14; Mark 11:22-25; Galatians 5:6-10)

1 TIMOTHY 6:17-19

Charge them that are rich in this world, that they be not highminded, nor trust in uncertain riches, but in the living God, who giveth us richly all things to enjoy; That they do good, that they be rich in good works, ready to distribute, willing to communicate; Laying up in store for themselves a good foundation against the time to come, that they may lay hold on eternal life.

~ *PRAYER* ~

Father, I thank You that You richly give me all things to enjoy. You are my unfailing provider. I do not trust in uncertain riches. I trust in You. I will not think of myself more highly than I ought. All that I have, I have because of You. I recognize that I am a steward, not a proprietor. Therefore, I will do good with what You have given me. I remain ever ready to give and to bless others. I choose to lay up for myself a good foundation against times to come and lay hold on eternal life.

—— *DECLARATION OF FAITH* ——

As I am well supplied in this present world, I will remain self-controlled. I will not allow myself to become arrogant or put my trust (or hope) in uncertain riches.

My trust (hope) is in God alone, who richly provides me with good things of every kind to enjoy.

I am not only rich in possessions but rich in good deeds as well, being ever-generous and always willing to share.

Through my acts of generosity, I lay up for myself an abundance of treasures in heaven as a firm foundation for my future. In this, I have taken hold of the life that is truly life—the very life that God desires for me to live.

(Genesis 12:1-3; 13:2; 2 Timothy 1:7; Jeremiah 9:23,24; Romans 8:32; 2 Peter 1:3; Ecclesiastes 5:18,19; 2 Corinthians 8:2-5,9; 9:5-11; 1 John 3:16-18; Philippians 4:15-19; Matthew 6:19-33)

CHAPTER FORTY-TWO

HEBREWS

Hebrews 6:10-15

For God *is* not unrighteous to forget your work and labour of love, which ye have showed toward his name, in that ye have ministered to the saints, and do minister. And we desire that every one of you do show the same diligence to the full assurance of hope unto the end: That ye be not slothful, but followers of them who through faith and patience inherit the promises. For when God made promise to Abraham, because he could swear by no greater, he sware by himself, Saying, Surely blessing I will bless thee, and multiplying I will multiply thee. And so, after he had patiently endured, he obtained the promise.

~ PRAYER ~

Father, my primary thought in all things is to honor You. You are truly the first love of my life. All of my tithing and giving is first of all to honor You and secondly to receive Your blessings. I am aware that You take notice of all that I have done and that You do not forget. I know that You always have a harvest in store for me and that You always fulfill Your promises. Therefore, I will remain patient and steady in faith. I will not vacillate in waves of doubt but stand confident in Your Word. Your blessing is upon me and nothing can change that. I am destined to receive every promise You have given.

—— DECLARATION OF FAITH ——

God is not unjust. He does not disregard the work that I have done in the kingdom or overlook the love that I have shown Him in my giving. Therefore, I will continue to do so with my whole heart, in full assurance of His faithfulness to the very end.

I refuse to become indifferent, faithless, and stagnant, believing that the circumstance reigns over the Word and thus giving up on my faith.

Instead, I am an imitator of those who through faith and patience (endurance and persistence) continually inherit God's promises.

I follow after the faith of father Abraham, who waited patiently for several years before He received the promise. Like Abraham, I will never give in to unbelief and never give up on God.

(Romans 3:4; 4:1-25; 1 Thessalonians 1:3; 1 Corinthians 15:58; Galatians 3:6-29; 6:9; Colossians 2:2,3; Hebrews 10:35-11:1, 6,8-10,17-19; 2 Corinthians 5:7; James 1:2-8)

HEBREWS 7:1-6

For this Melchisedec, king of Salem, priest of the most high God, who met Abraham returning from the slaughter of the kings, and blessed him; To whom also Abraham gave a tenth part of all; first being by interpretation King of righteousness, and after that also King of Salem, which is, King of peace; Without father, without mother, without descent, having neither beginning of days, nor end of life; but made like unto the Son of God; abideth a priest continually. Now consider how great this man *was*, unto whom even the patriarch Abraham gave the tenth of the spoils. And verily they that are of the sons of Levi, who receive the office of the priesthood, have a commandment to take tithes of the people according to the law, that is, of their brethren, though they come out of the loins of Abraham: But he whose descent is not counted from them received tithes of Abraham, and blessed him that had the promises.

~ PRAYER ~

Father, I acknowledge Jesus as my high priest in the order of Melchisedec. I do not hesitate to give Him a tenth of my spoils. I recognize that I have the promises and that the blessing of Abraham has been placed upon my life. I am blessed to be a blessing. I will follow Abraham's lead and freely give of my spoils as a blessing for my priest.

──────── *DECLARATION OF FAITH* ────────

I am a tither. I honor Jesus and tithe to Him through my church. He is my high priest in the order of Melchisedec. He is my king of peace and righteousness. It is He who holds the promises. Therefore, I will honor Him with my tithes and receive His promises into my life.

(2 Corinthians 1:19-22; Isaiah 9:6; Malachi 3:6-12)

HEBREWS 10:34-36

For ye had compassion of me in my bonds, and took joyfully the spoiling of your goods, knowing in yourselves that ye have in heaven a better and an enduring substance. Cast not away therefore your confidence, which hath great recompense of reward. For ye have need of patience, that, after ye have done the will of God, ye might receive the promise.

~ *PRAYER* ~

Father, I choose to be a cheerful giver. I joyfully allow the spoiling of my goods to bless my church. I know that none of my giving is in vain. My generosity produces for me a better and more enduring substance in heaven. Therefore, I will not cast away my confidence which has great recompense of reward. By faith and patience, after I have done the will of God, I receive the promise!

──────── *DECLARATION OF FAITH* ────────

I freely give for I know that I shall receive back much more in return. I will not throw down my faith, because I know in due time I will reap and be richly rewarded. I am resolved to persevere through any and every difficulty, not looking at the circumstance but with my eyes fixed on the promise. I know that once I have fulfilled the requirements of the promise, I will receive it in its full measure.

(1 Timothy 6:12; James 1:2-8,22-25; Psalm 119:109-116, 138,140; 2 Corinthians 1:20; 4:13,17,18; 5:7; Mark 11:13,14,20-25;)

HEBREWS 11:1-3

Now faith is the substance of things hoped for, the evidence of things not seen. For by it the elders obtained a good report. Through faith we understand that the worlds were framed by the word of God, so that things which are seen were not made of things which do appear.

~ *PRAYER* ~

Father God, I clearly see that by faith You created the worlds. You called those things that be not as though they were. This is the example that You have set before me. The charge that You have given me is to live my life in the same way. I will obey that charge, Father. I shall walk by faith and not by sight. I know that faith is the substance of the things I hope for and the evidence of the things I do not see. Therefore, no matter what the testimony of the circumstances is, I will remain confident that I shall have the things that I say.

———— *DECLARATION OF FAITH* ————

My faith is the substance of the things I hope for. It is the evidence that I have what I do not see. Through faith I maintain a good report. I know that when I believe the promise with my heart, and speak it from my mouth, it shall manifest in my life.

(Mark 11:22-24; 2 Corinthians 1:19-22; 4:13; Romans 10:8-10)

HEBREWS 11:6

But without faith *it is* impossible to please *him*: for he that cometh to God must believe that he is, and *that* he is a rewarder of them that diligently seek him.

~ *PRAYER* ~

Father, I choose to do that which is pleasing in Your sight. I choose to live a life of faith. I believe in You with all of my heart, and I know that You reward me as I diligently seek You. I am destined to receive blessings beyond measure!

──── *DECLARATION OF FAITH* ────

I diligently seek the Lord and walk by faith in every area of my life. My focus is not on adverse circumstances, but on the promise of God. I know that what I see is not the whole truth. I choose to believe in and live by what I do not see, and my Father rewards me abundantly for it.

(2 Corinthians 5:7; 4:13; Mark 11:22-24; Romans 4:16-21)

HEBREWS 13:5,6

Let *your* conversation *be* without covetousness; *and be* content with such things as ye have: for he hath said, I will never leave thee, nor forsake thee. So that we may boldly say, The Lord *is* my helper, and I will not fear what man shall do unto me.

~ *PRAYER* ~

Father, I thank You that You never leave me nor forsake me. Therefore, I am content no matter what my situation may be. I will not allow myself to become covetous and desirous of that which belongs to another. I already have all of the best that heaven has to offer. I do not worry about creditors or competitors. I boldly say that You are my helper, Lord. I will not fear what man can do to me.

──── *DECLARATION OF FAITH* ────

I keep myself free from the love of money and remain happy and content in the Lord no matter what my circumstance may be, for God has promised that He will never leave me nor forsake me. Therefore, I can say with unwavering confidence, "The Lord is my helper; I will not be afraid. What can man do to me?"

(1 Timothy 6:6-10; Philippians 4:10-13; Deuteronomy 31:6-8; Romans 8:31; Psalm 27:1)

CHAPTER FORTY-THREE

JAMES

— ✦ —

JAMES 1:2-4

My brethren, count it all joy when ye fall into divers temptations; knowing *this*, that the trying of your faith worketh patience. But let patience have *her* perfect work, that ye may be perfect and entire, wanting nothing.

~ *PRAYER* ~

Father, in You I find joy in the midst of trials. I know that the trying of my faith produces patience; and when patience has conceived, she produces a tremendous harvest. I will let patience have her perfect work so that I may be perfect and complete, wanting nothing.

── *DECLARATION OF FAITH* ──

I consider it pure joy whenever I find myself facing trials and temptations (to give up on my faith) of every kind; for I know that the testing of my faith produces in me an enduring patience; and once this patience becomes an unfailing part of my character (when I am mature and complete in it), I will lack no good thing in my life.

(Acts 5:41; Matthew 21:19-22; 2 Peter 1:6; Romans 5:3-5; Mark 11:22-25; Hebrews 6:12; Psalm 119:109-116)

JAMES 1:5-8

If any of you lack wisdom, let him ask of God, that giveth to all *men* liberally, and upbraideth not; and it shall be given him. But let him ask in faith, nothing wavering. For he that wavereth is like a wave of the sea driven with the wind and tossed. For let not that man think that he shall receive any thing of the Lord. A double minded man *is* unstable in all his ways.

~ *PRAYER* ~

Father, I thank You that whenever I need wisdom, You grant it to me liberally and without restraint. You do not find reasons to hold Your wisdom from me. I have asked for it, and I believe You have given it. I do not waver and find reasons to think otherwise. I know that just because I don't see something, it doesn't mean that I don't have it. In Jesus' name, I receive everything that I pray for. I will keep my mind single, Father, and always trust in Your Word.

———— *DECLARATION OF FAITH* ————

Wisdom is precious to me and knowledge is pleasant to my soul. The Lord grants me wisdom liberally whenever I ask for it. He never finds reason to hold it from me. Therefore, in all that I do, I will seek His wisdom and walk a sure path toward inevitable victory.

I refuse to be double-minded. I do not reason against the promises, nor do I allow circumstances to form the basis of what I believe. I believe the promise. Period. I will not allow doubts to progress in my mind. No matter what situation I find myself in, I will be steady as a rock.

(Proverbs 2:10-12; Mark 11:22-24; 2 Corinthians 5:7; Hebrews 6:12)

JAMES 1:22-25

But be ye doers of the word, and not hearers only, deceiving your own selves. For if any be a hearer of the word, and not a doer, he is like unto a man beholding his natural face in a glass: For he beholdeth himself, and goeth his way, and straightway forgetteth what manner of man he was. But whoso looketh into the perfect law of liberty, and continueth *therein*, he being not a forgetful hearer, but a doer of the work, this man shall be blessed in his deed.

~ PRAYER ~

Father, I choose to be a doer of Your Word and not a hearer only. I believe I am who You say that I am, and I can do what You say I can do. I dwell within the perfect law of liberty, and I continue therein. I am not a forgetful hearer but a doer of the Word, and I am blessed in all that I do.

——— DECLARATION OF FAITH ———

I remain quick to listen, slow to speak, and slow to anger, for anger does not bring about the righteous life that God desires for me to live. Therefore, I rid myself of all immorality, casting from my life the wickedness that is so prevalent in society today; and I humbly receive the Word planted within my spirit, which is able to deliver me.

I am not just a hearer but also a doer. I listen carefully to procure understanding so that I can do exactly what the Word is guiding me to do.

I am not like the man who hears the Word but does not act upon it. I do not see my face in a mirror and then walk away forgetting who I am. To the contrary, I listen to the Word—building an image within me of who I am and what I have in Christ—not just to know it but also to live it. I look intently into the perfect law of liberty (in Christ), and I am faithful to what I have learned.

The Word has become the life that I live; and as I live it, not forgetting who I am and what I have in Christ, I am blessed in all that I do.

(Proverbs 10:19; 14:17; 16:32; 17:27; Hebrews 12:1,2; Isaiah 55:11; Colossians 3:8-10; Matthew 7:24-27; John 13:12-17; 15:5-8; Luke 6:43-49; James 2:12,13)

JAMES 2:5

Hearken, my beloved brethren, Hath not God chosen the poor of this world rich in faith, and heirs of the kingdom which he hath promised to them that love him?

~ PRAYER ~

Father, I know that the poor do not dwell in Your kingdom. As soon as they enter, they suddenly become rich. You supply every need and shower them with Your abundance. Therefore, no matter what I am facing, I will stand in faith and enjoy the abundance of Your unfailing supply.

———— DECLARATION OF FAITH ————

I love God with all of my heart and do my very best to see all things through His eyes.

He has chosen me to be well supplied through faith and to inherit the kingdom that He has promised me.

(Deuteronomy 6:5; Isaiah 55:6-13; Matthew 6:19-33; 1 Timothy 6:17; 2 Corinthians 8:9; Luke 12:13-21)

JAMES 2:14-18

What *doth it* profit, my brethren, though a man say he hath faith, and have not works? can faith save him? If a brother or sister be naked, and destitute of daily food, And one of you say unto them, Depart in peace, be *ye* warmed and filled; notwithstanding ye give them not those things which are needful to the body; what *doth it* profit? Even so faith, if it hath not works, is dead, being alone. Yea, a man may say, Thou hast faith, and I have works: show me thy faith without thy works, and I will show thee my faith by my works.

~ PRAYER ~

Father, I realize that You intend for me to work to produce profit in my life. I am not the fool who thinks that prayer alone will get him the things that he needs. You prosper what I set my hand to do, not what I sit around and expect to be given. I am a man/woman of active, working faith. I work under the power of Your anointing, and I produce mass abundance for Your glory!

—— *DECLARATION OF FAITH* ——

I do more than just pray for the needs of the poor; I see to their needs as well. I give of my substance with a willing and cheerful heart, seeing to it that their needs are met through my deeds and not just my words.

In the same way, I maintain a working faith. I do not just give mental assent to the truth of the Word but act on it, bearing an abundance of righteous fruit in my life. My faith only has value in the fruit that it produces.

Even father Abraham was counted as righteous because of what he did when he offered Isaac on the altar. Therefore, like him, my faith and my actions work together, and my faith is made complete by the fruit that I produce.

Through active and working faith, I have become the righteousness of God in Christ Jesus. I am now the very friend of God. This could only happen by my actively receiving what God has for me.

I was justified by actively receiving what God has for me, and I now live my life in this earth in the same way that I received justification: by active, working faith.

(2 Corinthians 4:13; 5:7,21; 8:2-5; 9:5-11; 1 John 3:16-18; James 1:22-25; Matthew 7:17-19; John 1:12; 15:5-8,16; 16:23,24; 2 Chronicles 20:7; Colossians 2:6-8)

JAMES 4:10

Humble yourselves in the sight of the Lord, and he shall lift you up.

~ *PRAYER* ~

Father, I humble myself in Your sight. I place my complete trust in Your ability to prosper and promote me. I know that You shall lift me up and raise me to the position You have called me to.

—— *DECLARATION OF FAITH* ——

As I remain humble in the presence of my Father, He exalts me to a life full of joy and endless victory.

(1 John 5:14,15; 1 Peter 1:22-25; 5:5-7;Hebrews 12:1; Psalm 119:109-116)

CHAPTER FORTY-FOUR

1 PETER

1 PETER 3:8-11

Finally, *be ye* all of one mind, having compassion one of another, love as brethren, *be* pitiful, *be* courteous: Not rendering evil for evil, or railing for railing: but contrariwise blessing; knowing that ye are thereunto called, that ye should inherit a blessing. For he that will love life, and see good days, let him refrain his tongue from evil, and his lips that they speak no guile: Let him eschew evil, and do good; let him seek peace, and ensue it.

~ PRAYER ~

Father, I place love at the forefront of all of my endeavors. I choose to remain courteous and considerate of others. I do not render evil for evil or railing for railing, but I choose to be a blessing. For this is the reason I am called: to inherit Your blessing that I may be a blessing to others. Therefore, I will refrain my tongue from speaking negative and evil things. I am a lover of life, and I will see good days. I pursue peace with all of my heart. I shun all evil and do good.

—— DECLARATION OF FAITH ——

I live in harmony with my brothers and sisters in Christ. I am sympathetic of their every need and love them as members of my own family. I remain courteous and respectful toward them and show compassion for them at all times. I do not repay evil with evil or insult for insult, but am always of a mind to bless them. I see things through the eyes of my Father and constantly pursue ways to bless people regardless of how they treat me. To this I have been called; and in doing so (blessing others), I plant the seeds that produce a harvest of blessings in my own life.

I am a lover of life who continually sees good days. I refrain my tongue from speaking negative things. I speak the truth at all times and never allow lies and deceit to become a part of me. I turn away from evil and only do that which is good. I am a seeker of peace and pursue it with all of my will.

I am the righteousness of God in Christ Jesus my Lord.

His eyes never leave me, and I rest in His embrace. He is my shield of protection in this life. His ears are always opened to my prayers so that He can fulfill His Word on my behalf.

(John 17:20-26; Ephesians 4:1-6; 1 John 4:7-21; 5:14,15; Romans 12:9-21; Galatians 6:7-9; Psalm 5:11,12; 34:12-16; 2 Corinthians 5:21; Deuteronomy 33:12; Genesis 15:1; Isaiah 55:11; Jeremiah 1:12)

CHAPTER FORTY-FIVE

3 JOHN

3 JOHN 2

Beloved, I wish above all things that thou mayest prosper and be in health, even as thy soul prospereth.

~ *PRAYER* ~

Father, You have made Your will evident to me. Your wish is that I prosper and remain in good health even as my soul prospers. With You as my partner, Your wish shall come true.

——— *DECLARATION OF FAITH* ———

I know the heart of my Father. He is a good Father and wishes above all things that I prosper and remain healthy, even as my soul prospers.

(Psalm 35:27; 103:1-5; 112:1-10; Deuteronomy 8:18; 28:1-14; Galatians 3:13,14; Genesis 12:1-3; 13:2; Isaiah 53:4,5; 2 Corinthians 9:5-11; 1 Peter 2:24; Colossians 2:19; 1 Thessalonians 3:12)

CHAPTER FORTY-SIX

REVELATION

REVELATION 2:9a

I know thy works, and tribulation, and poverty, (but thou art rich)

~ PRAYER ~

Father, from this day forward I will see things as You see them. I will not look to the circumstances or the situation I am in. I do not live by what I see but what I do not see. I know that You are with me to prosper what I set my hand to do. Your blessing is upon me and nothing can change that. From now on I will recognize that in You I am not poor—I AM RICH! In Jesus' name, amen!

──── DECLARATION OF FAITH ────

Jesus is aware of my situation. He is concerned that I understand what He has provided for me, and that in Him, I have been made rich (wealthy; well supplied).

(Psalm 23:1-6; 1 Corinthians 1:30; 2:6-16; 2 Corinthians 8:9; Matthew 5:10-12; 13:11,15,16; Isaiah 54:17; Romans 2:17; Revelation 3:9; 2 Timothy 1:7; James 1:12; 1 John 5:4,5)

TOPICAL INDEX

Abundance; laws of abundance and increase; God's will that you have more than enough:

Genesis 12:1-3; 13:2; 15:1; 15:13,14; 24:34,35; 26:12-14; 27:28,29; 30:27-30; 36:6,7; 49:25,26; Deuteronomy 6:10-12; 8:10-18; 11:13-15; 24:19-22; 28:1-13; Joshua 22:8; 1 Chronicles 4:9,10; 29:1-14; 2 Chronicles 17:3-6; 20:20-25; 32:27-30; Job 1:3; 22:21-30; 42:10-12; Psalm 1:1-3; 35:27; 37:12-27; 84:4-12; 85:12,13; 104:24; 112:1-10; 115:11-16; 126:5,6; Proverbs 3:9,10; 10:3-5; 10:22; 11:16; 11:24-26; 12:11; 13:2; 14:20,21; 15:6; 21:5; 21:20; 28:13; 28:19,20; Ecclesiastes 6:1,2; 9:16; 11:1-6; Isaiah 1:19,20; 32:17-20; 55:8-13; Jeremiah 9:23,24; 29:11; 33:7-9; Ezekiel 44:30; Zechariah 8:12,13; Matthew 6:19-33; 13:11,12; 25:14-30; Mark 4:14-20; Luke 6:27-38; 12:32-34; 15:17-24; 19:11-26; John 15:1-8; 1 Corinthians 9:9-11; 2 Corinthians 8:7-9; 8:12-14; 9:6-15; Galatians 3:13,14; 6:4-10; Ephesians 4:28; Philippians 4:10-19; James 2:14-18.

Angels; God's ministers who prepare the way for your prosperity:

Genesis 24:40; 48:15,16; Exodus 23:20-30; Psalm 34:6-10; 91:11; Ecclesiastes 5:4-6; Luke 6:27-38; 15:17-24; 1 Corinthians 9:9-11; Hebrews 1:13,14.

Anointing; God's power within you to create wealth:

Genesis 12:1-3; 13:2; 13:5,6; 24:34,35; 26:12-14; 27:28,29; 30:27-30; 39:2-6; 39:20-23; Leviticus 26:3-9; Deuteronomy 8:10-18; 11:13-15; 15:7-11; 28:1-13; 29:9; 33:11; 2 Samuel 6:11,12; 1 Chronicles 4:9,10; 22:11-13; 29:1-14; 2 Chronicles 32:27-30; Job 22:21-30; 29:1-25; Psalm 1:1-3; 23:1-6; 37:12-27; 84:4-12; Proverbs 3:9,10; 8:18-21; 10:15; 12:14; 13:4; 13:11; 14:20,21; 14:23; Ecclesiastes 9:10,11; Ezekiel 44:30; Joel 2:18-27; Zechariah 8:12,13; Luke 11:17-26; 12:32-34; 19:11-26; 2 Corinthians 9:6-15; Philippians 4:10-19; 2 Thessalonians 1:11,12; James 2:14-18;

Blessing of Abraham; God's promises to bless you with the same blessing He gave to Abraham:

Genesis 12:1-3; 13:2; 13:5,6; 15:1; 24:34,35; 26:2-5; 28:3,4; 48:15,16; Deuteronomy 6:10-12; 8:10-18; Isaiah 51:2,3; Galatians 3:6-9; 3:13,14; Hebrews 6:10-15; 7:1-6; 10:34-36; James 2:14-18.

Budgeting; keeping a careful accounting of your spending:

Genesis 39:2-6; Deuteronomy 8:10-18; 23:5; 28:1-13; 2 Chronicles 32:27-30; Job 22:21-30; Psalm 1:1-3; Proverbs 3:9,10; 11:16; 21:5; 21:17; 21:20; 22:16; 23:20,21; 27:23,24; 28:8; 29:3; Joel 2:18-27; Matthew 6:19-34; 19:21; Luke 16:9-13; Acts 20:32-35; 1 Corinthians 9:9-11; 2 Corinthians 9:6-15; Philippians 4:10-19.

Children; God's promises to bless your children financially:

Genesis 26:2-5; 28:3,4; 49:25,26; Deuteronomy 6:10-12; 11:18-21; 28:1-13; 1 Chronicles 29:28; Job 29:1-25; Psalm 37:12-27; 112:1-10; 113:7,8; 115:11-16; 128:1-4; 147:10-15; Proverbs 8:32-35; 13:22; Jeremiah 33:7-9; Matthew 7:7-11; Luke 11:5-10.

Counsel; choosing and listening to the right financial instruction:

Judges 18:5; Job 29:1-25; Psalm 1:1-3; Proverbs 3:13-17; 8:10,11; 8:32-35; 10:22; 13:18; 21:5; 23:22,23; 24:30-34; Micah 4:11-13; John 14:26,27; Galatians 6:4-10.

Courage; having no fear regarding your finances:

Genesis 15:1; Leviticus 26:3-9; Deuteronomy 2:7; 28:1-13; Joshua 1:7-9; 1 Chronicles 17:23-27; 22:11-13; 2 Chronicles 17:3-6; 20:20-25; Psalm 3:1-8; 23:1-6; 34:6-10; 37:12-27; 112:1-10; 115:11-16; Proverbs 22:13; Isaiah 32:17-20; 55:8-13; Jeremiah 17:5-8; Joel 2:18-27; Micah 4:11-13; Zechariah 8:12,13; Matthew 6:19-34; 25:14-30; Luke 10:18,19; 12:16-21; 12:32-34; 19:11-26; 1 Corinthians 15:58; Hebrews 13:5,6; Revelation 2:9.

Covenant; the sealed contract where God pledges His resources toward your prosperity:

Genesis 12:1-3; 13:2; 15:1; 15:13,14; 48:15,16; Leviticus 26:3-9; Deuteronomy 8:10-18; 28:1-13; 29:9; 1 Kings 3:11-13; 2 Chronicles 20:20-25; Psalm 112:1-10; 147:10-15; Proverbs 22:9; Jeremiah 33:7-9; Zechariah 8:12,13; Luke 6:20; 15:17-24; Galatians 3:6-9; 3:13,14; 6:4-10.

Crisis; what to do in the event of financial disaster:

Genesis 39:20-23; Numbers 23:19,20; Deuteronomy 2:7; 1 Samuel 2:7-9; Job 29:1-25; 36:15,16; Psalm 3:1-8; 23:1-6; 34:6-10; 41:1,2; 68:19; 78:18-29; 104:20; 126:5,6; Proverbs 10:22; 11:1; 15:6; 15:16,17; 15:27; 17:5; Ecclesiastes 7:11-14; 11:1-6; Micah 4:11-13; Mark 4:14-20; Luke 6:20; 6:27-38; 11:5-10; 11:17-26; 12:16-21; John 14:26,27; 20:29; Romans 8:32; 2 Corinthians 6:10; 8:2-5; 9:6-15; Philippians 4:10-19; Hebrews 10:34-36; 13:5,6; James 1:5-8; Revelation 2:9.

Debt; living debt free:

Genesis 15:13,14; Leviticus 26:3-9; Numbers 30:2; Deuteronomy 8:10-18; 15:4-6; 28:1-13; Psalm 37:12-27; Proverbs 6:1-5; 12:24; 22:7; 22:26,27; Jeremiah 33:7-9; Hebrews 10:34-36.

Destiny; your financial future in the Lord:

Genesis 12:1-3; 31:13; Leviticus 19:9,10; Deuteronomy 28:1-13; Psalm 23:1-6; Proverbs 12:24; Jeremiah 29:11; Luke 12:16-21; John 14:26,27; 1 Corinthians 15:58; Ephesians 1:3; 4:28; 1 Timothy 6:17-19; Hebrews 6:10-15; 11:6.

Employment; getting the right job; living in accordance with your calling:

Genesis 12:1-3; 13:2; 24:34,35; 27:28,29; 30:27-30; 39:2-6; 39:20-23; Leviticus 26:3-9; Deuteronomy 28:1-13; Joshua 1:7-9; 1 Chronicles 22:11-13; Psalm 112:1-10; 115:11-16; Proverbs 3:13-17; 3:27,28; 8:12; 12:9; 13:4; 22:29; 24:30-34; Ecclesiastes 5:3; 5:18,19; 9:10,11; Isaiah 51:2,3; Matthew 6:19-34; 7:7-11; 25:14-30; John 14:26,27; Romans 8:32; Galatians 6:4-10; Colossians 1:9-12; 2 Thessalonians 1:11,12; 1 Timothy 4:14,15; James 4:10; 1 Peter 3:8-11.

Favor; God's anointing that causes people to go out of their way to do nice things for you:

Genesis 8:22; 12:1-3; 26:12-14; 27:28,29; 30:27-30; 39:2-6; 39:20-23; Exodus 3:21,22; 12:36; Leviticus 26:3-9; Numbers 6:22-27; Deuteronomy 15:7-11; 28:1-13; Ruth 2:12; 2 Chronicles 20:20-25; Job 29:1-25; Psalm 5:12; 41:1,2; 84:4-12; 106:3-5; 128:1-4; Proverbs 3:4-10; 8:32-35; 19:6; 22:1; Ecclesiastes 9:10,11; Isaiah 55:8-13; Luke 6:20; 6:27-38; Romans 5:17; 1 Corinthians 9:9-11; 2 Corinthians 9:6-15; Philippians 4:10-19.

Fear (See Courage)

Giving and receiving (See Seedtime and Harvest)

Greed; avoiding a greedy pursuit of gain; maintaining a spirit of generosity:

Deuteronomy 23:19,20; 1 Kings 3:11-13; Psalm 78:18-29; Proverbs 15:27; 21:20; 21:25,26; 23:4,5; 28:22; 30:8,9; Matthew 6:19-34; Luke 6:27-38; 12:13-15; 12:16-21; Acts 20:32-35; 1 Timothy 6:6-10; 6:17-19.

Guidance; following the right financial advice:

Genesis 26:2-5; 36:6,7; Judges 18:5; 2 Chronicles 20:20-25; Psalm 1:1-3; 23:1-6; 37:12-27; 112:1-10; Proverbs 3:4-10; 11:1; 12:14; 20:4; 21:5; 22:13; Joel 2:18-27; Luke 11:5-10; 11:17-26; John 14:26,27; 2 Corinthians 6:10; James 1:22-25.

Humility; humbling yourself and putting God first in your finances:

Exodus 12:36; Deuteronomy 8:10-18; 1 Chronicles 4:9,10; 29:1-14; Job 22:21-30; Proverbs 6:1-5; 11:1; 16:16; 16:19; 22:4; James 1:22-25; 4:10.

Investing (See Saving and Investing)

Leadership; your call to be a leader in your community:

Genesis 24:34,35; 39:2-6; 39:20-23; Deuteronomy 15:4-6; 28:1-13; Judges 18:5; 1 Samuel 2:7-9; Job 29:1-25; Proverbs 8:18-21; 12:9; 12:24; 22:7.

Litigation; what to do when you are threatened with law suits, etc.:

Genesis 15:13,14; 39:20-23; Exodus 3:21,22; 12:36; Leviticus 26:3-9; Numbers 23:19,20; Deuteronomy 2:7; 11:18-21; 23:5; 28:1-13; 33:11; Joshua 1:7-9; 1 Samuel 2:7-9; 1 Kings 3:11-13; 2 Chronicles 20:20-25; Job 1:10; 29:1-25; 36:15,16; Psalm 3:1-8; 23:1-6; 34:6-10; 37:12-27; 41:1,2; 52:1-9; 68:19; 78:18-29; 104:20; 112:1-10; 126:5,6; 147:10-15; Proverbs 10:22; 11:1; 12:9; 15:6; 15:16,17; 15:27; 17:5; 18:20,21; 25:21,22; Ecclesiastes 7:11-14; 11:1-6; Isaiah 41:10-13; 54:17; Joel 2:18-27; Micah 4:11-13; Malachi 3:8-12; Matthew 12:25-29; Mark 4:14-20; Luke 6:20; 6:27-38; 10:18,19; 11:5-10; 11:17-26; 12:16-21; John 14:26,27; 20:29; Romans 8:32; 2 Corinthians 6:10; 8:2-5; 9:6-15; Philippians 4:10-19; Hebrews 10:34-36; 13:5,6; James 1:5-8; Revelation 2:9.

Negotiation; creating win/win situations with the people you do business with:

Deuteronomy 29:9; Joshua 1:7-9; Judges 18:5; Nehemiah 2:20; Job 29:1-25; Psalm 5:12; 62:9-12; 84:4-12; 112:1-10; Proverbs 8:10,11; 11:1; 14:23; 16:11; 20:10; 20:14,15; 22:1; 28:8; John 14:26,27; Colossians 4:1; 1 Thessalonians 4:10-12; 1 Peter 3:8-11.

Partnership with God:

Genesis 12:1-3; 26:2-5; 39:20-23; Judges 18:5; 2 Samuel 6:11,12; Job 29:1-25; Psalm 1:1-3; 37:12-27; 115:11-16; Micah 4:11-13; Zechariah 8:12,13; Malachi 3:6-12; John 20:29; 2 Corinthians 8:2-5; Galatians 6:4-10; James 2:14-18; 4:10; 3 John 2.

Planning; knowing how to schedule, forecast, and prepare for every financial venture:

Deuteronomy 8:10-18; 2 Chronicles 32:27-30; Job 22:21-30; Psalm 1:1-3; Proverbs 3:4-10; 14:20,21; 21:5; 24:3,4; 24:27; 27:23,24; Ecclesiastes 9:10,11; Jeremiah 29:11; Matthew 24:45-47; Acts 20:32-35; 1 Corinthians 9:9-11; Philippians 4:10-19; James 1:2-4.

Profit; God's will that you be a profitable servant as opposed to being a wicked and slothful servant:

Genesis 12:1-3; 13:2; Deuteronomy 8:10-18; 28:1-13; 78:18-29; Proverbs 3:4-10; 3:13-17; 14:20,21; 14:23; 16:11; 20:4; 20:14,15; 20:16; 21:5; Ecclesiastes 5:9-11; 7:11-14; Matthew 25:14-30; Luke 19:11-26; Acts 20:32-35; 1 Corinthians 13:3; Galatians 3:13,14; Ephesians 4:28; 1 Thessalonians 4:10-12; 1 Timothy 4:14,15; 6:6-10; James 2:14-18.

Promotion; the edge you need to be promoted on the job and in every other area of life:

Genesis 12:1-3; 24:34,35; 26:12-14; 39:2-6; 39:20-23; Deuteronomy 8:10-18; 15:4-6; 28:1-13; Judges 18:5; 1 Samuel 2:7-9; Job 29:1-25; Psalm 112:1-10; Proverbs 8:18-21; 12:9; 12:24; 21:25,26; 22:7; James 4:10.

Protection; living under God's secure covering in times of trouble:

Genesis 15:1; 49:25,26; Deuteronomy 28:1-13; Job 1:10; Psalm 3:1-8; 23:1-6; 37:12-27; 52:1-9; 84:4-12; 112:1-10; Proverbs 23:4,5; Ecclesiastes 6:1,2; Isaiah 32:17-20; Joel 2:18-27; Malachi 3:8-12; Matthew 6:19-34; Luke 12:13-15; 12:32-34; 1 Peter 3:8-11; Revelation 2:9.

Provision; having all that you need for every financial endeavor:

Genesis 12:1-3; 13:2; 13:5,6; 27:28,29; 28:20-22; 30:27-30; 36:6,7; 48:15,16; 49:25,26; Deuteronomy 2:7; 6:10-12; 8:10-18; 11:13-15; 14:22; 15:4-6; 18:4,5; 24:19-22; 28:1-13; 1 Chronicles 29:1-14; 2 Chronicles 32:27-30; Job 8:6,7; 22:21-30; 29:1-25; 36:15,16; Psalm 23:1-6; 34:6-10; 37:12-27; 62:9-12; 68:19; 78:18-29; 84:4-12; 104:24; 115:11-16; 126:5,6; 147:10-15; Proverbs 3:4-10; 6:6-11; 10:3-5; 11:24-26; 20:13; 21:20; 21:25,26; 23:4,5; 28:19,20; 30:8,9; Ecclesiastes 7:11-14; Jeremiah 17:5-8; 29:11; 33:7-9; Joel 2:12-14; 2:18-27; Malachi 3:8-12; Matthew 6:19-34; 19:21; Luke 6:20-23; 12:16-21; 16:9-13; 2 Thessalonians 3:6-10; 1 Timothy 6:6-10; 6:17-19.

Purpose; knowing God's purpose for you and fulfilling it:

Deuteronomy 8:10-18; 16:17; Judges 18:5; 1 Kings 3:11-13; 1 Chronicles 29:1-14; Psalm 23:1-6; 34:6-10; 37:3-5; Proverbs 6:6-11; 8:12; 22:16; Ecclesiastes 5:3; 5:18,19; Isaiah 51:2,3; 55:8-13; Luke 19:11-26; John 15:1-8; Galatians 6:4-10; 2 Thessalonians 1:11,12.

Restoration; God's promises to restore what the enemy has stolen; recovery from financial disaster:

Exodus 3:21,22; Joshua 22:8; Job 8:6,7; 42:10-12; Psalm 23:1-6; 41:1,2; 126:5,6; Proverbs 6:30,31; Joel 2:18-27; Matthew 12:25-29; Luke 12:32-34.

Saving and investing; God's blessing that fills your storage places and accounts:

Genesis 13:2; 26:12-14; Deuteronomy 8:10-18; 23:5; 28:1-13; 2 Chronicles 31:6-10; 32:27-30; Job 22:21-30; Psalm 1:1-3; 147:10-15; Proverbs 3:4-10; 6:6-11; 11:16; 12:27; 13:11; 13:22; 15:6; 19:17; 21:5; 21:20; 27:23,24; 28:8; Joel 2:18-27; Malachi 3:8-12; Matthew 6:19-34; 19:21; Luke 12:16-21; 16:9-13; 19:11-26; John 16:23-27; 1 Corinthians 9:9-11; 2 Corinthians 9:6-15; Philippians 4:10-19; 1 Timothy 6:17-19.

Seedtime and harvest; giving and receiving:

Genesis 8:22; 26:12-14; 28:3,4; Leviticus 26:3-9; 27:30; Deuteronomy 11:13-15; 14:22; Psalm 37:12-27; 62:9-12; 85:12,13; 126:5,6; Proverbs 3:4-10; 6:6-11; 11:11; 17:8; 18:20,21; 21:20; 28:13; Ecclesiastes 5:3; 6:1,2; 11:1-6; Isaiah 32:17-20; 55:8-13; Jeremiah 4:3; Joel 2:18-27; Zechariah 8:12,13; Malachi 3:8-12; Matthew 17:19-21; 25:14-30; Mark 4:14-20; 12:41-44; 1 Corinthians 9:9-11; 2 Corinthians 9:6-15; Galatians 6:4-10; 1 Peter 3:8-11.

Tithes and offerings:

Genesis 8:22; 12:1-3; 28:20-22; Leviticus 23:10; 26:3-9; 27:30; Deuteronomy 14:22; 16:17; 18:4,5; 1 Chronicles 29:1-14; 2 Chronicles 31:6-10; Psalm 37:12-27; 112:1-10; Proverbs 3:4-10; 3:27,28; 6:6-11; 11:24-26; 14:20,21; 18:16; 19:17; 20:25; 21:20; 21:25,26; 22:9; 28:27; Ecclesiastes 5:9-11; 11:1-6; Isaiah 55:8-13; Jeremiah 4:3; Ezekiel 44:30; Zechariah 8:12,13, Malachi 3:8-12; Matthew 6:19-34; 7:7-11; 19:21;

Luke 6:27-38; 2 Corinthians 8:2-5; 8:7-9; 8:12-14; 9:6-15; Galatians 6:4-10; Hebrews 7:1-6.

Trusting in God and not money, credit ratings, the economy, or other circumstances:

Genesis 26:2-5; 28:20-22; 49:25,26; Numbers 23:19,20; Deuteronomy 11:13-15; 28:1-13; Ruth 2:12; 2 Samuel 7:28,29; 2 Chronicles 20:20-25; Job 22:21-30; 29:1-25; Psalm 5:12; 34:6-10; 37:3-5; 52:1-9; 62:9-12; 78:18-29; 84:4-12; 112:1-10; 115:11-16; 128:1-4; 147:10-15; Proverbs 3:1-10; 11:1; 11:24-26; 11:28; 22:4; 22:13; 28:27; Ecclesiastes 5:9-11; 5:12,13; 7:11-14; 9:10,11; 11:1-6; Isaiah 55:8-13; Jeremiah 17:5-8; Micah 4:11-13; Matthew 6:19-34; Luke 11:17-26; 12:16-21; 16:9-13; John 14:26,27; Acts 20:32-35; Philippians 4:10-19; 1 Timothy 6:6-10; 6:17-19; James 1:5-8; 4:10.

Wisdom for financial decisions:

Genesis 24:34,35; Deuteronomy 8:10-18; 15:7-11; 18:4,5; 28:1-13; 29:9; Joshua 1:7-9; 1 Kings 2:3; 3:11-13; 1 Chronicles 22:11-13; 29:28; Job 29:1-25; Psalm 23:1-6; Proverbs 3:1-10; 3:13-17; 3:27,28; 6:1-5; 6:6-11; 8:10,11; 8:12; 8:18-21; 8:32-35; 10:3-5; 10:15; 10:22; 11:16; 12:11; 13:18; 13:22; 14:24; 15:19; 16:16; 16:19; 17:18; 18:9; 18:16; 20:14,15; 21:17; 21:20; 23:4,5; 23:22,23; 24:3,4; 24:27; 25:21,22; 27:23,24; 29:3; Ecclesiastes 7:11-14; 9:10,11; 9:16; Jeremiah 9:23,24; Matthew 24:45-47; John 14:26,27; Ephesians 1:3; Colossians 1:9-12; James 1:5-8.

Work ethic; how God prospers what you set your hand to do:

Genesis 26:12-14; 39:2-6; 39:20-23; Leviticus 26:3-9; Deuteronomy 2:7; 15:7-11; 23:19,20; 24:19-22; 28:1-13; 33:11; Ruth 2:12; 1 Kings 2:3; 1 Chronicles 22:11-13; 29:1-14; 2 Chronicles 26:5; 31:20,21; Job 1:10; 29:1-25; Psalm 1:1-3; 52:1-9; 62:9-12; 112:1-10; Proverbs 6:6-11; 10:3-5; 12:11; 12:14; 12:24; 12:27; 13:4; 13:11; 14:20,21; 14:23; 15:19; 16:11; 18:9; 19:15; 20:4; 21:6; 22:13; 22:29; 24:27; 28:19,20; Ecclesiastes 5:12,13; 9:10,11; 10:18; 11:1-6; Matthew 25:14-30; Luke 19:11-26; Acts 20:32-35; 1 Corinthians 15:58; 2 Corinthians 6:10; Galatians 6:4-10; Ephesians 4:28; 1 Thessalonians 4:10-12; 2 Thessalonians 2:16,17; 3:6-10; Hebrews 6:10-15; James 1:22-25; 2:14-18.

PRAYER OF SALVATION

God loves you—no matter who you are, no matter what your past. God loves you so much that He gave His one and only begotten Son for you. The Bible tells us that "...whoever believes in him shall not perish but have eternal life" (John 3:16 NIV). Jesus laid down His life and rose again so that we could spend eternity with Him in heaven and experience His absolute best on earth. If you would like to receive Jesus into your life, say the following prayer out loud and mean it from your heart.

Heavenly Father, I come to You admitting that I am a sinner. Right now, I choose to turn away from sin, and I ask You to cleanse me of all unrighteousness. I believe that Your Son, Jesus, died on the cross to take away my sins. I also believe that He rose again from the dead so that I might be forgiven of my sins and made righteous through faith in Him. I call upon the name of Jesus Christ to be the Savior and Lord of my life. Jesus, I choose to follow You and ask that You fill me with the power of the Holy Spirit. I declare that right now I am a child of God. I am free from sin and full of the righteousness of God. I am saved in Jesus' name. Amen.

If you prayed this prayer to receive Jesus Christ as your Savior for the first time, please contact us on the Web at **www.harrisonhouse.com** to receive a free book.

Or you may write to us at

Harrison House

P.O. Box 35035

Tulsa, Oklahoma 74153

ABOUT THE AUTHOR

James R. Riddle is a successful entrepreneur, educator, and Bible teacher. He is a member of Abundant Living Faith Center in El Paso, Texas, and has been working closely with Charles Nieman Ministries since 1987. He is also an honors graduate from the University of Texas at El Paso with a degree in English: Creative Writing. *The Complete Personalized Promise Bible* series is the result of an intensive three-year study of the entire Bible that James Riddle undertook.

To contact James Riddle,
please write to:

James R. Riddle
P.O. Box 972624
El Paso, Texas 79997
or via his Web site
www.jamesriddle.net

Every Promise Personalized in Chronological Order!

Over 1,800 promises from God are found in this remarkable book. Promises to bless, encourage, and instruct you. God knew in this world you would need His Word and His Promises to live in victory. But if you don't know what those promises are, you will not have a basis for your faith or a solid foundation to put your trust in.

The Complete Personalized Promise Bible takes you through *every single promise* in the Bible, from Genesis to Revelation. In chronological order, each promise is recorded from various Bible translations and includes a personalized, Scripture-based declaration of faith. Also included is an introduction to each book of the Bible explaining the basis for God's promises for that book. By studying these promises and praying them back to the Father God, you will establish your faith for those promises to be a part of your life.

This book...is amazing! It is a great blessing to our congregation. *The Complete Personalized Promise Bible* is a book every home should have in its spiritual library.
>   —Charles Nieman
>   Pastor and Author of *Becoming a Master Asker*
>   Abundant Living Faith Center
>   El Paso, Texas

James Riddle's book, *The Complete Personalized Promise Bible*...makes the Word of God real, applicable, and vital to each child of God. As one uses this study aid they will...realize...that He desires His children to have successful, fulfilling lives.
>   —Pastor Tommy Barnett
>   Phoenix First Assembly of God
>   Phoenix, Arizona

Perfect as a devotional or in prayer time, *The Complete Personalized Promise Bible* will help God's Word to become so rooted in your spirit that you will not be able to turn from the truth or give up, no matter how difficult your situation is. God has made a way for you to overcome!

For more information visit www.promisebible.com.
ISBN-10: 1-57794-537-9
ISBN-13: 978-1-57794-537-6

ISBN-10: 1-57794-537-9
ISBN-13: 978-1-57794-537-6

The COMPLETE
PERSONALIZED
PROMISE
BIBLE

Every Promise *in the* Bible

from Genesis *to* Revelation

Written Just *for* You

JAMES RIDDLE

For Women Only and in Topical Format!

The Bible is filled with over *1,800 promises* from God to bless, encourage, and instruct us. Why would God give so many promises? He knew in this world we would need them. But if you don't know what those promises are, you will not have a basis for your faith or a solid foundation to put your trust in.

The Complete Personalized Promise Bible for Women takes you through *every single promise* in the Bible, listed in topical format for easy reference. Each topic includes an introduction explaining why those promises are important to you. Each promise is recorded from various Bible translations and includes a personalized, Scripture-based declaration of faith. By studying these promises and praying them back to the Father God, you will establish your faith for those promises to be a part of your life.

Let God's Word become so rooted in your spirit that you will not be able to turn from the truth or give up, no matter how difficult your situation is. God has made a way for you to overcome!

Topics include:

- Unique Abilities
- His Angels
- To Care for Your Children
- You Are His Chosen One
- Comfort and Encouragement
- To Give You the Desires of Your Heart
- Favor
- To Fight for You
- Freedom
- Friends

- Guidance
- Healing
- Long Life
- A Good Marriage
- To Make You a Good Parent
- Peace
- Answers to Your Prayers
- Strength
- Wisdom
- And much more

For more information visit www.promisebible.com.
ISBN-10: 1-57794-664-2
ISBN-13: 978-1-57794-664-9

ISBN-10: 1-57794-664-2
ISBN-13: 978-1-57794-664-9

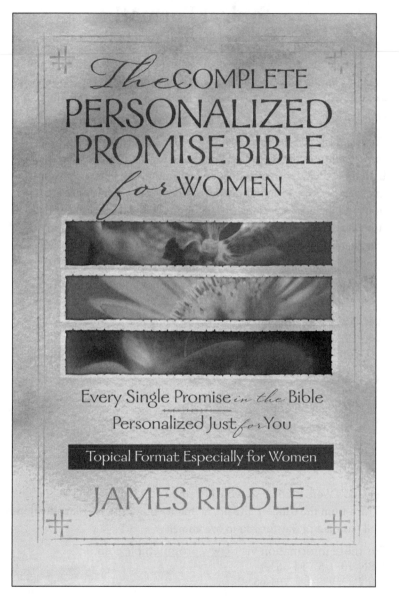

Just for Men and in Topical Format!

The Bible is filled with over *1,800 promises* from God to bless, encourage, and instruct us. Why would God give so many promises? He knew in this world we would need them. But if you don't know what those promises are, you will not have a basis for your faith or a solid foundation to put your trust in.

The Complete Personalized Promise Bible for Men takes you through *every single promise* in the Bible, listed in topical format for easy reference. Each topic includes an introduction explaining why those promises are important to you. Each promise is recorded from various Bible translations and includes a personalized, Scripture-based declaration of faith. By studying these promises and praying them back to the Father God, you will establish your faith for those promises to be a part of your life.

Topics include:

- An Anointing
- You Are His Chosen One
- Courage and Boldness
- To Give You the Desires of Your Heart
- A Destiny
- Favor
- To Fight for You
- Forgiveness
- Guidance
- Healing

- Honor and Rewards
- Joy and Happiness
- Long Life
- A Good Marriage
- To Make You a Good Parent
- Peace
- Strength
- Success
- Wisdom
- And much more

Let God's Word become so rooted in your spirit that you will not be able to turn from the truth or give up, no matter how difficult your situation is. God has made a way for you to overcome!

For more information visit www.promisebible.com.

ISBN-10: 1-57794-663-4
ISBN-13: 978-1-57794-663-2

ISBN-10: 1-57794-663-4
ISBN-13: 978-1-57794-663-2

The COMPLETE PERSONALIZED PROMISE BIBLE for MEN

Every Single Promise *in the* Bible *from*

Personalized Just *for* You

Topical Format Especially for Men

JAMES RIDDLE

www.harrisonhouse.com

Fast. Easy. Convenient!

- ◆ New Book Information
- ◆ Look Inside the Book
- ◆ Press Releases
- ◆ Bestsellers
- ◆ Free E-News
- ◆ Author Biographies

- ◆ Upcoming Books
- ◆ Share Your Testimony
- ◆ Online Product Availability
- ◆ Product Specials
- ◆ Order Online

For the latest in book news and author information, please visit us on the Web at www.harrisonhouse.com. Get up-to-date pictures and details on all our powerful and life-changing products. Sign up for our e-mail newsletter, *Friends of the House,* and receive free monthly information on our authors and products including testimonials, author announcements, and more!

Harrison House—
Books That Bring Hope, Books That Bring Change

THE HARRISON HOUSE VISION

Proclaiming the truth and the power
Of the Gospel of Jesus Christ
With excellence;

Challenging Christians to
Live victoriously,
Grow spiritually,
Know God intimately.

The
Lost Girls
of Ireland

BOOKS BY SUSANNE O'LEARY

THE SANDY COVE SERIES
Secrets of Willow House
Sisters of Willow House
Dreams of Willow House
Daughters of Wild Rose Bay
Memories of Wild Rose Bay
Miracles in Wild Rose Bay

The Road Trip
A Holiday to Remember